STOPPARD:
THE MYSTERY AND THE CLOCKWORK

STOPPARD:

THE MYSTERY AND THE CLOCKWORK

RICHARD CORBALLIS

AMBER LANE PRESS ● OXFORD

━━━━━━━━━━━━━━━━━━━━━━━━━━━━━━━━

METHUEN ● NEW YORK

Published in 1984 by
Amber Lane Press Limited
9 Middle Way
Oxford OX2 7LH

First published in 1984 in the
United States of America by
Methuen, Inc.
733 Third Avenue
New York, N.Y. 10017

ISBN 0 906399 46 7 (Amber Lane edition, cased)
 0 906399 47 5 (Amber Lane edition, paper)
 0 416 01011 3 (Methuen edition, cased)
 0 416 00981 6 (Methuen edition, paper)

Library of Congress Cataloging in Publication Data
Corballis, Richard.
 Stoppard, the mystery and the clockwork.
 Bibliography: p.
 1. Stoppard, Tom—Criticism and interpretation.
I. Title.
PR6069.T6Z62 1984   822'.914   84-91151
ISBN 0-416-01011-3 (U.S.)
ISBN 0-416-00981-6 (U.S.: pbk.)

Text set in Bembo.
Printed and bound in Great Britain at
The Pitman Press, Bath

822.914
S8832c

Contents

Acknowledgements

The first draft of this book was written in Canberra in 1979, while I was a Summer Fellow at the Humanities Research Centre of the Australian National University. I am very grateful to the staff of the Centre—especially Chris Eade and Ian Donaldson—for their help and hospitality. To my wife Penny, who coped with three boisterous children and a new job while I was away, I owe an even greater debt.

My research was assisted by a grant from the University of Canterbury and by the labours of Hugh Brazier, Victoria Baird, Celia Burry, Joanne Boloski, Lorraine North and Liz Yates. Mary Theo, Julie Barton, Dorothy Nicolls and Julia Hobby typed and retyped the manuscript with never a grumble and scarcely an error.

Judith Scott of Amber Lane Press helped me considerably in the latter stages of my labours. The steady stream of press-clippings and other ephemera which she directed my way was particularly useful.

An earlier version of Chapter 3 was published in *Ariel* Volume XI Number 2 (1980) under the title: 'Extending the Audience: The Structure of *Rosencrantz and Guildenstern Are Dead*'. I am grateful to the Board of Governors of the University of Calgary for permission to reproduce it here.

The extensive extracts from the works of Tom Stoppard are quoted with the kind permission of Faber and Faber Ltd (London) and Grove Press Inc. (New York). I acknowledge also the considerable assistance which I received from Frank Pike and Brian Dickson (Faber) and Robin Simmen (Grove) in the compiling of my bibliography of Stoppard's works.

Finally I wish to thank Tom Stoppard himself for his unfailingly courteous replies to my numerous footling queries.

Richard Corballis

A note on the references (or lack of them)

The bewildering array of available editions has led me to abandon any attempt to provide precise references for my quotations from Stoppard's works. Virtually all my quotations from the critics are likewise unglossed. In all cases, however, the name of the critic in question (or of the article where no author is specified) is given in the text, and a glance at the Bibliography will establish the source (though not, of course, the page number) of the reference. Where the name [Ronald] Hayman appears in the text the reference is always to his book, *Tom Stoppard*.

1 Introduction

Let Us Go Then, You and I . . .

Many theatre-goers find it difficult to appreciate the essential substance of a play. Like Donne surveying his mistress for the first time in the flesh in 'Air and Angels', they get dazzled by the surface effects. Or, to adopt a more commonplace metaphor, they fail to see the wood for the trees. The New Zealand director, Raymond Hawthorne, tells the story of a person who went to see Roger Hall's play, *Middle Age Spread*—hardly a challenging piece—and could comment afterwards only on the type of coffee-service used in the last scene. A good many people come away from Stoppard's plays with the same reaction writ large. Even the editors of *Theatre Quarterly* complained—in 'Ambushes for the Audience'—that the plays up to and including *Jumpers* 'don't really make clear statements'. The surface brilliance inhibits appreciation of the underlying design.

This brilliance is primarily linguistic. The anxiety, acknowledged in 'Ambushes for the Audience', to 'inject some sort of interest and colour into every line', causes Stoppard to toss off puns and epigrams at a rate unequalled even by Oscar Wilde. So prodigal is his talent for word-play that he does not need to parade it as Wilde generally does; Stoppard is often content to let puns and quibbles lie submerged in a welter of other verbiage, as in this example from the Player's big speech about death in Act II of *Rosencrantz and Guildenstern Are Dead*:

> I had an actor once who was condemned to hang for stealing a sheep—or a lamb, I forget which—so I got permission to have him hanged in the middle of a play . . .

C. W. E. Bigsby is certainly correct when he claims that

Stoppard 'believes in the primacy of words' and is therefore an 'aesthetic reactionary', at odds with the *avant-garde* theatre, which 'is de-emphasizing language, stressing performance over text, preferring group composition to the insights of the individual author'. But it would be wrong to pursue this argument too far, as did Clifford D. May, who concluded a feature article for the American journal *Newsweek* thus:

> 'Words, words. They're all we have to go on', says Guildenstern in Stoppard's 'R & G'. The way Tom Stoppard uses them, they're all that's needed.

No, words are not all we have to go on when we are interpreting Stoppard. The vivid words are accompanied (most of all in *Jumpers*, least of all in *The Real Thing*) by vivid action. And Stoppard himself told Ronald Hayman that in the last analysis he was 'in it because of the theatre rather than because of the literature'. The action is always carefully contrived to supplement the text; no scope is left for improvization, which is why Bigsby's remarks remain valid. But action there certainly is—of a vivid and intricate kind which is more akin to the activities of conjurors and circus performers than to orthodox stage business.

So the audience for a Stoppard play is likely to be straining its ears for submerged word-play and feasting its eyes on zany spectacle. And there is scarcely ever a moment of tranquillity in which to reconcile the evidence of these two senses and to arrive at an appreciation of the overall significance of the play. It is in predicaments like this one that academic criticism, which issues from a peculiarly tranquil environment, can be of real help to the ordinary theatre-goer, although Stoppard's own scepticism about academics— expressed in 'Playwrights and Professors' and elsewhere— suggests that he would be reluctant to concede this point. Unfortunately, most of the criticism so far devoted to Stoppard has failed to achieve the kind of overview that is required; instead it has tended to confine itself to the surface of the plays, where it has identified still more examples of cleverness, notably the imitation and/or parody of other playwrights, both ancient and modern.

This book, written in the extraordinary tranquillity of a South Pacific university, sets out to define the basic ground-plan upon which the extravagant language and spectacle have been raised. Believing as I do that criticism is at its most useful when it provides bold generalizations for readers to kick against until their own more subtle interpretations emerge, I have oversimplified my case to the point of arguing that the design of every published Stoppard play is essentially the same. There is always a collision between two worlds: a world of 'mystery' and uncertainty, which is the real world, and a world of 'clockwork', abstraction and artifice, which is an unreal dream world—a world, Stoppard insists, to be avoided.

Before we proceed to elaborate and test this hypothesis, however, we must confront Stoppard's own remarks about the structure of his plays. At first glance many of them seem very damaging to my case. Here, for example, is what he had to say in 'Ambushes for the Audience' about the genesis of *Rosencrantz and Guildenstern Are Dead:*

> The chief interest and objective was to exploit a situation which seemed to me to have enormous dramatic and comic potential . . . What was actually calculated was to entertain a roomful of people with the situation of Rosencrantz and Guildenstern at Elsinore. The chief thing that added one line to another line was that the combination of the two should retain an audience's interest in some way . . .

No gestures here in the direction of design or meaning. Indeed until very recently Stoppard strenuously resisted the notion that his plays—indeed *any* plays—constituted an ordered, planned attempt to demonstrate some idea or moral. To Hayman he insisted that 'you write away into a tunnel, you have a corpse on the floor, and you don't know who it is or what to do with him, and suddenly you say HIGGS!!!' Again, this time in 'But for the Middle Classes', he wrote:

> . . . the most widespread misapprehension about playwrights (apart from the misapprehension that they have access to unlimited free tickets for their plays) is that they set out to say something and then say it, in short that a play is the end product of an idea.

In unguarded moments, however, Stoppard occasionally went close to betraying this portrait of himself as an inspired improviser. To Hayman, for example, he conceded that one of his 'twin preoccupations' was 'to make the play say what you want it to say'. (The other preoccupation was 'having the audience on the play's side'.) And in 'Ambushes for the Audience' he acknowledged that his work might be shaped by subconscious choices.

Kenneth Tynan sensed these contradictions at once, and pointed out that not only the plays but also Stoppard's responses to interviewers seemed to have been carefully planned. And in three recent interviews Stoppard himself has finally removed his improviser's mask. To Joost Kuurman he acknowledged that 'It starts with an idea . . . one has an idea for a play and then works out some kind of form for it'. Nancy Shields Hardin elicited a similar admission. And when David Gollob and David Roper questioned him about his contention that 'the ideas are the end-product of the play, not the other way round', he confessed that this was 'a sort of "travelling pose"' which 'has the overstatement of most epigrams'. In fact, he added, 'What you were quoting stopped being applicable round about the time I started writing *Jumpers*. There the play was the end-product of an idea as much as the converse'. This implies of course that *Rosencrantz and Guildenstern Are Dead* and the other plays written prior to *Jumpers* must still be regarded as plays in which 'the ideas are the end-product of the play'. But Stoppard went on to explain to Gollob and Roper that the only thing different about these earlier plays was that many commentators found the *wrong* ideas in them:

> After I had written *Rosencrantz and Guildenstern* I en-countered over the next few years all kinds of inter-pretations of the events of the play, and it seemed to me that the play had somehow created all these ideas in the mind of the watcher and so they were in that sense the end-product of a play about two Elizabethan cour-tiers trapped by the action of *Hamlet*.

So provided we keep close to the notion of 'two Elizabethan courtiers trapped by the action of *Hamlet*' we would seem to be justified in regarding this play too as 'the end-product of an idea'.

Stoppard has also let slip some very useful hints about the structural devices which he adopts in order to bring out these ideas. To Hayman he expressed admiration for:

> . . . a Beckett joke which is the funniest joke in the
> world to me. It appears in various forms but it consists
> of confident statement followed by immediate refuta-
> tion by the same voice . . . That sort of Beckettian
> influence is much more important to me than a mere
> verbal echo of a line or a parallelism at the end of
> *Jumpers* . . .

A little later in the same interview he explained how this debt
to Beckett affects the structure of his plays: 'What I'm always
trying to say is "Firstly, A. Secondly, minus A."' Or, as he
was forever putting it in his early interviews, 'I write plays
because it's the only respectable way of contradicting myself'. The same idea is expressed thus in 'Ambushes for the
Audience':

> What there is, is a series of conflicting statements made
> by conflicting characters, and they tend to play a sort of
> infinite leap-frog. You know, an argument, a refuta-
> tion, then a rebuttal of the refutation, then a counter-
> rebuttal . . .

As Stoppard conceives it here, this intellectual leap-frog is
infinite: 'There is never any point . . . at which I feel *that* is
the speech to stop it on, *that* is the last word'. Many critics
have concurred with this self-assessment and have proceeded
to depict a Stoppard 'withdrawing in style from the chaos'
(Tynan) in order to tease his audiences with a dizzying
succession of 'views from a revolving door' (Levenson) that
testify to his acceptance of the Einsteinian premise that:

> Here and now . . . is a time and place defined by an
> infinite number of converging factors, each heading
> towards it at the speed of light and steadily slowing
> down to nothing before passing through it and speeding
> up again. (Clive James)

And yet towards the end of 'Ambushes for the Audience' we
find Stoppard claiming to have 'a consistent idea of good and
bad in the way human beings treat each other', averring that
Jumpers (his latest play at that stage) 'goes against Marxist-
Leninism in particular and against all materialistic philosophy' and roundly declaring that 'a materialistic view of
history is an insult to the human race'. Encouraged by Mel
Gussow to think in more abstract terms, in 'Stoppard Refutes

Himself, Endlessly', he posited the notion of 'an absolute "ceiling view of a situation"' and even countenanced the existence of God.

All this evidence tends to confute the relativistic portrait painted by James and others. To some extent the contradiction can be resolved historically. In 1977 (International Prisoner of Conscience Year) Stoppard produced two works with an explicit political commitment: *Professional Foul* and *Every Good Boy Deserves Favour*. The same commitment is evident in two subsequent plays (*Night and Day* and *Cahoot's Macbeth*) and with the benefit of hindsight it is possible to trace it back as far as *Jumpers*. James, Tynan, Levenson and company were on the scene too early to appreciate this new development, although Tynan, who had been able to see the manuscript of *Every Good Boy Deserves Favour*, sensed impending change.

But while it would be convenient to believe that Stoppard suffered a sudden conversion from playboy to man-of-conscience, this does not seem to be the whole truth. In 1978, in an interview with Milton Shulman in *The New York Times*, he claimed, 'I was always morally, if not politically, involved'. As usual this statement conflicts with a host of others, the most famous of which is probably the Wildean observation which recurs in many of the early interviews: 'I should have the courage of my lack of convictions', and it may be that in these critical statements, as in the plays, we are up against 'a sort of infinite leap-frog'. But it is probably significant that in the recent interview with Gollob and Roper, where Stoppard sloughed off a number of his old masks, he claimed to have shared 'for years and years, and years before Anderson ever existed' the moral involvement which George Anderson learns in the course of *Professional Foul*. Unfortunately, in this same interview Roper interrupted before Stoppard could answer Gollob's leading question about the relationship of Stoppard's professed idealism and 'an opposite but more characteristic feature of your writing, which is the relativism of everything'.

At all events, nobody raised, as I was, in a milieu over which Karl Popper once presided will rest satisfied with a notion of infinite leap-frog. Before we accept it we must test every hypothesis which pretends to create order out of the chaos. My own hypothesis, which is offered in a Popperian spirit for others to falsify, would reduce Stoppard's infinite series—argument, refutation, rebuttal, counter-rebuttal—to a set of variations on the first two terms: argument and refutation, or 'A' and 'minus A'. The plays, like the masques of the early Stuart court, are binary in form. More important, I reckon that from the start the plays provide evidence of Stoppard's moral involvement in that there is almost always a last word; the refutation generally triumphs over or at least generates more sympathy than the argument, which means, of course, that the counterpart to 'A' has a positive value of its own and should therefore be labelled 'B' rather than 'minus A'. Specifically I contend that in all Stoppard's work an abstract, artificial view of the world ('A') is pitted against the flux of reality ('B'), and the audience is invited to eschew the 'clockwork' of the former in favour of the 'mystery' of the latter.

These labels of 'mystery' and 'clockwork' are drawn from Stoppard's own writings. In Act II of *Jumpers* George complains, unjustifiably as it turns out, that Archie's disciple, McFee, 'never put himself at risk by finding mystery in the clockwork'. Elsewhere the terms occur separately. Clockwork is sometimes introduced quite literally into the plays; clocks of one kind or another feature prominently in *Enter a Free Man, If You're Glad I'll be Frank, Travesties, Dirty Linen, The Real Thing* and *The Dog It Was That Died*. In all cases their purpose is to underscore the inhuman regimentation of the characters with whom they are associated; one cannot 'impose moral terms on clockwork dancers', as Stoppard observed in 'A Case of Vice Triumphant'.

Mysteries are also prevalent in Stoppard's plays. Why do the coins keep coming down heads? Who is the real Inspector Hound? Whose mother is Mother in *After Magritte*? Who killed McFee? And just as the literal clocks are merely the outward and visible or audible signs of an inward and very unspiritual state of mind, so these shallow and/or melo-dramatic puzzles serve to direct our attention to more fundamental mysteries concerning the situations, the aspira-tions and even the achievements of Stoppard's heroes. For Rosencrantz and Guildenstern truth is never more than 'a permanent blur in the corner of your eye'; George Moore knows that God exists but fails dismally in his attempts to prove it; Lenin gets every bit as tangled in his efforts to define the proper function of the arts, and ends lamely by complaining that 'one's duty is infernally hard'; and the moral of *Dirty Linen* is most easily expressed negatively: mind your own business.

Even in the more polemical works that Stoppard has produced since 1977 there tends to be a curious lack of definition about the status and achievements of the central characters. In *Every Good Boy Deserves Favour* and *Cahoot's Macbeth* he emphasizes what the heroes stand against rather than what they stand for. *Professional Foul* elaborates more carefully the cause of individual liberty to which Professor Anderson is converted in the course of the play, but somehow the smuggling of a thesis—note that Hollar's manuscript is only a thesis and not an overtly political document—seems an inadequate objective correlative to the anguish experienced by the principal characters. And in *Night and Day* the relish with which Ruth and Milne lambast the crassness of popular journalism almost overwhelms Guthrie's final assurance that 'it's worse in places where everybody is kept in the dark'.

This vagueness or 'mystery' at the core of the plays has often been mistaken for emptiness, and Stoppard has been dismissed as a siren rather than a serious artist (Roberts) and 'a grin without a cat' (Wardle). Stoppard's own flippant insistence upon his lack of convictions has not helped, of course. A number of critics—rather more than Dougald McMillan supposes—have sprung to Stoppard's defence, but most of them have had some difficulty in defining just what Stoppard stands for. At one extreme we have David Camroux propounding, with zest and good humour, the difficult notion that Stoppard's heroes are 'metaphysical egocentrics' and that the plays champion a humanity which 'is a metaphysical property not a sociological one'. Much more accessible is Jim Hunter's contention that Stoppard's works—

> . . . urge us to keep jinking, on the move, sceptical and free. Irrationality, in Stoppard, becomes heroic: it even becomes the best hope for the survival of reason . . . It isn't the dogmas, in fact, which imply absolutes, but the flux itself.

And Hunter proceeds to quote George's argument, in Act II of *Jumpers*, that 'life itself is the mundane figure which argues perfection at its limiting curve'. 'Irrationality', 'the flux itself', 'life itself': these are some of the notions that are comprehended in my term, 'mystery'.

I am principally concerned with Stoppard's stage plays, to each of which a separate chapter is allotted. But before we launch into the dizzy world of the *gesamtkunstwerke* it may help to consider briefly representative examples of the work which Stoppard has written for other media. These lack at least one of the dimensions present in the stage plays and are therefore easier to dissect.

The bulk of this other work, which includes fiction and plays for radio and television, is treated in Appendix I of this study. But his only novel, *Lord Malquist and Mr Moon*, and his prize-winning plays for radio, *Albert's Bridge* (Prix Italia, 1968) and television, *Professional Foul* (British Television Critics' Award, 1977) will be considered at this point in order both to demonstrate Stoppard's versatility and, more importantly, to give an initial indication of some ways in which his work has developed over the years.

'Lord Malquist and Mr Moon': Simple Juxtaposition

The juxtaposition of 'mystery' and 'clockwork' is clearly exhibited in Stoppard's novel. The principal 'clockwork' character is Lord Malquist, the dandified earl, who has removed himself from 'the chaos of life', preferring to be a stylist, a 'man of inaction who would not dare roll up his sleeves for fear of creasing the cuffs'. As this quotation suggests, Malquist's contempt for reality is most obviously indicated by his impeccable dress; but there is another pointer which is, for our purposes, even more significant. Malquist is writing 'a monograph on *Hamlet* as a source of book titles'. The mention of *Hamlet* immediately calls to mind *Rosencrantz and Guildenstern Are Dead*, which is indeed the novel's 'sister' work, and the nature of the subject brilliantly evokes the 'clockwork' universe which Malquist shares with the actors in the play-within-that-play. For to study *Hamlet* merely as a source of book titles is to study art entirely for art's sake, at two removes from reality.

The other titular character, Moon, is trying to write a book of a very different kind. It is a history of the world which will demonstrate the 'grand design' which underlies human existence. The project is a futile one, of course. In the background, the death and burial of the great statesman (whom Hayman identifies specifically as Churchill) constitutes 'the last flourish of an age whose criteria of greatness are no longer applicable', and ushers in a new age devoid of both greatness and design. And the foreground of Moon's world is no more reassuring. Lions roam the parks of London; cowboys ride the streets; Lord Malquist, in eighteenth-century garb, rides round in a coach which is controlled, stylishly but quite incompetently, by a black Irish Jew; a scrounging Irishman, who denies being an Irishman, claims to be the risen Christ; Moon's wife (Jane) and her maid (Marie) give every indication that they have turned the house into a brothel; etc., etc. Moon's desultory endeavours to find method in this madness avail him nothing. At one point he calms his rising panic by gazing out of the window at a picture-book vista of a large lawn and lake, with green hills in the distance. After a withering interview with O'Hara the coachman, Moon registers to the fact that the scene was an artificial one painted on a piece of plyboard which covers the kitchen window—shades of Magritte here. A little later, Moon seems to find relief by a different, and very Stoppardian, method:

> Jane squealed and threw . . . an eighteenth-century gilt mirror which exploded round his head, violent as plate glass bursting out of a train window. Moon exhaled as if his body were one big lung. The spring unwound itself, proportion was re-established. He rocked blind in the great calm, his mouth loose, his legs gone. He knew what it was to solve the world.

In Stoppard's works, mirrors, train windows and the like reflect the chaos of existence. Order can be achieved by smashing the glass, however, and so when Jane breaks the mirror over Moon's head he seems to discover a logical world. But as usual his experience of *Nirvana* is short-lived;

he is soon back in the real world, forced to contend with a cut eye and the self-proclaimed 'Risen Christ'.

And so it goes on. Moon never succeeds in getting through the looking-glass for more than a moment. His bewilderment is reinforced by continual allusions to T. S. Eliot's 'Love Song of J. Alfred Prufrock'.* Moon is always seen in terms of the repressed Prufrockian 'I' of Eliot's poem; only once—upon losing his virginity to Lady Malquist late in the novel—does he see himself as the liberated 'you', but this moment of triumph is followed at once by his 'return to the world.'

Moon's last resort is his bomb. He hopes that an explosion will shock mankind

> . . . into a moment of recognition—*bang!*—so that they might make a total re-assessment, recognise that life has gone badly wrong somewhere, the proportions have been distorted . . .

But Moon's protest ends, as one might expect, not with a bang but a whimper. It transpires that his bomb is not a bomb at all but a self-inflating giant balloon with an obscene message on it. When the balloon bursts, pieces of red rubber flap down into Trafalgar Square, reminding us of the various rolls and scraps of paper that have served as another of the book's symbols of life's 'mystery'.

Once his attempt at violence has failed, Moon is, like Guildenstern, doomed. The cause of his death? A bomb. The explanation for the bombing? None whatsoever. Moon is killed quite accidentally in a case of mistaken identity. The incomprehensible 'mystery' of life has finally claimed him as its victim. At first glance this death of a realist may appear to contravene the preference for 'mystery' over 'clockwork' which I reckon to be Stoppard's staple theme. But the actual fates of the parties concerned matter less than the degree of sympathy which they generate. Indeed, Stoppard insisted to

---

* 'Prufrock' is a favourite poem of Stoppard's and it provides the basis for the early story, 'Life, Times: Fragments' (see Appendix I). Of Stoppard's subsequent works *Lord Malquist and Mr Moon* and *Jumpers* probably owe most to the poem but in *Night and Day* the oscillation between Ruth and 'Ruth' is comparable to the I/you distinction in 'Prufrock'.

Gollob and Roper that the death of a character 'confirms the truth which he becomes a martyr to'. In *Lord Malquist and Mr Moon* our sympathies are with Moon throughout, just as they are with Rosencrantz and Guildenstern in the dramatic companion-piece. Malquist, like the Tragedians in the play, is too much of an automaton to generate real sympathy, even though his sense of style provokes some admiration. Anyway, Malquist too is doomed at the end of the book; he is bankrupt and destitute with 'nowhere to retreat to any more'. And his disciple, Jane, appears to have got herself into an irreversible yoga position, though more matter-of-fact-sounding things seem to be going on behind closed doors a few pages later.

So the commitment to reality is already unmistakable in this early work. One distinctive feature that we should note, however, is that Stoppard had to beat his theme out very thinly in order to accommodate it to a full-length work. Malquist, the epitome of 'clockwork', and Moon, the epitome of 'mystery', live in separate worlds. 'I am an island, Mr Moon, and when the bell tolls it tolls for thee', observes Malquist at the very start of the novel, and what follows proves him absolutely right. There is, then, a curious lack of conflict between characters, both here and in *Rosencrantz and Guildenstern Are Dead*, where, as we shall see, the link which the Tragedians provide between the Moon-like world of Rosencrantz and Guildenstern and the Malquist-like world of the *Hamlet* cast is, in the last analysis, a somewhat factitious one.

'Albert's Bridge': Enter the Straddler

The later plays move some way towards finding common ground for the interplay of 'mystery' and 'clockwork'. At first this is done by the introduction of a character who straddles both realms. In Stoppard's first radio play, *If You're Glad I'll be Frank*, Frank almost achieves this, although his conversion from 'clockwork' to 'mystery' is a whirlwind affair with uncertain consequences. The whole business is too slight to form the basis for significant conclusions.

One of the developments evident in *Albert's Bridge*, Stoppard's next play for radio, is the expansion of the role of the straddler, and this makes it much easier for the audience to judge the relative merits of 'the mystery' and 'the clock-work'. Here the central character is, or quickly becomes, a 'clockwork' figure. To Albert everyday life is bafflingly complex. These, for example, are his reflections on the life of a factory man:

> . . . his bits and pieces scatter, grow wheels, disinte-grate, change colour, join up in new forms which he doesn't know anything about. In short he doesn't know what he's done, to whom.

Albert grasps at any means of escaping this 'mystery'. We hear that after obtaining his degree (in philosophy, a disci-pline which Stoppard told Mark Amory he regards as 'taking place in a large plastic bubble' and which therefore features as the epitome of 'clockwork' in a number of his plays) he tried to stay on in the cosy, cloistered world of the university, but, as he ruefully observes, 'they wouldn't have me'. The next avenue of escape that comes Albert's way is a holiday job as one of four painters on a railway bridge above Clufton Bay. The bridge—'the fourth biggest single-span, double-track, shore-to-shore railway bridge in the world bar none'—embodies a logic which is not to be found in life. It is—

> . . . separate—complete—removed, defined by princi-ples of engineering which makes (sic) it stop at a certain point, which compels a certain shape, certain joints—the whole thing utterly fixed by the rules that make it stay up.

Albert would prefer to spend his life on the Eiffel Tower because it is less functional, but the bridge is a good second-best, and when the City Engineer, Fitch, produces a rigorously 'clockwork' scheme for cutting costs by sacking, or rather redeploying, the other three painters and using a more durable paint, Albert is delighted to be left alone on the job. He quickly becomes so absorbed by it that he severs all links with reality. His wife, Kate, pleads with him and resorts to smashing crockery to bring him back to earth, but all to no avail; Albert works longer and longer hours until he ends up spending a whole night on the bridge. So Kate leaves him, taking their little daughter with her.

Albert has now become a completely 'clockwork' figure, an unfeeling automaton like the Player in *Rosencrantz and Guildenstern Are Dead*. The 'mystery' of reality is kept before our eyes, however, by the introduction of the straddler figure—a character called Fraser who climbs up on to the bridge in order to commit suicide. Like Albert he has felt oppressed by 'the flying splinters of a world breaking up at the speed of procreation without end', and, again like Albert, he finds that when he gets away from it all on the bridge 'the proportions have been re-established' and his 'confidence is restored, by perspective'. So he does not commit suicide. But he also declines to stay on the bridge and become a 'clockwork' figure like Albert; he goes back down into 'the big blooming buzzing confusion' of reality. Again it overwhelms him; again he climbs the bridge to commit suicide; and again the view from the bridge reassures him. He seems doomed to this perpetual shuttling between the two worlds, and one can see here a primitive version of the bridging role performed by Dotty in *Jumpers* and by a number of other characters in Stoppard's later plays.

Although his predicament seems ludicrous, Fraser does have a serious function. His ambivalence puts him in a position to criticize Albert's absolute embrace of 'clockwork': 'You see yourself as the centre, whereas I know that I am not placed at all'. Moreover, his sense of dilemma imbues him with a human warmth which accentuates, by contrast, the cold impersonal nature of Albert, who can hardly wait for Fraser to make his suicide-leap and leave him alone on his beloved bridge.

Thus Fraser (and to a lesser extent Kate) alienates us from Albert to the point where we are ready to accept his destruction. It results not so much from an intrusion of reality from without as from an excess of 'clockwork' within—an overwinding of the spring, as it were. Because Albert alone works much more slowly than the four painters who were employed at first, the old non-durable paint ahead of him begins to deteriorate long before he can cover it with the new durable paint. So Fitch, much embarrassed that he did not foresee this, leads an army of 1,800 temporary painters up on to the bridge for a day. They aim to finish the first durable coat so that Albert can begin again, painting durable over durable. But the army of temporary painters, all marching in step and whistling 'Colonel Bogey', proves too much for the bridge, which collapses, bringing Albert, Fraser, Fitch and the 1,800 abruptly down to earth.

'Professional Foul': Humanizing the Framework

Professional Foul, commissioned by the BBC, was Stoppard's sixth television play, but his first real success in this medium. It won the British Television Critics' award for the best play of 1977, and Peter Barkworth, who played Professor Anderson, was named best television actor of the year.

The play is a savage indictment of Czechoslovakia's repressive regime. The degree of political commitment took many by surprise. While Stoppard's earlier plays are, as I argue, all 'committed' to the extent that they advocate immersion in the 'destructive element' (life's 'mystery') rather than a recourse to closed 'clockwork' systems, they provide no obvious evidence of any specific political involvement. Even *Travesties*, in which Lenin plays a principal role, is something much grander than a mere political play. Indeed, as he explained to Janet Watts and others, Stoppard used to be extremely sceptical about the possibility of political art. But *Professional Foul* obviously heralds a change of mind, to which *Every Good Boy Deserves Favour*, *Night and Day* and *Cahoot's Macbeth* bear further witness.

Beneath the more polemical surface of these plays, however, 'mystery' and 'clockwork' continue to do battle. Indeed in *Every Good Boy Deserves Favour* the conflict is as absolute and clear-cut as ever it was; 'clockwork' communists confront 'mysterious' dissidents, and young Sacha eventually finds himself straddling the gap between the two. But in *Professional Foul* and *Night and Day* the characters are less exaggerated, more human than in his earlier works, so that there is a sort of melting-pot of ordinary mortality in which 'mystery' and 'clockwork' may interact. In fact this realistic approach dates back to *Artist Descending a Staircase* (1972), a much underrated radio play (see Appendix I).

It is obvious at once that *Professional Foul* is a more crowded work than any we have analysed so far. The big cast provides Stoppard with an opportunity to examine subtle gradations of 'mystery' and 'clockwork'. Thus, whereas *Albert's Bridge* depicted just two 'clockwork' systems (Fitch's and Albert's), both equally mechanical, *Professional Foul* contains at least five systems, each of which has its own peculiar quantity and quality of 'clockwork'. These five can be roughly classified into three groups. Firstly, there is a pair of philosophical arguments: Stone's abstract demonstration of the necessary ambiguity of language, and McKendrick's rather similar case for the ambiguity of moral principles. Secondly, there is a pair of inflexible codes: the rules of football and the laws of Czechoslovakia. Lastly, there is Hollar's insistence, which is finally taken up by Anderson, on the inalienable rights of the individual.

These different abstractions are disposed of in different ways. Stone's is simply unnecessary, since experience, in the form of the interpreters' difficulties with his paper, the misunderstandings which mark Anderson's dealings with the Czech police at Pavel Hollar's apartment, and the argument between Stone and the Frenchman at the dinner-table, speaks louder than his obscure logic on the subject. McKendrick's attempt to apply catastrophe theory to ethics is similarly irrelevant, since the argument means nothing until it is put into practice, and when Anderson does put McKendrick's logic into practice by abandoning his loyalty to his hosts (the Czechs) and smuggling out a subversive document in McKendrick's bag, McKendrick is outraged:

ANDERSON: . . . I'm afraid I reversed a principle . . .
MCKENDRICK: You utter bastard.
ANDERSON: I thought you would approve.
MCKENDRICK: Don't get clever with me . . .

Stone and McKendrick are in effect contained by a play-within-the-play (the *Colloquium Philosophicum*) and their attitudes are as rigid and artificial as those of all Stoppard's other players.★

The rules of football are of more use than the logic of either Stone or McKendrick. They are designed for a practical purpose, and when Broadbent challenges them by perpetrat-

★For a summary of the significance of the play-within-the-play in Stoppard see the opening of Chapter 9.

ing a 'professional foul' on Deml he gains nothing, since the Czechs score from the resultant penalty. No real obloquy seems to attach itself to Broadbent, however; here as else-where the play endorses what McKendrick scornfully calls 'utilitarian values' and 'acts of expediency'.

At the very moment when Broadbent's misdemeanour occurs the Czech police are busy carrying out a 'professional foul' of a different kind on the dissident, Pavel Hollar. They plant foreign currency in his apartment in order to give themselves a pretext on which to arrest him. This foul, of course, is to be deplored, as are the laws of Czechoslovakia. These laws may look logically akin to the rules of football, but whereas the latter, like the artificial logic of the players' world in *Rosencrantz and Guildenstern,* are designed exclusive-ly for role-players and may therefore be as inflexible as the role in question, the former have to embrace real people, and must therefore be flexible enough to accommodate the rights of the individual from which, as Hollar insists and Anderson comes to recognize, they ultimately derive.

It is the fifth category of 'clockwork' that is the most important and the most interesting. In fact the arguments of Pavel Hollar, which Anderson repeats in his improvised and curtailed address to the *Colloquium Philosophicum* near the end of the play, are not really 'clockwork' at all but 'mystery' masquerading as 'clockwork'. Both characters champion the inalienable rights of the individual and, for all the philo-sophical jargon with which Hollar and (more noticeably) Anderson invest them, there is ultimately no attempt to deny that these rights are merely 'fictions acting as incentives to the adoption of practical values'. The point is thrice made that the best guide to the nature of the real rights of man is not some abstract theory but the instinct of a child. The abstractions of Hollar and Anderson are just systematizations of the practical values, the utilitarianism (for Anderson is the J. S. *Mill* Professor of Ethics), the 'acts of expediency', the 'yob ethics', the desire for 'tits and bums' as well as for higher civilization, and the preference for football over philosophi-cal discourse that our instincts recommend to us.

Hollar and Anderson are, in the last analysis, realists no less than Moon. But they put a braver face on their realism in order to join battle with the 'clockwork' enemy. The result is drama of a much more intensive kind than is to be found in, say, *Enter a Free Man* or *Albert's Bridge*. For the same reason *Jumpers* and *Travesties* prove ultimately more engaging than *Rosencrantz and Guildenstern Are Dead*. George Moore and Lenin, like Hollar and Anderson, are essentially just ordinary men—Stoppard told Amory that George might equally well have been a playwright or a vicar—striving to dignify their native intuitions with a logical facade. Guthrie in *Night and Day* is a similar figure but he is not developed to anything like the same extent and the play suffers as a result.

The way these characters twist and turn in their attempts to justify their beliefs contributes much humour to the plays but it is always the rich humour of comedy rather than the cold, clear humour of farce. Indeed, considerable pathos is generated from time to time. Anderson is one of the most engaging characters in this group, though he looks very unpromising to begin with—an Oxbridge don with a scholastic air, a somewhat fastidious appearance and a fear of flying, who is acutely embarrassed when he is discovered reading a girlie magazine and again when he becomes the object of Hollar's personal appeals (from which he escapes into abstract theorizing). McKendrick, described as 'a rougher sort of diamond', who writes articles for girlie magazines and who claims to be 'empirical', looks a much more promising specimen. But first appearances prove deceptive, and the moulding of a flexible hero from such unpromising material gives considerable impact to the play.

I hope that the limits and co-ordinates of the following discussion are now clear. In every play we shall be looking for a clash between 'mystery' and 'clockwork', but we shall expect this clash to become more subtle and dramatic—less obvious and masque-like—as time goes by.

2 Enter a Free Man
Enter a Chained Playwright

Stoppard sketched the early stages of his career as a play-wright in 'The Definite Maybe', a whimsical little article published in Volume 78 of *The Author* (1967). He records that in 1958 he began a piece for *The Observer*'s drama competition, but it 'petered out after a dozen pages that were not unlike *Look Back in Anger*'. Then in 1960 he completed a play which he called *A Walk on the Water*. There was talk of a London season in 1962 but nothing came of it and the play (somewhat adapted) was eventually premièred on television late in 1963. It was staged for the first time in 1964, not in England, however, but in Hamburg, where it was received with some hostility. Back in England it was televised again (in 1964) as *The Preservation of George Riley*, and then, after another false alarm in 1966, it finally reached the stage in 1968 under a new title: *Enter a Free Man*. By this time *Rosencrantz and Guildenstern Are Dead* was firmly ensconced in the National Theatre repertoire, Stoppard's version of Mrozek's *Tango* had completed its season at the Aldwych, and *The Real Inspector Hound* was scheduled for performance at the Criterion.

Each time there was a prospect of performance Stoppard tinkered with the text of *Enter a Free Man* and so it might be argued that the published version, which was prepared for the 1968 season, should be regarded not as his first stage play but as his fourth, or even his fifth if one counts *The Gamblers*—'a one-acter not unlike *Waiting for Godot*' that was written shortly after the first draft of *A Walk on the Water* and was staged by amateurs in Bristol in 1965. Stoppard told Giles Gordon, however, that the 1968 text of *Enter a Free Man* was 'basically the play I wrote in 1960', and the tentative way in which the clash between 'mystery' and 'clockwork' is handled confirms that it is essentially an apprentice piece.

The play focusses on an ordinary man, George Riley, his ordinary daughter, Linda, and their extraordinary dreams. Linda dreams of a 'fair-y prrince', a 'knight in sil-ver arm-our', a '*sheek* . . . dark and handsome and love-lay'. In the first act she believes that her hero has at last arrived:

> *We-ell*, I was in the desert one day, you see, and all of a sudden, before I knew *where* I was, I heard the thunder of horsepower and a strong brown arm *scooped* me up and as we roared into the sunset he co-vered me with burn-ing kiss-es and put me on his pillion!

In fact Linda has merely encountered a rather shady young man at the fancy goods counter in Woolworths where she works but like most of Stoppard's 'clockwork' characters she prefers to eschew reality in favour of a play- (or in this case a Rudolf Valentino film-) within-the-play. Even when life breaks in upon her dreams she contrives to keep it at a distance by clinging close to her beloved radio.

The particular disillusionment that awaits Linda is the discovery that her motorcycle knight is already married. Moreover, he has given her a false name; the extent of her delusion is established above all by her pathetic admission, 'I didn't even know his name'.

Linda's father dreams of being a free man. At one level it is domestic freedom that he craves; like Albert he wants to leave his wife and daughter but he cannot afford to do so because his sole income is the pocket-money that Linda gives him every weekend. But this desire for domestic freedom is not the be-all and end-all; George wants this limited freedom in order to be able to pursue a greater one—the freedom to plant his 'footprints, footprints that will never be erased' on some 'uncharted untrod path'. For George fancies himself as an inventor. When the play opens he already has a number of useless inventions to his credit, such as a device for producing indoor rain, which also produces indoor thunderstorms; a bottle-opener for which the appropriate bottle-tops have yet to be invented; and a pipe that will never go out as long as it is smoked upside down. A fourth invention, which stands somewhat apart from the others because it has no pretensions to usefulness, is a clock. It plays 'Rule Britannia!' instead of

striking twelve. Like so many of Stoppard's characters,
George is associated quite literally with 'clockwork'.

The problem with all George's inventions (except perhaps
the clock) is that they are impractical. Or, to put it the other
way round, George is too theoretical, too philosophical. He
likes to quote Descartes and Rousseau, and to think of
himself as someone removed from life,

> . . . with home as a little boat, anchored in the middle of
> a big, calm sea, never going anywhere, just sitting, far
> from land, life.

His resistance to reality extends to the point of giving his
friends new names for purely aesthetic reasons. Thus Constance, Richard and Victor become Persephone, Able and
Carmen respectively. Conversely he anathematizes sport,
which for Stoppard is typically an activity undertaken only
by down-to-earth realists.

The play probes George's propensity for abstraction by
tracing the fate of an invention so simple that it comes to
symbolize the very quintessence of 'clockwork' abstract
thought. The absolute *simplicity* of George's re-usable envelope is stressed throughout the play. But ultimately, of
course, it proves to be absolutely impracticable as well. The
indoor rain machine does work up to a point; a pipe *can* be
smoked upside-down; bottle-tops might be invented to fit
George's bottle-opener; but a ripped envelope is altogether
beyond redemption.

The idea is finally exploded by a character called Harry,
whom George had hoped to make his partner in the re-usable
envelope business. Harry is an attractive rogue comparable to
Linda's 'fair-y prrince' (though he prefers horses to motor-
bikes), and the parallel between the respective predicaments
of father and daughter is consolidated when George is
reminded that, despite his high hopes of Harry, he 'didn't
even know his name . . .' (The fact that Linda is George's
chief critic and vice versa constitutes another link between
the two plots.)

The two types of 'clockwork' that Stoppard explodes in
Enter a Free Man come up for explosion again and again in the
later plays. Linda's romantic version anticipates the philanderings of Birdboot in *The Real Inspector Hound*, the

dreams of Ruth in *Night and Day*, and Henry in *The Real Thing*; and it is not too far removed from either Dotty's romantic yearnings in *Jumpers* or the MPs' lust for Maddie in *Dirty Linen*. George's philosophical version, on the other hand, looks towards Joyce and Tzara in *Travesties*, Archie in *Jumpers*, Stone and McKendrick in *Professional Foul*, the orthodox Russians in *Every Good Boy Deserves Favour*, the Czechs in *Cahoot's Macbeth*, Albert in *Albert's Bridge*, the Post Office in *If You're Glad I'll be Frank*, Moon in *The Real Inspector Hound* and even the Player in *Rosencrantz and Guildenstern Are Dead*. Incidentally, the lack of proportion between these two lists indicates the relative unimportance of love, sex and marriage in Stoppard's work. Hound, who, after turning critic in the latter stages of *The Real Inspector Hound*, inveighs against 'the shower of filth and sexual allusion foisted on to an unsuspecting public in the guise of modernity at all costs', would approve.

In many ways, then, *Enter a Free Man* anticipates the shape of things to come. In one important respect, however, it does not.

According to Stoppard (who is almost as critical of this play as Shaw was of his first effort: *Widowers' Houses*) it is the characterization that is at fault. He confessed to Hayman that he lacked any 'mental acquaintance with the characters . . . they're only real because I've seen them in other people's plays. I haven't actually met any of them myself'.

Stoppard acknowledges a special debt to Arthur Miller's *Death of a Salesman* and Robert Bolt's *Flowering Cherry* (which itself leans heavily on *Death of a Salesman*). A number of other influences have been suggested—Peter Shaffer, Peter Nichols, Ionesco, N. F. Simpson and Lewis Carroll (by Kerensky), Ibsen's *Wild Duck* (by Hayman), and Tony Hancock (by Hunter)—and it seems to me that another play by Miller, *A View From the Bridge*, might be added to the list. The relationship between Linda and her motor-cyclist is very like the affair between Miller's Catherine and Rudolpho, and George Riley's disapproval is in some ways similar to, if much less intense than, Eddie's. I would suggest that *Death of a Salesman* provided the basis for Stoppard's main plot (George's story) while *A View From the Bridge* suggested the subplot (Linda's story). *Flowering Cherry* showed how these two plots might be interwoven. Like *Enter a Free Man* it depicts in parallel the self-deceptions of a father and his daughter, although Bolt gives less attention to his daughter figure than Stoppard does.

All this derivativeness does indeed reduce the impact of the play. Still more damaging, however, is the discrepancy that arises from the fact that Stoppard furnished a comedy with materials lifted out of tragedies. One of the chief ways in which tragedy is usually said to differ from comedy is in the complexity of its characterization. We need to be able to feel for a tragic hero like Willy Loman at the same time as we recognize and criticize his mistakes. On the other hand, comedy (and, to an even greater extent, farce, towards which Stoppard's comedies always tend), normally employs flat characters or types, who can be unequivocally punished or rewarded at the end of the play.

Now when Stoppard turned the romantic, pastoral dreams of Cherry and Willie into the cerebral speculations of George Riley he propelled his central character into the simpler world of comedy. George's crazy ideas can never be affecting in the way that Cherry's and Willie's are. But at the same time Stoppard tried to retain for George the kind of 'tattered dignity' that characterizes his tragic prototypes. So we are asked to sympathize with George at the same time as we deride him. The discrepancy becomes fully apparent at the end of the play, where Stoppard very obviously fudges his final verdict on George and Linda. At first Linda seems sadder and altogether wiser as a result of her experience but then she comes out with this remark about the policeman who told her that her boyfriend was married: 'Nice policeman he was. Brown eyes. I could go for him'. And George, though he agrees to go to the Labour Exchange and seek a real job, still feels that he was 'meant to be an inventor'. This ambivalence is underscored elsewhere in the text. Constance, alias Persephone, encourages George's fantasies. Apparently she believes that journeys into the underworld of dreams are necessary to mitigate the harshness of reality. And, for all her murmurings against her father, Linda seems to feel this too; in fact she makes the point more explicitly and more memorably than Persephone ever does:

> There's two of everyone. You see, you need that . . .

and if the two of him's the same, I mean if he's the same
in the pub as he is with us, then he's had it.

This is a curious speech. It sounds authoritative and it gains
further impact from the fact that it is repeated when Act I
returns to the point at which it began. On the other hand,
Linda has a vested interest in the sort of double life that she
defends here, and it is significant that she does not repeat
these ideas after her disillusionment in Act II. Even more
significant perhaps is the fact that two independent observers
deny the need for a double life; Able feels lost and wants to
get back to his ship, while Florence thinks that it is too late to
run away on romantic odysseys to exotic places like South
America.

In fact I wonder if Linda's 'two of everyone' speech really
means very much. Why should there be just *two* of everyone
rather than three or five or seventy-six? Stoppard seems to
have asked himself this question before proceeding to
another play. His subsequent heroes are so complex, so
unsure of themselves that their beliefs—and even identities—
remain shrouded in 'mystery'. At the same time Stoppard
takes care to distinguish between these muddled but very
human characters and their single-minded 'clockwork' antagonists.

In *Enter a Free Man* he fails to make this distinction. George
and Linda are basically single-minded like the later villains,
but on to their 'clockwork' is grafted a crude semblance of
complexity. The suggestion of complexity is enough to stop
us from laughing dismissively at their crazy dreams but it is
so patently factitious that our sympathy is also inhibited.
Thus George and Linda combine elements of what will
become the Stoppard hero and the Stoppard villain, and the
play as a whole ends up as an uneasy compromise between
the tragedies on which it is based and the comedies towards
which Stoppard's genius quickly led him.

3 Rosencrantz and Guildenstern Are Dead
The Spectator as Hero

Although *Rosencrantz and Guildenstern Are Dead* is still perhaps Stoppard's best-known, most-performed and most-studied play, a surprising number of critics continue to echo Andrew Kennedy's complaint, in 'Old and New in London Now', that 'there is something forced and jejune about much of the overt rhetoric of ideas' which it contains.

Not all have proceeded to dismiss the play as brusquely as Robert Brustein; a sizeable contingent has tried to salvage it as a specimen of what Normand Berlin calls 'Theatre of Criticism'. They argue that it is a play about other plays—those of Beckett, Albee, Genet, Osborne, Pinter, Pirandello, (and James Saunders surely, although this debt has never been properly investigated), as well as Shakespeare—rather than a direct comment on life. Perhaps. Certainly Stoppard throws around the vocabulary of modernism in a highly self-conscious fashion. But although the overt themes of the play may look derivative, forced and jejune on the page, I have always found them effective and even moving in the theatre, where subtlety is not always a virtue. Moreover, I cannot go along with the suggestion that these themes are communicated by sheer rhetoric; on the contrary, I believe that Stoppard has contrived a very sophisticated dramatic structure for the articulation of his ideas.

It is clear at a glance that Stoppard's play turns Shakespeare's inside out, so that, in the Player's words, we see 'on stage the things that are supposed to happen off'. Thus the exits marked for Rosencrantz and Guildenstern in *Hamlet* become exits for all the other characters in Stoppard. Now at one level this obviously constitutes a simple technical device for putting Rosencrantz and Guildenstern in Hamlet's place at the centre of the play so that the action of *Hamlet* can be seen in a different perspective. As Harold Hobson explained in his article, 'Tom Stoppard—Master of Dramatic Invention' (*The Christchurch Press*, 3 May, 1977):

> Shakespeare looked at the matter from Hamlet's viewpoint, with the Prince in the centre and everything revolving round him. How would these events appear to someone not at their centre, but on the periphery; someone such as Guildenstern or Rosencrantz? This is the question that Stoppard answers. To Rosencrantz and Guildenstern what happens in Shakespeare's play seems totally baffling and incomprehensible.

This is certainly part of the story, but it rather implies that Stoppard tinkered, albeit ingeniously, with an established dramatic masterpiece for no better reason than that 'it was there'. I hope to show that the play is based upon a much more substantial foundation than this, and that the inversion of the *Hamlet* action is merely a symptom of a thoroughgoing inversion of conventional assumptions about life.

These profounder concerns are immediately suggested by the fact that not all the occasions on which Stoppard has inverted *Hamlet* can be explained by the desire to substitute Rosencrantz and Guildenstern for Hamlet at the centre of the action. Why *show* us 'Hamlet, with his doublet all unbraced . . .' instead of having Ophelia describe him in this guise? (And, indeed, why include the episode at all—or any of the episodes from *Hamlet* in which Rosencrantz and Guildenstern play no part?) Similarly, why turn 'To be or not to be' from speech to mime? And why have Hamlet retreating from Polonius during the 'crab' speech instead of vice versa, which is the conventional arrangement? These subsidiary inversions are designed, I think, to provide tangible support for the play's basic theme, which is that modern life requires an inversion of the assumptions which, in Stoppard's view at any rate, underlie *Hamlet*.

The key to Stoppard's play seems to me to lie in the recognition of a hard-and-fast distinction between the world of Rosencrantz and Guildenstern and the world of the players-within-the-play, i.e. the Tragedians and the *Hamlet* cast. Let us, for reasons which will presently appear, begin by ignoring the Player, Alfred and the rest of their troupe, and concentrate on Rosencrantz and Guildenstern, on the one

hand, and the *Hamlet* cast, on the other. There seem
to be no points of contact whatever between them. Even
when Rosencrantz and Guildenstern are supposed to be
involved in the *Hamlet* action Stoppard has contrived to make
them look completely detached from the other characters'
business. Thus, in the middle of Act II, when Stoppard
depicts the discussion between Claudius, Gertrude, Rosencrantz and Guildenstern that occupies the early part of Act
III, Scene 1 in *Hamlet*, he keeps Guildenstern apart from the
others for as long as he can and, more importantly, turns
Rosencrantz's responses to Gertrude's questions into deliber-
ate untruths. Rosencrantz lies again (in Stoppard but not in
Shakespeare) over the matter of Hamlet's arrest following the
murder of Polonius, and it is clear that in Stoppard Hamlet is
captured *in spite of* Rosencrantz and Guildenstern's endeavours rather than because of them. The *Hamlet* action
seems to go its own way under its own momentum, while
Rosencrantz and Guildenstern stand about on the fringes,
more like spectators than participants.

It is, I surmise, in order to emphasize their role as
spectators that Stoppard has incorporated into his play scenes
from *Hamlet* in which Rosencrantz and Guildenstern are
spectators pure and simple. Time and again we find them
downstage, observing the scenes from *Hamlet* which are
going on upstage. At times they express their awareness of
the passive role they are playing: 'I feel like a spectator', says
Rosencrantz late in Act I. At other times they put this
awareness to spectacular effect: 'Next!' shouts Rosencrantz in
Act II, presumably imitating a director auditioning actors—a
role more obviously assumed by Guildenstern much earlier,
when he tells the miserable Alfred, 'We'll let you know'. All
this seems to suggest that Stoppard regards Rosencrantz and
Guildenstern as an extension of the audience. The pair deliver
many of their speeches directly to the audience, the most
spectacular case in point occurring in Act II when Rosencrantz yells, 'Fire!' at the audience and, when they don't
move, observes contemptuously: 'They should burn to death
in their shoes'. The published text is designed for performance in theatres with a proscenium arch and footlights; in
more adaptable spaces I imagine Stoppard would approve if
Rosencrantz and Guildenstern were to mingle with the

audience on occasions, just as Moon and Birdboot do in *The Real Inspector Hound*.

This brings us back to the point that Rosencrantz and Guildenstern, on the one hand, and the cast of *Hamlet*, on the other, are strictly juxtaposed. Rosencrantz and Guildenstern are portrayed as an extension of the audience and therefore as 'real' people; the *Hamlet* characters, by virtue of the onstage audience (added to the offstage one), are made to appear all the more stagey, 'clockwork' and 'unreal'. It is noteworthy that on the one occasion when Hamlet tries to communicate with the audience he fails to penetrate the invisible fourth wall of the conventional stage:

> HAMLET *comes down to the footlights and regards the audience.*
> *The others watch but don't speak.* HAMLET *clears his throat*
> *noisily and spits into the audience. A split second later he claps*
> *his hand to his eye and wipes himself. He goes back upstage.*

The conversion of 'To be or not to be' from speech to mime robs Hamlet of another chance to communicate directly with his audience.

With this distinction in mind let us examine these two sets of characters in more depth. The world of Rosencrantz and Guildenstern is manifestly bizarre; absurdity permeates both their voluntary activities (spinning coins, playing word-games, establishing the points of the compass and the time of day) and their involuntary ones (muddling their names, tripping over words, losing their trousers). Beneath this Beckettian veneer lie the customary Beckettian problems. Somewhat arbitrarily perhaps, I tend to isolate three of them, all of which gain in intensity as the play proceeds. First there is the problem of comprehending a world devoid of essence. Guildenstern begins bravely by attempting to use syllogisms to deduce the nature of his situation from *a priori* premises. But his efforts produce meaningless results:

> Syllogism the second: one, probability is a factor which operates within natural forces. Two, probability is not operating as a factor. Three, we are now within un-, sub- or supernatural forces. Discuss . . . Now—counter to the previous syllogism: tricky one, follow me carefully, it may prove a comfort. If we postulate, and we just have, that within un-, sub-, or supernatural forces *the probability is* that the law of probability will not

operate as a factor, then we must accept that the
probability of the first part will not operate as a factor,
in which case the law of probability *will* operate as a
factor within un-, sub- or supernatural forces. And since
it obviously hasn't been doing so, we can take it that we
are not held within un-, sub- or supernatural forces after
all; in all probability, that is . . .

So deduction proves fruitless and we soon find that it has
given way to induction in the form of 'pragmatism' and
learning 'by experience'. This obviously represents a decline
of confidence. This process culminates in the abandonment
of the attempt to understand early in Act III:

> I've lost all capacity for disbelief. I'm not sure that I
> could even rise to a little gentle scepticism.

Hereafter the two are reduced to desperate appeals: 'What
for?', 'What's it all about?', 'But why?' and 'We've done
nothing wrong!'. Ultimately, then, Rosencrantz and Guildenstern's situation proves to be incomprehensible. They are
in the alarming situation of the two men who see the
unicorn, and this is not far removed from the dilemma of the
celebrated 'Chinaman of the T'ang Dynasty' who 'dreamed
he was a butterfly, and from that moment . . . was never
quite sure that he was not a butterfly dreaming it was a
Chinese philosopher'. In this context, where there are no
answers, the game of questions that they love to play begins
to look extremely apt as well as amusing.

Rosencrantz and Guildenstern cannot understand their
predicament, nor can they control it. Their attempts to do so
constitute the second of the serious issues which seem to me
to underlie the play's trivial veneer. The coin-tossing episode
provides Guildenstern with an early indication that 'the
fortuitous and the ordained' are no longer 'related . . . into a
reassuring union which we recognized as nature'. Nevertheless, he is capable of speculating a few moments later that the
encounter with the Tragedians may have been dictated by
chance rather than fate. And even when his conviction of an
ineluctable destiny becomes stronger towards the end of Act
I he is prepared to regard the prospect with equanimity:

> There's a logic at work—it's all done for you, don't
> worry. Enjoy it. Relax. To be taken in hand and led,
> like being a child again, even without the innocence, a

child—It's like being given a prize, an extra slice of
childhood when you least expect it, as a prize for being
good . . .

Early in Act II Guildenstern is still capable of some optim-
ism, though the logic of the first sentence rather undercuts
that of the third and fourth in this speech:

> Wheels have been set in motion, and they have their
> own pace, to which we are . . . condemned. Each move
> is dictated by the previous one—that is the meaning of
> order. If we start being arbitrary it'll just be a shambles:
> at least, let us hope so. Because if we happened, just
> happened to discover, or even suspect, that our spon-
> taneity was part of their order, we'd know that we were
> lost.

But later in this scene even Rosencrantz is conscious of his
lack of free will:

> We have no control. None at all . . . for all the
> compasses in the world, there's only one direction, and
> time is its only measure.

At the beginning of Act III, when the pair find themselves on
a boat, apparently free from the shackles of the court and the
world of *Hamlet*, they experience a brief upsurge of confidence:

> GUIL: One is free on a boat. . . . Free to move, speak,
> extemporize . . .

But this moment of hope is succeeded at once by an even
deeper sense of doom. Guildenstern remembers that they
'have not been cut loose' from *Hamlet*; they 'are taking
Hamlet to England'. And Rosencrantz comes up to report
that Hamlet is indeed on board the ship. So Guildenstern is
forced to conclude that,

> Our truancy is defined by one fixed star, and our drift
> represents merely a slight change of angle to it . . .

Somewhat later he betrays an even deeper pessimism:

> We've travelled too far, and our momentum has taken
> over; we move idly towards eternity, without possibility
> of reprieve or hope of explanation . . . Where we went
> wrong was getting on a boat. We can move, of course,
> change direction, rattle about, but our movement is
> contained within a larger one that carries us along as
> inexorably as the wind and current . . .

It is at this point, when Guildenstern's awareness of their predicament is at its most profound, that he makes a supreme final effort to defy the logic containing them by performing a spontaneous act designed to prove that he is still 'Free to move, speak, extemporize . . .' In a gesture obviously akin to Moon's attempt to blow up London with his bomb (and reminiscent also of Mathieu's more effective defiance of the existential dilemma at the end of Sartre's *Roads to Freedom*) he stabs the Player and triumphantly refutes the notion of an ordaining destiny:

> If we have a destiny, then so had he—and if this is ours, then that was his—and if there are no explanations for us, then let there be none for him.

But it was a trick dagger—just as Moon's bomb was a trick bomb—and the Player rises to his feet again to destroy Guildenstern's last illusion of freedom.

Once they have lost their free will, Rosencrantz and Guildenstern must inevitably die for that is what happens to them in *Hamlet*. And the third great problem they have to grapple with in Stoppard's play concerns the nature and significance of death. Again there is an important progression in their attitudes. In Act I death is a subject for frivolous disquisition: Rosencrantz wonders why 'the fingernails grow after death, as does the beard'. Rosencrantz's treatment of death in Act II is even sillier, but this time his intentions seem to be serious, and Guildenstern adds a chilling afterword:

> Death followed by eternity . . . the worst of both worlds. It *is* a terrible thought.

He supplements this reflection with an impassioned debunking of the stage-deaths depicted in the dress-rehearsal of 'The Mousetrap':

> No, no, no . . . you've got it all wrong . . . you can't act death. The *fact* of it is nothing to do with seeing it happen—it's not gasps and blood and falling about—that isn't what makes it death. It's just a man failing to reappear, that's all—now you see him, now you don't, that's the only thing that's real: here one minute and gone the next and never coming back—an exit, unobtrusive and unannounced, a disappearance gathering weight as it goes on, until, finally, it is heavy with death.

At the end of the play Guildenstern reacts similarly with less passion, as befits his reduced circumstances, but still with 'an edge of impatience', to another spate of 'romantic' stage-deaths, and then proceeds to act out his own definition:

> Well, we'll know better next time. Now you see me, now you—
> [*And disappears*]

To Rosencrantz and, more particularly, Guildenstern, death is no more meaningful than life; it is simply the negation of existence—*l'être et le néant,* nothing more. Thus through the experience of Rosencrantz and Guildenstern Stoppard conveys to his audience these themes, all of them commonplace in the literature of existentialism: that life is a 'mystery' which can be neither understood nor controlled; and that death, far from being imbued with romance and significance, is mere negation—the absence of existence.

In the juxtaposed 'stage' world of *Hamlet* things are, of course, quite different. All the characters seem to know what they are doing and they do it completely and efficiently, notwithstanding the obstacles which Rosencrantz and Guildenstern put in their way from time to time. This applies to their deaths no less than to their lives; the final holocaust, as depicted by the Players is full of expression and meaning, and in the speech with which (in the revised second edition) Stoppard concludes his play Horatio is able to give a satisfactory explanation of each death.

There are in the play several explicit and even spectacular demonstrations of the coherence of the *Hamlet* world *vis à vis* the shambles of Rosencrantz and Guildenstern's. Here is one of the more explicit ones. Guildenstern is reacting to a scene from *Hamlet* which the pair have just witnessed:

> And yet it doesn't seem enough; *to have breathed such significance.* Can that be all? And why us?—anybody would have done. *And we have contributed nothing.* (my emphasis)

Now for an example that is more spectacular than explicit. Late in Act I Rosencrantz and Guildenstern, after a series of unsuccessful attempts, suddenly get their names right at the very moment when Hamlet crosses the stage. But as soon as he disappears the old confusion returns. Coherence is evidently dependent on the presence of some member of the *Hamlet* cast. Likewise, in Act I the run of 'heads' ceases, and the law of probability reasserts itself, simultaneously with the commencement of the *Hamlet* action. And in Act III the appearance of Hamlet from behind his umbrella seems to be the factor which enables Rosencrantz to give a suddenly lucid summary of their situation.

Thus the worlds of Rosencrantz and Guildenstern on the one hand, and the cast of *Hamlet* on the other, are juxtaposed in much the same way as the worlds of Moon and Malquist in Stoppard's novel. There is, however, a slight fuzziness about the juxtaposition in the play. I have argued that Rosencrantz and Guildenstern are, like Beckett's Vladimir and Estragon, whom they so much resemble, Everyman figures whose predicament epitomizes the existential dilemma common to modern man. Their involvement in *Hamlet* is the factor which sharpens the outlines of this dilemma. Guildenstern seems to see things this way when he remarks:

> All your life you live so close to truth, it becomes a permanent blur in the corner of your eye, and when something nudges it into outline it is like being ambushed by a grotesque. A man standing in his saddle in the half-lit half-alive dawn banged on the shutters and called two names . . .

The summons to enter the world of *Hamlet* was the factor which nudged truth into outline.

It is possible, however, to see Rosencrantz and Guildenstern's situation in a much more particular light. According to this interpretation they may once have been ordinary, 'real' people like the audience, but from the moment when they are summoned to Claudius's court they come under an extraordinary spell which divorces them from the audience (who are thus enabled to laugh at them more freely than I should like to think possible).

In the most cogent analysis of the play that I have yet encountered, Jonathan Bennett insists that Rosencrantz and Guildenstern, far from representing mankind in general, remain the peculiar 'nobodies' that Shakespeare created. Bennett, whose discipline is philosophy, would, I imagine, be quick to point out that my reading of the play is illogical in that the force which confronts and ultimately subdues Rosencrantz and Guildenstern is not the 'mystery' of life but the 'clockwork' of *Hamlet*. What overtakes them at the end of the play is not so much 'real' death as absorption into the world of the play-within-the-play. When Guildenstern complains that he has 'lost all capacity for disbelief' he is not just confessing that he has ceased trying to understand his predicament but, perhaps more obviously, consenting to the 'willing suspension of disbelief' that is supposed to characterize orthodox playgoers. And when he disappears with the exclamation, 'Now you see me, now you [don't]' he may be using a phrase which he has associated with 'real' death, but the phrase itself is a very artificial one, drawn from the parlance of conjurors and magicians. In short, Rosencrantz and Guildenstern, while they may have been 'real' people before the banging on the shutters, are, or quickly become, 'clockwork' characters in the course of the play. They are more like the Moon of *The Real Inspector Hound* than the Moon of Stoppard's novel.

While conceding the logic of this interpretation, I obstinately prefer to remain illogical. I *feel* for Rosencrantz and Guildenstern just as I feel for Vladimir and Estragon, and indeed for Hamlet, that most 'existential' of Shakespeare's heroes. In addition to the evidence already cited for my case let me just add a further observation about the ending of the play. As originally written (and published in the first Faber edition) it features a new Rosencrantz and Guildenstern (the two Ambassadors), who are as puzzled as their predecessors about what has happened in *Hamlet*; and offstage we, and they, hear more banging on shutters and calling of names. Clearly the whole business is about to happen over again. This indicates that the experience of Rosencrantz and Guildenstern was *not* peculiar. Stoppard suppressed this ending, of course, but I think that the logic which dictated it remains in the revised version.

Having thus salvaged the notion of a masque-like juxtaposition of 'mystery' (Rosencrantz and Guildenstern) and 'clockwork' (the *Hamlet* cast), we can now turn to the Tragedians, who straddle the gap between these two worlds in the manner of Fraser in *Albert's Bridge*.

At first the Tragedians seem to inhabit the same world as Rosencrantz and Guildenstern. They get involved in the absurd coin-spinning, complain that they have no control, and join in the empty speculation about chance and fate. With this 'existential' attitude goes an inverted form of theatre:

> We keep to our usual stuff, more or less, only inside out. We do on stage the things that are supposed to happen off. Which is a kind of integrity, if you look on every exit being an entrance somewhere else.

They are prepared to portray *flagrante delicto* and they even countenance audience participation. All this goes under the title of realism. And since Rosencrantz and Guildenstern too are doing on stage the things that are supposed to happen off—in *Hamlet*—this passage provides another reason for considering them as 'real' characters. But soon the Tragedians' style changes. Guildenstern persuades them to present an orthodox play rather than one of their inverted 'performances', and the Player seems suddenly to change from a 'real' person to an actor, 'Always in character', like the *Hamlet* cast. This association with *Hamlet* is immediately cemented when, in place of the expected play by the Tragedians, Stoppard gives us a scene from *Hamlet*. It is as if the Tragedians have been somehow metamorphosed into the cast of *Hamlet*.

This transubstantiation effect is employed again frequently in Acts II and III. A small example is Rosencrantz's mistaking Alfred for Gertrude just before the dress-rehearsal of 'The Mousetrap'. Much more significant is Stoppard's handling of this rehearsal, which forms the centre-piece of his play in much the same way as the final performance forms the centre-piece of Shakespeare's. In extending the play-within-the-play beyond the truncated version given by Shakespeare, Stoppard has turned it into a paraphrase of *Hamlet*. This at once serves to bind the Tragedians all the more firmly into the world of *Hamlet*. Moreover, when, early on, the Player calls, 'Gentlemen! . . . It doesn't seem to be coming. We are not getting it at all . . .' he seems to be alluding not to the rehearsal itself but to the incursions made into it by Hamlet, Ophelia, Claudius and Polonius. Once again the Tragedians and the *Hamlet* cast interweave, and the Player fails to distinguish between them. The intermingling of these two groups culminates in the closing moments of the play. Stoppard's stage directions tell the story:

> ALFRED, *still in his queen's costume, dies by poison: the*

PLAYER, *with rapier, kills the* 'KING' *and duels with a fourth*
TRAGEDIAN, *inflicting and receiving a wound* . . . *Immediate-*
ly the whole stage is lit up, revealing, upstage, arranged in the
approximate positions last held by the dead TRAGEDIANS, *the*
tableau of court and corpses which is the last scene of Hamlet.

I hope it is clear from this account that the Tragedians do not
do what we might reasonably have expected them to do; they
do not shuttle back and forth between the 'mystery' and the
'clockwork' in order to provide common ground for the
'real' characters of Rosencrantz and Guildenstern and the
'artificial' characters of Hamlet and company throughout the
play. Instead, they make one decisive shift, late in Act I, from
the 'real' to the 'artificial'. Thus they are never really in a
position to mediate between the two worlds, and the play is
consequently less dramatic than it might have been. Nevertheless, the Tragedians do serve a number of useful purposes.
Firstly, their abandonment of the world of Rosencrantz and
Guildenstern underscores the intensifying sense of isolation
which the pair feel as the play proceeds. It should be noted
that the full effect of the change in the Tragedians is not felt
until the middle of Act II, which is when Guildenstern is
becoming particularly anxious about the other problems
which I have defined. Secondly, by removing the Tragedians
from the 'real' world of Rosencrantz and Guildenstern Stoppard has not completely deprived himself of a link between
this world and the 'clockwork' world which the Tragedians
now inhabit alongside the cast of *Hamlet*. For although there
is now a *psychological* rift between the Tragedians and the
protagonists, the two groups continue to encounter each
other *physically*, so that, on this level at least, there persists a
sense of drama rather than sheer juxtaposition. In fact one of
the main functions of the Tragedians is to develop the
abstract antithesis between the world of *Hamlet* and the
world of Rosencrantz and Guildenstern into a physical
confrontation full of fear and menace. In Acts II and III the
Tragedians act as surrogates for the *Hamlet* cast—surrogates
who, because of their freedom from a pre-existing
Shakespearean text, can activate or dramatize the clash
between the two worlds. This sense of physical menace first
becomes strong just prior to 'The Mousetrap' rehearsal. The
confrontation between Rosencrantz and the Player here is a

replay of their Act I confrontation, but this time the Player rather than Rosencrantz comes off best, and Rosencrantz emerges hurt and frightened. What follows is even more alarming:

> *He makes a break for an exit. A* TRAGEDIAN *dressed as a* KING *enters.* ROS *recoils, breaks for the opposite wing. Two cloaked* TRAGEDIANS *enter.* ROS *tries again but another* TRAGEDIAN *enters, and* ROS *retires to midstage.*

This note of menace is maintained during the rehearsal, particularly at its climax: the death of the two spies, who are stage replicas of Rosencrantz and Guildenstern. At this point Rosencrantz and Guildenstern are only half-aware of the resemblance between them and the spies and therefore of the threat posed to them by the spies' deaths; but the replay of these deaths in Act III finally convinces them that they are doomed. The context of this replay, incidentally, provides a good example of the way in which Stoppard uses the Tragedians to flesh out the threats posed to Rosencrantz and Guildenstern by the *Hamlet* plot: Rosencrantz and Guildenstern read the death-warrant which Hamlet has prepared for them, and immediately they are threatened physically by the Tragedians:

> *One by one the* PLAYERS *emerge, impossibly, from the barrel, and form a casually menacing circle round* ROS *and* GUIL *who are still appalled and mesmerized.*

The impossibility of this appearance of six people from a single barrel draws attention to the 'unreal', 'clockwork' nature of the Tragedians' world.

So Stoppard uses the Tragedians in *Rosencrantz and Guildenstern Are Dead* to make tangible the forces threatening his protagonists in order to provide a modicum of action in a play which deals largely with the inner man. But a much more important function of the Tragedians is to elucidate the basic clash between the real and the artificial on which the play depends. This task of elucidation begins almost as soon as the Tragedians appear at Claudius's court in Act II. In the midst of his plangent account of the spectatorless perform- ance given in response to Guildenstern's commission in Act I the Player lets slip a crucial definition: 'We're *actors*—we're the opposite of people!' At this point it is the Player who seems to be out of his element, but it very soon becomes apparent that in the world of *Hamlet* it is the 'actors' who are at home and the 'real' people like Rosencrantz and Guildenstern who are lost. Later in Act II this point emerges clearly from an exchange (modelled on a passage early in James Saunders' *Next Time I'll Sing to You*) between Guildenstern and the Player:

> GUIL: But we don't know what's going on, or what to do with ourselves. We don't know how to *act*.
> PLAYER: Act natural . . .

The emphasis on the word 'act' in Guildenstern's speech indicates that Stoppard is still using it in its technical sense; he is maintaining the dichotomy between people and actors. The Player now proceeds to define the kind of world that actors inhabit:

> There's a design at work in all art—surely you know that? Events must play themselves out to aesthetic, moral and logical conclusion [*sic*] . . . we aim at the point where everyone who is marked for death dies.
> . . . It is *written* . . . We follow directions—there is no *choice* involved. The bad end unhappily, the good unluckily. That is what tragedy means.★

This world, unlike the 'real' world of Rosencrantz and Guildenstern, has form and meaning, and death is an accepted part of its design. To be sure, for the Tragedians, as for Rosencrantz and Guildenstern, 'there is no *choice* involved', but in the case of the Tragedians there is a transparent logic behind this lack of choice, and anyway, the death that is ordained for them is only a mock death:

> Do you know what happens to old actors? . . . Nothing. They're still acting.

Guildenstern reacts with derision to this ordered, artificial view of the world, especially to its stylized version of death:

> Actors! The mechanics of cheap melodrama! That isn't *death*! . . . You scream and choke and sink to your

---

★ The Player is, of course, echoing Wilde's Miss Prism, who defines fiction in similar terms early in Act II of *The Importance of Being Earnest*. This is perhaps the point at which to observe that Wilde too was fascinated by Rosencrantz and Guildenstern. Clearly Stoppard's debt to Wilde extends beyond *Travesties*.

knees, but it doesn't bring death home to anyone—it doesn't catch them unawares and start the whisper in their skulls that says—'One day you are going to die.' . . .

This verbal disagreement is bolstered visually by the confrontation between the 'real' Rosencrantz and Guildenstern and their replicas, and particularly by the contrast, here and at the end of Act III, between the 'dramatic' death acted out by the spies and the 'real' death defined by Guildenstern.

This mention of Guildenstern in isolation from Rosencrantz brings me to my last observation about the basic design of this play, which is that the two protagonists are not interchangeable. Rosencrantz's relative obtuseness is indicated by Stoppard in his introductory stage direction:

> The run of 'heads' is impossible, yet ROS betrays no surprise at all—he feels none. However, he is nice enough to feel a little embarrassed at taking so much money off his friend. Let that be his character note.
> GUIL is well alive to the oddity of it. He is not worried about the money, but he is worried by the implications; aware but not going to panic about it—his character note.

That Stoppard maintained this distinction throughout the play is clear enough. Helene Keyssar-Franke sums up the matter thus:

> They are men conceived on an existential pattern, but for Rosencrantz the protest against the loss of hope is a cry in the wind; for Guildenstern it becomes the full tragic perception.

At this point a caveat should be sounded concerning the word 'existential'. Stoppard, notwithstanding an earlier claim, in 'The Definite Maybe', that he was interested in Rosencrantz and Guildenstern as 'existential immortals' (whatever that means) as early as 1964, insisted in 'Ambushes for the Audience' that he—

> . . . didn't know what the word 'existential' meant until it was applied to *Rosencrantz*. And even now [1974] existentialism is not a philosophy I find either attractive or plausible.

Luckily he goes on to say that 'the play can be interpreted in existential terms, as well as in other terms', and most critics have been happy to plump for the existential label.

Of course, it is a trifle ironic that Guildenstern should emerge as an existential hero when several modern critics have applied the same label to Shakespeare's Hamlet. And perhaps Rosencrantz is a little like Shakespeare's Horatio. Stoppard was not unaware of this resemblance, I think; it is probably significant that he made Guildenstern assume the mask of Hamlet in Act I (although there are echoes of Beckett's *Endgame* hereabouts as well). But this kinship between Guildenstern and Hamlet does not mean that the play need never have been written. Stoppard realized that the 'death of tragedy' in our century meant that *Hamlet* had to be redefined. The same urge was felt by other men of the theatre in the 1960's. David Warner played Hamlet as an unheroic alienated young intellectual in Peter Hall's 1965 production for the Royal Shakespeare Company; Nicol Williamson portrayed a very down-to-earth prince at the Round House in 1969 and subsequently on film; and Charles Marowitz went further in producing a *Hamlet* collage with a hero who 'is a slob' and can 'never pull his finger out'. But whereas all these kept more or less to Shakespeare's text, Stoppard pushed the idea to its logical extreme and created an original masterpiece.

4 The Real Inspector Hound
The Dangers of Wish-Fulfilment

In *The Real Inspector Hound*, as in *Rosencrantz and Guildenstern Are Dead*, the distinction between 'mystery' and 'clockwork' is expressed in terms of one set of characters who mirror, in this case quite literally, the audience, and a second set who are actors in a play-within-Stoppard's-play. But this time the protagonists, Moon and Birdboot, move clearly out of reality into abstraction—according to a logic which is likewise clearly defined—and are duly punished. In other words, although *The Real Inspector Hound* is nowhere near as profound a play as *Rosencrantz and Guildenstern Are Dead*, it does have a more clear-cut structure.

Much more explicit is the link between the protagonists and the audience. Stoppard does it with mirrors, although in practice he has been content to dispense with the mirror and simply place Moon and Birdboot in the audience (as I have suggested might be done with Rosencrantz and Guildenstern):

> The first thing is that the audience appear to be confronted by their own reflection in a huge mirror . . . back there in the gloom—not at the footlights—a bank of plush seats and pale smudges of faces. The total effect having been established, it can be progressively faded out as the play goes on, until the front row remains to remind us of the rest and then, finally, merely two seats in that row—one of which is now occupied by MOON.

Moon behaves like any ordinary member of an audience. He jiggles around in his seat, flips through his programme, and then, when he sees Birdboot behind him, indulges in a constrained wave. Birdboot comes down and sits next to Moon in the second of the two seats specified, and now we have some snatches of dialogue which reflect, albeit in exaggerated form, the sort of conversation that two ordinary theatre-goers, or rather two ordinary critics, might be expected to hold before the start of a play.

Moon and Birdboot, then, represent the 'real' world of the audience even more patently than do Rosencrantz and Guildenstern. And the play-within-the-play which they have come to see is an even more blatant piece of well-made artifice than was Stoppard's *Hamlet*. The opening speech, delivered into the telephone, represents the ultimate in artificial exposition and, just as Stoppard stressed the unreality of *Hamlet* by devices such as the translation of speech into mime, so here he has Mrs Drudge begin by giving voice to what should obviously be a stage-direction:

> Hello, the drawing-room of Lady Muldoon's country residence one morning in early spring? . . . *Hello!*—the draw—Who? Who did you wish to speak to? I'm afraid there is no one of that name here, this is all very mysterious and I'm sure it's leading up to something, I hope nothing is amiss for we, that is Lady Muldoon and her houseguests, are here cut off from the world, including Magnus, the wheelchair-ridden half-brother of her ladyship's husband Lord Albert Muldoon who ten years ago went out for a walk on the cliffs and was never seen again—and all alone for they had no children.

So far we have the same distinction as in *Rosencrantz and Guildenstern Are Dead* between the real world of Moon and Birdboot (and the audience) and the artificial world of the play-within-the-play. But by the time Mrs Drudge speaks, an important difference between this play and its predecessor has already begun to emerge. The difference lies in the depiction of the 'real' characters, Moon and Birdboot, who, not content to remain at the level of the 'real', have begun to develop little fantasy-worlds of their own.

Moon, who is his newspaper's second-string drama critic (as Stoppard himself once was), is obsessed by jealousy of the number-one critic, Higgs. As the play-within-the-play hiccoughs along it becomes clear that Moon is less intent on it than on his own dream-play, which is modelled on roughly similar lines, featuring as it does such concepts as Revenge, Jealousy and Murder: 'Sometimes I dream that I've killed him'.

Meanwhile Birdboot is rapidly sinking into his own dream-play about the various women in his life. Early on he reveals his infatuation for the actress playing Felicity, but the moment Cynthia makes her entrance he transfers his attentions to her. At the same time in the play-within-the-play Simon Gascoyne is similarly transferring his allegiance from Felicity to Cynthia. This stage-parallel to Birdboot's experience stresses how stagey his behaviour, and Moon's, is becoming.

Immediately following the end of Act I of the play-within-the-play Stoppard shows us how completely preoccupied with their private fantasies Moon and Birdboot have become by having them launch into a dialogue on separate tracks. This is a favourite device of Stoppard's, which can be found elsewhere in this play and in several of the others.

> MOON: Camps it around the Old Vic in his opera cloak
> and passes me the tat.
> BIRDBOOT: Do you believe in love at first sight?
> MOON: It's not that I think I'm a better critic—
> BIRDBOOT: I feel my whole life changing—
> MOON: I am but it's not that.
> BIRDBOOT: Oh, the world will laugh at me, I know . . .
> MOON: It is not that they are much in the way of shoes to
> step into . . .
> BIRDBOOT: . . . call me an infatuated old fool . . .
> MOON: . . . They are not.
> BIRDBOOT: . . . condemn me . . .
> MOON: He is standing in my light, that is all.
> BIRDBOOT: . . . betrayer of my class . . .
> MOON: . . . an almost continuous eclipse, interrupted by
> the phenomenon of moonlight.
> BIRDBOOT: I don't care, I'm a gonner.
> MOON: And I dream . . .
> BIRDBOOT: The Blue Angel all over again.
> MOON: . . . of the day his temperature climbs through
> the top of his head . . .
> BIRDBOOT: Ah, the sweet madness of love . . .
> MOON: . . . of the spasm on the stairs . . .
> BIRDBOOT: Myrtle, farewell . . .
> MOON: . . . dreaming of the stair he'll never reach—
> BIRDBOOT: . . . for I only live but once . . .
> MOON: Sometimes I dream that I've killed him.

BIRDBOOT: What?
MOON: What?

They manage to pull themselves together at this point and return to 'reality', but at the end of the second act of the play-within-the-play they are both back in their dream-worlds, on separate tracks, and it is no surprise that they are both soon involved in the stage-action.

Early in the play Moon dropped a very pompous hint about the way in which this involvement should be interpreted. Referring ostensibly to Simon's first entry he spoke of—

> . . . the classic impact of the catalystic [sic] figure—the outsider—plunging through to the centre of an ordered world and setting up the disruptions—the shock waves—which unless I am much mistaken, will strip these comfortable people—these crustaceans in the rock pool of society—strip them of their shells and leave them exposed as the trembling raw meat which, at heart, is all of us.

Stoppard does use this device of the catalytic figure from time to time. Pavel Hollar in *Professional Foul* is a good example. His impact removes Anderson's shell and causes him to face reality. Similarly, in *Dirty Linen*, the arrival of French brings matters to a head. More often, however, Stoppard introduces characters who look like catalysts but who end up being catalysed. Foot and Holmes in *After Magritte* and Bones in *Jumpers* imagine that they are going to strip off a few shells but find to their surprise that they are the real 'crustaceans'.

In *The Real Inspector Hound* the case is altered again. No shells are removed, except perhaps from Hound and Simon, who are discussed more fully below. Instead, Moon and Birdboot *assume* shells, become 'crustaceans', when they leave their seats in the audience and involve themselves in the play-within-the-play.

After a false start by Moon, modelled on the old joke about the unscheduled ringing of the telephone on stage, it is Birdboot who takes to the boards first. As we might expect, he finds himself replacing Simon Gascoyne in a truncated replay of the play-within-the-play's first two acts. Thus he acts out with the stage-characters, Felicity and Cynthia, the transfer of emotions which he has experienced *vis à vis* the actresses playing these roles. Eventually he is shot just as Simon had been at the end of Act II, but before this happens he is able to apprise Moon of the fact that the body which has been lying unidentified on the stage up to this point (like the body of Marie in *Lord Malquist and Mr Moon* and that of McFee in *Jumpers*) is the body of Higgs, Moon's superior. This brings Moon on to the stage, apparently in the role of Inspector Hound, who had made an appearance during Act II of the play-within-the-play. Of course, it is clear from the glimpses we have had of Moon's fantasizing so far that the role of murderer suits Moon better than the role of detective. And, sure enough, in a very significant passage of dialogue, near the end of the play, it is revealed that Moon is *not* the real Inspector Hound:

> MAGNUS: I put it to you!—are you the real Inspector Hound?!
>
> MOON: You know damn well I'm not! What's it all about?
>
> MAGNUS: I thought as much.
>
> MOON: I only dreamed . . . sometimes I dreamed—
>
> CYNTHIA: So it was you!
>
> MRS DRUDGE: The madman!
>
> FELICITY: The killer! . . .

There is some doubt as to whether Moon really did kill Higgs, of course. The faltering manner in which he protests his innocence to Birdboot suggests guilt but, since Magnus eventually turns out to be the third-string critic, Puckeridge (Macafferty in the first edition), it is possible that Moon was framed, in which case we have the prospect of a circular argument: Moon, posing as Inspector Hound, is accused of Higgs's murder by Puckeridge, who claims to be the *real* Inspector Hound, along with a number of other things; but Puckeridge himself may be the murderer rather than the real Inspector Hound, in which case presumably Moon *was* the real Inspector Hound . . . Or perhaps neither of them is the real Inspector. The actor who played this part in the first instance, before Moon and Magnus-alias-Albert-alias-Puckeridge got in on his act, is still around at the end, sitting in Moon's seat in the audience. Given my distinction between the abstract (on stage) and the real (in the audience), he would seem to have an extra dimension to his claim to be the *real* Inspector Hound. As a critic he is notably more sensible than Moon was. And his neighbour (the actor who played Simon until Birdboot usurped his role) is likewise more sensible than Birdboot. On the few occasions when Moon and Birdboot manage to focus on the play they laud it absurdly in jargon-ridden language. Hound and Simon, on the other hand, while still prone to jargon, are at least capable of seeing that the play is 'a complete ragbag' and that 'some of the cast seem to have given up acting altogether'. But I suppose that this is hardly sufficient evidence on which to conclude that Simon and Hound's movement away from the stage has turned them into realists. Stoppard's most obvious and important motive for transferring them to the audience was to fill the seats of Moon and Birdboot and prevent their escape from the stage. Any deeper significance in the handling of Simon and Hound is not clearly spelled out.

Perhaps this is a weakness in the play. In performance, however, things have become so gloriously farcical at this point that there is every justification for piling on the complications without pausing to give a theoretical justification for them. (Much the same sort of thing happens at the end of *Dirty Linen*; Maddie, who has previously spoken in direct, realistic English unaccountably switches to artificial Italian for her curtain-speech.) I am content to leave such details unexamined but I do want to stress that the main thrust of the plot—the hoisting of Moon and Birdboot with their own petards—accords with Stoppard's usual practice of foiling, discouraging or criticizing all attempts to escape from the 'mystery' of life into a 'clockwork' world of dreams. As he himself put it, in 'Ambushes for the Audience', the play is 'about the dangers of wish fulfilment'.

5 After Magritte
Stranger Than Fiction

As Hersh Zeifman has noted, in what is perhaps the best general article yet written on Stoppard, there is a pun embedded in the very title of *After Magritte*. The tableau that confronts the audience at the outset has obviously been constructed quite deliberately 'after' (in the manner of) Magritte, an artist whom Stoppard greatly admires. We see a dimly-lit room where most of the furniture has been stacked against the upstage wall, except for an ironing-board and one chair. On the chair stands Reginald Harris, who wears nothing but thigh-length green rubber fishing waders over black evening dress trousers and black patent leather shoes. (In the première production, at the Ambiance Lunch-hour Theatre Club he was given a formal shirt-front and cuffs as well.) He is blowing into a lampshade which hangs above his head. On the ironing-board lies Mother, covered by a white bath towel, with a tight-fitting black rubber bathing cap on her head. Her right foot rests against the iron, and she has a black bowler hat—a very Magrittean detail this—perched on her stomach. On the floor, crawling about vaguely and picking up little metal objects from time to time, is Thelma, who is dressed in a full-length ballgown, with her hair expensively 'up'. The other important eccentricity is that alongside the lampshade hangs a fruit basket, attractively overflowing with apples, oranges, bananas, a pineapple and grapes.

It is all very Magrittean on the surface—very like Magritte's *L'Assassin Menacé* in fact, as Wendell V. Harris has pointed out—but there the resemblance ends, for, in Bigsby's words,

> Stoppard is no surrealist. The *tableau* . . . is not a
> surrealist image designed to liberate the imagination, to

energize the subconscious, but a teasing problem in logic, a conundrum to be unravelled . . .

The unravelling involves providing naturalistic explanations for all the apparent absurdities. This is how Stoppard does it. The furniture has been piled against the wall to provide room for Thelma and Harris to practise ballroom-dancing, this being necessary after a fiasco at the Cricklewood Lyceum. The fact that they are about to go out for an evening's dancing accounts for the elements of formal dress they are wearing. Harris's lack of a shirt is explained by the fact that it needs ironing. This in turn explains the ironing-board. The iron has to be plugged into the hanging lightshade. This cannot be done until the bulb is extracted, and the bulb is still too hot to handle, which is why Harris is up on a chair blowing on it. The light has been turned off of course, and there is no other bulb in the room, so the stage is unlit. Mother, who is about to have a bath and therefore wears a towel and bathing-cap, has been receiving massage on the ironing-board from Thelma, who has hurt her back and therefore cannot attend to Mother on the floor. The rubber waders worn by Harris were put on to protect his good clothes and to preserve himself from electrocution when he was changing a bulb in the bathroom just prior to the start of the play. Thelma is on the floor looking for her shoes in the dim light. The metal objects which she picks up are the contents of the original counterweight to the hanging lamp-shade. Now that the counterweight has been broken the basket of fruit has been hung in its place. The bowler hat on Mother's stomach is there for use as a supplement to the basket of fruit when the lampshade becomes heavier after the insertion of the iron plug.

Gradually, then, the whole bizarre spectacle comes to make sense to the audience. We see, as Harris puts it, that 'There is a perfectly logical reason for everything'—indeed that 'The activities in this room today have broadly speaking been of a mundane and domestic nature bordering on cliché'. And as soon as the spectacle has been explained it is quickly dismantled, so that by the middle of the play, when Foot and Holmes arrive, everything is in place and the only surviving oddity is the fruit basket. Moreover, Stoppard goes on to

remove any lingering doubts we may have about Reginald
Harris and his family by having all three characters agree that
a Magritte exhibition which they have just visited (for no
better reason than that some of the paintings contained tubas)
was rubbish because it wasn't life-like. In short, the oddity of
the opening tableau is not a surrealist construct 'after' (in the
manner of) Magritte, but a faithful mimesis of a slice of life
which occurred in the Harris household 'after' (subsequent
to) a visit to a Magritte exhibition.

All this becomes clear to the audience—but not to P.C.
Holmes, who was looking through the window when things
were at their most Magrittean early in the play. He saw not
only the extraordinary opening tableau but also its hilarious
sequel in which Mother's foot was burned as the iron
warmed up. To Holmes, as we later find out, Mother's
tight-fitting black rubber bathing cap suggested the head of 'a
bald nigger', and her posture while clutching her burned foot
suggested that she had only one leg. When Harris brought
butter to apply to Mother's foot he applied it to the wrong
one—the one hanging down—so that from the back there
was still no indication of a second leg.

Holmes duly fetches his superior, Foot, and the two of
them arrive, apparently in the role of catalytic figures. They
charge Harris and Thelma with performing 'without anaes-
thetic an illegal operation on a bald nigger minstrel about
five-foot-two or Pakistani' or, as Foot subsequently puts it,
with 'offering cut-price amputations to immigrants'.

Foot's fervid and treacherous imagination has been at work
ever since an elderly lady reported seeing 'the talented though
handicapped doyen of the Victoria Palace Happy Minstrel
Troupe' hopping past her house in Ponsonby Place, holding
a broken crutch, and leaving 'one or two tell-tale coins on the
pavement'. He has proceeded to conjure up a vision of a
robbery in which the said one-legged minstrel—

> . . . emerged from his dressing-room in blackface, and
> entered the sanctum of the box-office staff; whereupon,
> having broken his crutch over the heads of those good
> ladies, the intrepid uniped made off with the advance
> takings stuffed into the crocodile boot which, it goes
> without saying, he had surplus to his conventional
> requirements.

He winds up his account by postulating that Harris, who received a parking ticket in Ponsonby Place and was seen to drive away at about the same time as the thief was spotted, may have kept a rendezvous with the minstrel and driven off with him in his car.

When Foot arrives at the house to press charges, however, the Magrittean oddities of the opening tableau have, as we have seen, all disappeared, with the exception of the hanging fruit-basket. So his opening exclamation, 'What is the meaning of this bizarre spectacle?!!' falls devastatingly flat. He has struck the one moment when the room does *not* look bizarre. He hangs on to his 'clockwork' dream ever more tenuously for a little while, and exhibits some very 'clockwork' mannerisms, like the stagey aside just after his entrance; but eventually a call from the station convinces him that no robbery has in fact taken place. To revert to the terminology of Moon in *The Real Inspector Hound*, the catalytic figure has been catalysed; instead of stripping others of their shells he has had his own removed.

What then did the elderly lady in Ponsonby Place actually see? She saw something which Harris, Thelma and Mother also saw when they were there, and which all three have been interpreting and reinterpreting in wildly different ways since the play began. All four saw Foot acting out the charade which he describes in two speeches at the end of the play:

> I'd been out with the boys from C Division till dawn, and left my car outside the house, thinking that I'd move it to a parking meter before the wardens came round—in my position one has to set an example, you know. Well, I woke up late and my migraine was giving me hell and my bowels were so bad I had to stop half way through shaving, and I never gave the traffic warden a thought till I glanced out of the window and saw your car pulling away from the only parking space in the road. I flung down my razor and rushed into the street, pausing only to grab my wife's handbag containing the small change and her parasol to keep off the rain . . .

> I got pretty wet because I couldn't unfurl the damned thing, and I couldn't move fast because in my haste to pull up my pyjama trousers I put both feet into the same

leg. So after hopping about a bit and nearly dropping
the handbag into various puddles, I just thought to hell
with it all and went back in the house. My wife claimed
I'd broken her new white parasol, and when I finally got
out of there I had a parking ticket. I can tell you it's just
been one bitch of a day.*

The one remaining piece of absurdity is thus satisfactorily
explained, and Stoppard marks the moment with a piece of
spoof symbolism: 'Lights!' cries Mother immediately after
Foot has finished speaking, and for the first time in the play
the room is adequately lit from above. But the symbolic
significance of the light is forgotten almost at once. The
audience is quickly distracted by the bizarre spectacle which
the light reveals. For from the moment when Thelma drapes
her ballgown over Harris in order to raise its hem, the set has
been reverting with ever-increasing speed to the Magrittean
aspect which it wore at the beginning. Finally we get the
following tableau:

> The row on the table reads from left to right:
> [(1) MOTHER, standing on her good foot only, on the wooden
> chair which is placed on the table; a woollen sock on one hand;
> playing the tuba.]
> [(2) Lightshade, slowly descending towards the table.]
> [(3) FOOT, with one bare foot, sunglasses, eating banana.]
> [(4) Fruit basket, slowly ascending.]
> [(5) HARRIS, gowned, blindfolded with a cushion cover over
> his head, arms outstretched, on one leg, counting.]
> [THELMA, in underwear, crawling around the table, scanning
> the floor and sniffing.]
> [HOLMES recoils into paralysis.]
> [The lampshade descends inexorably as the music continues to
> play; when it touches the table-top there is no more light.]
> [Alternatively, the lampshade could disappear down the horn
> of the tuba.]

Foot is not to be fooled again, however. Refusing to be
diverted by the absurdity of this spectacle, of which he forms
a part in any case, he turns on Holmes and rebukes him for

---

* This unlikely tale seems to be based on fact, as Stoppard explains in
'Ambushes for the Audience' and elsewhere. Incidentally, Foot must have
moved very quickly, since he saw Harris's car pulling away from the kerb
before he set out for the street and he arrived in time to be passed in the car
by the Harrises.

his fanciful reading of the opening tableau: 'Well, Constable, I think you owe us all an explanation'.

Clearly Foot has learnt the great Stoppardian lesson: that 'clockwork' dreams must be eschewed in favour of reality. Moreover, the terms in which the lesson is couched in this play underline the all-important point that reality may wear an aspect of 'mystery'. Truth can be stranger than fiction.

6 Jumpers
Ayery Nothings

The success of *Rosencrantz and Guildenstern Are Dead* in the
National Theatre production at the Old Vic put Stoppard in a
position to make heavy demands upon the company's generous resources for his next full-length play. And thus it was
that the surface of *Jumpers* came to be littered with so many
spectacular diversions: the trapeze, the acrobatics, the giant
television screen, the dermatograph, etc.

At first it might seem that we should demur in this case
from Bigsby's contention that Stoppard is an aesthetic reactionary who, 'at a time when *avant-garde* theatre is de-
emphasizing language, stressing performance over text, preferring group composition to the insights of the individual
author . . . believes in the primacy of words'. But on closer
inspection we find that the spectacle is not of the free-
wheeling, improvized kind; it is tightly prescribed and
closely geared to the significance of the words. And both
words and spectacle are governed by Stoppard's customary
theoretical framework. The outward and visible sign of this
framework is the triangular relationship of the three principal characters—Archie, George and Dotty. Their relationship is obviously akin to the eternal triangle depicted in
Lord Malquist and Mr Moon. In both works we see a confused
unworldly husband (Moon/George) competing with a slick
but perhaps effete admirer (Malquist/Archie) for the attentions of a beautiful young wife (Jane/Dotty). And, once we
take the point made in 'Ambushes for the Audience' that
Stoppard's plays 'tend to bear on life in an oblique, distant,
generalized way' so that the outward appearance of each
character matters less than what Stoppard calls the 'universal
perception' which he or she embodies, then we are in a
position to see that both these triangles are congruent with

the structure of *Rosencrantz and Guildenstern Are Dead,* in which the Tragedians move between the confused world of Rosencrantz and Guildenstern and the slick efficiency of Shakespeare's text. In all three plays we have a symbol of 'mystery' (Moon/George/Rosencrantz and Guildenstern), a symbol of 'clockwork' (Malquist/Archie/the *Hamlet* cast) and a straddler (Jane/Dotty/the Tragedians). A similar framework is to be found in *Albert's Bridge* and we shall glimpse it again in *Travesties.* But in *Jumpers* the basic triangle has sprouted an accretion in the form of Inspector Bones, and it will be as well to account briefly for his role in the play before turning back to the three principals. Bones's presence in the play is a symptom of the fact that really it contains two plots. The main plot depicts the rivalry between George and Archie for Dotty (and for philosophical supremacy). The subplot depicts Bones's attempts to solve the mystery which surrounds the death of Duncan McFee, who is shot in the opening moments of the play. The plots are kept distinct by two important circumstances: Bones knows nothing of philosophy, and George knows nothing of the murder, at least not until the end of Act II.

As several critics have observed, the subplot merely reflects the events and themes of the main plot at a more accessible level—the level of detective fiction. G. B. Crump, for example, comments that 'the mystery of McFee's murder is a metaphor for the essential mysteries of creation', which means that, however unfortunate the comparison may seem, Bones's search for a murderer corresponds to George's search for God. The parallel between Bones and George is cemented in a number of ways. The intrusion of George's recorded sound-effects into Bones's first encounter with Dotty constitutes a very obvious, and highly comic, linking device. More significant is the fact that both men are torn between their professional duties and the delights of Dotty. Moreover, for both Bones and George, Archie represents the principal antagonist: he removes McFee's body from Bones's sphere of activities just as he removes God from George's. Archie provides another link between the two men when he offers Bones the Chair of Divinity, which ranks with George's Chair of Ethics at the bottom of the academic pecking order. And both men finally fail in their quests; the murder remains unsolved and the existence of God unestablished, although I shall argue below that George manages to establish something of a presumption in His favour.

Bones may therefore be regarded as a kind of mundane reflection of George. He reduces George's problems and preoccupations to an everyday level—to their bare bones, as it were. This difference of level is indicated by Stoppard's handling of the recorded sound-effects. George uses them consciously and intelligently as part of a philosophical argument, but for Bones they are the sole means of communicating with Dotty. It is as if Bones exists at the level of pure instinct—the level of the beast whose mating-call is the first sound-effect to be heard—whereas George, although he would be the first to acknowledge the reality and importance of instincts, possesses superior faculties. Bones is not unlike Rosencrantz (and Moon), whereas George is more like Guildenstern. Guildenstern's self-consciousness made him a more profitable subject for analysis than the naive Rosencrantz. For the same reason George warrants closer scrutiny than Bones. Let us therefore turn to the main plot of *Jumpers* and its triad of characters: George, Dotty and Archie.

The action is divided into two acts and a coda, but it seems reasonable to regard the party scene at the beginning of Act I as a fourth part—a typically Stoppardian prelude. It contains the event from which the Bones subplot develops: the shooting of McFee. (In the National Theatre production George, posing as Spinoza, was seen to make the telephone call of complaint to the police which also assumes some importance in the subplot. This is not described in the published texts.) More important, the prelude features a series of tableaux that introduce in graphic terms the thematic antinomy which underlies the main action. First of all we get in juxtaposition a characteristically glib speech from Archie, acting for the moment as Master of Ceremonies at Dotty's party, and an equally characteristic snatch of incoherent song from Dotty. This contrast will turn out to be of crucial significance but at this stage the audience is unlikely to appreciate its importance if only because Archie is as yet unseen. It is the simpler and more spectacular encounter between Crouch and the Secretary that makes the first real assault upon our faculties. The poker-faced Secretary performs a strip-tease on a swing, which moves like a pendulum in and out of the spotlight. She seems to symbolize the austere logic, the 'mental acrobatics'*, the 'clockwork'— notice the image of the pendulum—of Archie, the Jumpers and the Radical Liberal Party to which they all belong. She turns out in fact to be the mistress of McFee, one of the Jumpers. And the nod which she directs at Archie when he first appears may indicate that she is in cahoots with him. Poor bewildered Crouch, the porter-turned-waiter, strays into the path of the swing unwittingly and is knocked over. His bewilderment anticipates the confusion experienced by Dotty, as she strives to retain her instinctive sense of mystery and romance, and to a lesser extent by George, as he strives, like Anderson in *Professional Foul*, to justify his instinctive sense of moral rectitude. And the physical crash which finally befalls Crouch prefigures Dotty's mental breakdown, as well as the demise of Pat and Thumper.

The second tableau, which is again vividly theatrical, juxtaposes Dotty and the Jumpers. Though they are not especially talented—a qualification which suggests by analogy the shortcomings of Archie's rationalism—the Jumpers perform well enough to convince Dotty that she cannot, as she at first claimed, sing better than they can jump. In fact at this stage of the play they are even capable of defying gravity for a few seconds by keeping their human pyramid intact after the shooting of McFee, one of the three Jumpers at the base of the structure. Once again we are prepared analogically for the triumph of Archie's reason over Dotty's romance.

Once these tableaux have been completed, Acts I and II proceed to depict events in the Moore household on the morning after the party. The significance of these events is best conveyed by successive analyses of the roles of the three principals. And although he is actually the last of the three to appear, we shall look first at Archie.

Sir Archibald Jumper, M.D., D.Phil., D.Litt., L.D., D.P.M., D.P.T. (Gym.) embodies the spirit of the Radical Liberal Party

---

* Martello uses this phrase to describe barren abstract art in *Artist Descending a Staircase*. Mrs Wahl's reference to 'the philosophical flying-trapeze' in Act I of *Undiscovered Country* provides another relevant gloss on this episode.

which has just come to power in a general election. The Party is dedicated to rationalism, or scientism as George calls it. This attitude is epitomized by their plan to rationalize the Church. Already the Radical Liberal spokesman for Agriculture has been made Archbishop of Canterbury and an unspecified building containing magnificent stained glass has been converted into a gymnasium. Archie himself, as his qualifications suggest, is something of a Renaissance Man; he has expertise in an impossibly wide range of fields that has been acquired by dedication to rational inquiry. This same dedication causes him and his colleagues to associate themselves with classical Greece and with 'the Athens of the North', Edinburgh. Archie's dedication to reason has led him, like A. J. Ayer, whom some regard as his real-life prototype, to embrace an extreme form of positivism, which Dotty defines thus:

> Things do not *seem*, on the one hand, they *are*; and on the other hand, bad is not what they can *be*. They can be green, or square, or Japanese, loud, fatal, waterproof or vanilla-flavoured; and the same for actions, which can be *disapproved of*, or comical, unexpected, saddening or good television, variously, depending on who frowns, laughs, jumps, weeps or wouldn't have missed it for the world. Things and actions, you understand, can have any number of real and verifiable properties. But good and bad, better and worse, these are not real properties of things, they are just expressions of our feelings about them.

Archie is capable of defending his position in glib and plausible terms but the play is at pains to point out that, at best, his interpretation of things is only skin-deep, like the superficial posturings of the Jumpers, and that, at worst— and this is what makes him a more disturbing character than Lord Malquist—this lack of depth can lead to tyranny after the manner of Henry II and Richard III or Hitler, Stalin or Nero or sundry military dictators of recent times.

Archie's shallowness is indicated in all sorts of ways, for instance by the fact that he needs only two minutes to prepare a philosophical paper. But it is the introduction of the dermatograph which demonstrates most forcibly that his scientism is, quite literally, only skin-deep. The machine is trundled on to the stage at the end of the first act and set in operation at the end of the second. Archie describes its function early in Act II:

> It reads the skin, electronically; hence dermatograph.
> . . . All kinds of disturbances under the skin show up on
> the surface. . .*

In the first (1972) edition of the play Stoppard insists that the dermatograph is still ambiguous, that there is a hint of erotic obsession as well as a genuine interest in medical research about Archie's close analysis of Dotty's skin. That this stage direction is cut from the second (1973) edition makes it all the more clear that Archie's eroticism, if it exists at all, is only skin-deep compared to George's. The knowledge to which George aspires includes 'knowing in the biblical sense of screwing', although he has been hampered latterly by the fact that, as he wistfully puts it, Dotty 'retired from consummation about the same time as she retired from artistry'. Archie is well aware that George's lusts are more earthy than his own:

> . . . you think that when I run my hands over her back I
> am carried away by the delicate contours that flow like a
> sea-shore from shoulder to heel—oh yes, you think my
> mind turns to ripe pears as soon as I press—

George's blood is stirred and he interrupts viciously at this point. However, Archie is undeterred and he completes his distinction by defining his own professional attitude:

> But to us medical men, the human body is just an
> imperfect machine. As it is to most of us philosophers.
> And to us gymnasts, of course.

The contrast between Archie's 'clockwork' aloofness and George's full-blooded sensuality is reflected on a more abstract plane in the contrast between Archie's scientism and George's faith in intuition, which leads him to insist that 'there is more in me than meets the microscope'. Like Professor Anderson in *Professional Foul*, with whom he also shares an interest in sport, a respect for instincts, and a

---

* Archie's analysis of the skin may involve a pun on the name of B. F. Skinner. Stoppard told Mel Gussow in 'Stoppard Refutes Himself, Endlessly' that *Jumpers* was 'an anti-Skinner play'.

conviction that rights are different from rules, George is better at criticizing the principles of his antagonists than at proving his own case. He establishes easily that 'if rationality were the criterion for things being allowed to exist, the world would be one gigantic field of soya beans', and again that Archie's positivism makes 'one man's idea of good . . . no more meaningful than another man's whether he be St Francis or . . .'—and it is Archie himself who completes the statement—'Hitler or Stalin or Nero'. But when it comes to establishing the existence of God or the validity of the proposition that 'Good and evil are metaphysical absolutes', George runs into all sorts of difficulties, both in theory (witness his ridiculous attempts to dictate a lecture on these topics at the beginning of Act I) and in practice (witness the apparent failure of providence which allows George unwittingly to kill his hare and his tortoise in the course of the play).

George's bewilderment is very like that of Rosencrantz and Guildenstern, and Moon in *Lord Malquist and Mr Moon*. Moon was always at his most confused when confronted by a mirror, and George has the same experience; he stares into a mirror while dictating his hopelessly bungled lecture. This mirror is an imaginary one so that when George looks into it he is actually looking straight at the audience. This establishes a bond between George and the audience that is reminiscent of the link between the audience and protagonists both in *Rosencrantz and Guildenstern Are Dead* and in *The Real Inspector Hound*.

But in the last analysis George is a much more positive character than Moon or Rosencrantz or Guildenstern. Rosencrantz hardly tries to control or understand his world; Moon makes a few desultory attempts but finally opts despairingly to make 'a great big bang that snuffs it out'; Guildenstern rises to what Helene Keyssar-Franke calls 'the full tragic perception' of his predicament but still fails to do anything about it. George, however, finally manages to turn his back on the mirror and put together a coherent and powerful justification of his faith in God and goodness.

Towards the close of Act I George dictates to the secretary a three-page chunk of argument which, apart from three retractions of potentially slanderous material, is a coherent whole, quite devoid of the tangles and confusions that marred his earlier pronouncements. He begins with a discussion of aesthetic judgements, which involves the three sound-effects (Mozartian trumpets, the trumpeting of an elephant and 'the sound made by a trumpet falling down a flight of stone stairs') of which, as we have seen, punning use is made in the sub-plot. His aim is to ridicule the positivists' contention that 'it could not be said that . . . any one set of noises was in any way superior to either of the other two'—to ridicule it, but not absolutely to refute it, since he cuts short his argument with the concession that the positivists' conclusion 'may, of course, be the case'. And now he moves on to the all-important field of ethics. George cavalierly concedes the positivists' point that 'the word "good" has . . . meant different things to different people at different times'; he maintains, in fact, that this 'is not a statement which anyone would dispute'. He then woos his audience with some hilarious juxtapositions of different moral values before summoning all his energy for the knock-out punch:

> What is surely . . . surprising is that notions such as honour should manifest themselves at all. For what *is* honour? What are pride, shame, fellow-feeling, generosity and love? . . . Whence comes this sense of some actions being better than others?—not more useful, or more convenient, or more popular, but simply pointlessly *better*? What, in short, is so good about *good*?

Professional philosophers, including Bennett, Henning Jensen and even Ayer, have not been very impressed by George's arguments, though Ayer admires *Jumpers* as a play and respects Stoppard. But there can be no doubting the excellence of George's rhetoric, and in the theatre this more than compensates for the inadequacy of his metaphysics. And the speech we have been examining is not just powerful in itself; it is also powerfully placed, constituting as it does the closing statement, the verbal climax, so to speak, of Act I. No doubt it was this passage in particular that Stoppard had in mind when he claimed in 'Ambushes for the Audience' that *Jumpers* was the first play in which he 'set out to ask a question and try to answer it, or at any rate put the counter-question'. George's intuitionism, as defined here, provides a most effective counter to Archie's scientism.

Unfortunately, George is not always so coherent or so eloquent. As we have seen, his earlier attempts to expound his views are vitiated by a series of gross linguistic blunders. And in Act II, although he manages a few telling points and evocative images, as when he likens his belief in God to being 'ambushed by some quite trivial moment—say the exchange of signals between two long-distance lorry-drivers in the black sleet of a god-awful night on the old A1', he never really gets back into top gear. And for a man bent on justifying the notion of providence George suffers an inordinate number of personal disasters in Act II. He loses his hare, his tortoise and his goldfish, and looks to be well on the way to losing his wife as well.

George is a complex and intriguing character. Bigsby notes that there is a curious paradox in his predicament—a paradox which—

> . . . resides in the fact that while he elaborates his defence of values . . . the world outside is renouncing all interest in the matter. Engaged only on a theoretical level, he implicitly compounds the forces which he deplores. Just as life inevitably evades his attempt to pin it down with words, his elaborate arguments sliding off into anecdote and parenthetical by-ways, so his grasp on the real world is seen to be tenuous at best.

George fails where Professor (George) Anderson and (George) Guthrie will later succeed; he cannot effect a marriage between theory and practice. He can praise the Good Samaritan while failing to emulate him by rescuing Dotty from her predicament. His extreme impracticality is manifested by his failure to see the body of the dead Jumper in Dotty's bedroom during Act I. As an academic he is, as he admits himself, at one remove from the centre of events. In this respect he is exactly like McKendrick in *Professional Foul*; both men have the right sort of ideas but they are, like the philosopher George Edward Moore, *naifs* who are better at expounding ideas than at putting them into practice. Both lack the sort of flexibility or pragmatism that enables Professor Anderson to combine principle and practice. But George Moore does give voice to the kind of principles on which right action might be based, and to that extent he represents a real advance on Rosencrantz, Guildenstern and Moon, all of whom were paralysed mentally as well as physically.

In *Jumpers* it is Dotty who appears to be paralysed. She is caught between the new 'clockwork' (represented by Archie) and the old 'mystery' (represented by George), and the tension has driven her 'dotty'. In the introductory tableau where she and the Jumpers are juxtaposed she demonstrates her inability to sustain the romantic celebrations of the moon which made her a much-loved star of the musical stage. Whenever she attempts to sing she finds herself unable to distinguish between one moon-song and another and her efforts peter out in confusion. In the middle of the first act she explains her predicament to George:

> It'll be just you and me under that old-fashioned, silvery harvest moon, occasionally blue, jumped over by cows and coupleted by Junes, invariably shining on the one I love; well-known in Carolina, much loved in Allegheny, familiar in Vermont; [*the screw turning in her*] *Keats's* bloody moon!—for what has made the sage or poet write but the fair paradise of nature's light—And *Milton's* bloody moon! rising in clouded majesty, at length apparent queen, unveiled her peerless light and o'er the dark her silver mantle threw—And Shelley's sodding maiden, with white fire laden, whom mortals call the—[*weeping*] *Oh yes, things were in place then!*

For the difference between this disordered 'then' and the chaotic 'now' we are offered a quite specific explanation, lifted and elaborated from Stoppard's earlier radio play, *Another Moon Called Earth*. After the introductory tableaux the very first action that we see is the television coverage of the first British landing on the moon. This turns a romantic image into something matter-of-fact and it is this which kills Dotty's old aptitude for moon songs. It also kindles an unwonted sadism in her: in Act II it is revealed that she has sacrificed the family goldfish in order to imitate the moon-men. This in turn is a symptom of a thorough-going revision of values that the moon-landing has wrought in her; now that 'Man is on the moon, his feet on solid ground',

> . . . he has seen us whole, all in one go, *little—local* . . .
> and all our absolutes, the thou-shalts and the thou-shalt-
> nots that seemed to be the very condition of our

existence, how did *they* look to two moonmen with a
single neck to save between them? Like the local
customs of another place . . .

As this quotation suggests, the implications of the landing
itself are graved deeper for Dotty by the circumstances in
which it takes place. The space-ship is damaged so only one
of the two astronauts can be lifted off the moon. The two
men, Captain Scott and Astronaut Oates, struggle until
Oates is knocked to the ground. This fracas makes the moon
an even less romantic place. At the same time it destroys one
of the great myths of English decency: the story of 'the first
Captain Oates, out there in the Antarctic wastes, sacrificing
his life to give his companions a slim chance of survival . . .'

Dotty follows the progress of the moon-landing on the
television set in her bedroom. From time to time she changes
channels and gets coverage of a procession to celebrate the
election victory of Archie's Rad-Lib Party. The television
screen on which the images appear is another of Stoppard's
distorting mirrors, and the alternating images define the
tension between 'mystery' and 'clockwork' in Dotty's dis-
torted mind. This tension is established by other means as
well. When Dotty calls out 'Darling!', George and Archie
both respond instinctively; indeed Dotty does show genuine
affection for both of them, though in very different ways.
With George she is sincere, confiding and emotional, while
with Archie she is gay and composed. By the end of Act II,
however, Archie's influence seems to have prevailed; Dotty
is trying to 'Forget Yesterday', and one of the last images we
have of her is the close-up of her skin projected on the
television screen by the dermatograph. (This image closes the
act in the first published edition but in the second it is moved
back a few pages.) We see her, as it were, through Archie's
eyes, and what we see closely resembles the unromantic
close-up of the moon which helped to bring on her dottiness
in the first place.

Act II therefore ends very dismally. Dotty has been
reduced to Archie's level, while George has, for the moment
at least, been reduced to Dotty's, his cry of 'Help! Murder!'
echoing her earlier appeals for attention, and his destruction
of Pat and Thumper recalling her murder of the goldfish—
and perhaps of McFee. And in the sub-plot Bones has had to

abandon his quest for McFee's murderer after Archie has discovered him in a compromising situation with Dotty.

At the same time, however, a more optimistic note has been introduced by Crouch, who has been pressed into service as a sort of *deus ex machina* or catastatic character to provide a modicum of approval for George's ideas and to reveal more fully the circumstances surrounding McFee's death, which turn out to be rather damaging for Archie. Crouch confides that McFee—or Duncan, as he prefers to call him*—had been going through a crisis and had intended entering a monastery (like a number of Stoppard's earlier heroes). The causes of this crisis were twofold. Firstly, at an abstract level, the astronauts fighting on the moon had led him to question the implications of the pragmatism or scientism to which he had been helping Archie to lend philosophical respectability. Secondly, at a personal level, he had begun to crack under the strain of a clandestine affair with George's secretary. This sounds very like a case of 'mystery in the clockwork', and if we assume, as I think we may, that the Secretary is somehow in league with Archie, then McFee's liaison becomes a double betrayal of his Vice-Chancellor, both in principle and in practice, so to speak. Archie certainly seems to suspect such a thing, to judge by these remarks to Bones:

> With the possible exception of McFee's fellow gymnasts, anybody could have fired the shot, and anybody could have had a reason for doing so, including, incidentally, myself. . . . McFee was the guardian and figurehead of philosophical orthodoxy, and if he threatened to start calling on his masters to return to the true path, then I'm afraid it would certainly have been an ice-pick in the back of the skull.

Crouch himself is a curiously ambiguous figure. His support for George's argument goes only so far: 'I grant you he's answered Russell's first point . . .—the smallest proper fraction is zero—*but* . . . the original problem remains in

---

* The allusion to *Macbeth*, which is backed up by a number of direct quotations, ultimately matters less, I think, than the suggestion of personal affection conveyed by Crouch's (and George's) use of McFee's first name. Archie's coldness is indicated by his preference for surnames.

identifying the *second* term of the series . . .' And in his
capacity as porter he threatens, unnecessarily as it turns out,
to remove two of the key props to George's argument, his
hare and his tortoise: 'No pets allowed in the flats'. Moreover, Crouch's very name suggests that he is a potential
'jumper' and supporter of Archie. But then it has been
observed (by Zeifman) that George too is a kind of 'jumper',
since his proof of the existence of God involves a Kierkegaar-
dian leap of faith. So the name betokens no definite allegiance.

The net result of Crouch's intervention late in Act II is to
warn the audience that Archie's triumph may not be as
absolute as it seems. At the same time we may begin to see
that George's collapse is less than total. Very early in the play
George insures himself against the debilitating effect of his
chronic linguistic ineptitude by insisting that there is a great
difference between language and meaning and that confusion
in the former does not necessarily signify confusion in the
latter. The unfortunate deaths of his pets do not scupper
George's religious instincts either, since he makes it clear that
the God he acknowledges is not the naively providential God
of religious observance. Moreover, long before he steps on
Pat (the tortoise) George has contemplated the case of a man
who accidentally crushes a beetle and has succeeded in
extracting moral significance from the event. And the killing
of Thumper (the hare), while it is distressing, does have a
positive aspect: it demonstrates the point, which is an integral
part of George's proof of the existence of God, that arrows
do reach their targets, so that Saint Sebastian need not have
died of fright.

And so as the Coda begins, the tension between Archie's
scientism and George's intuitionism has still to be finally
resolved. Technically this scene is a dream sequence devised
by George's fevered imagination, and the depiction of events
is certainly somewhat bizarre. But despite this dislocation in
the mode of presentation there is no real discontinuity in
either the themes or the characterization. It is particularly
remarkable that there is no change in the portrayal of George;
although the George of the Coda is his own projection of
himself he remains the same old impractical figure, who
refuses to intervene to save Clegthorpe from death. As far as

the ideas are concerned, the Coda may be considered as a direct continuation of the preceding two acts.

For the most part the Coda is quite flippant in tone—too flippant perhaps to serve the purpose for which it seems to have been designed: to recommend George's views and discredit Archie's. The discrediting of Archie is effected by a number of factors, for example by Archie's own nonsense-speech in defence of scientism, by the way in which he manipulates Captain Scott's defence of his conduct on the moon (in the first edition only), and by Clegthorpe's betrayal of Archie, which re-enacts McFee's betrayal, as it was described by Crouch in Act II. The killing of Clegthorpe, with its echoes of Richard III's murder of Hastings and Henry II's disposal of Thomas à Beckett, brings out Archie's tyrannical propensities, while the fact that the pyramid of Jumpers disintegrates as soon as Clegthorpe is shot out of it, instead of staying intact for a time as it did under similar conditions at the beginning of the play, seems to indicate that the morale of the Rad-Lib party is weakening. Dotty's song, which follows, is still fairly dotty, but we note that she is now longing for the happy days when she could hold a tune instead of persisting in her attempts to 'Forget Yesterday'. And indeed she *does* hold a tune for five verses; and the tune in question is 'Sentimental Journey', whose very title, coupled with the fact that Crouch sings it early in the play, suggests that there are still feelings lurking beneath her skin. Moreover, her line 'Two and two make roughly four' is a slogan for individual freedom, derived ultimately from Orwell's *1984*. In short, to quote Weldon B. Durham, Dotty seems to experience 'reintegration' in the Coda. When Dotty finishes, George takes over, and at last he manages to put together a defence of intuitionism which is as powerful and coherent as his big speech at the end of Act I. Even logical positivists, he contends,

> . . . *know* that life is better than death, that love is better than hate, and that the light shining through the east window of their bloody gymnasium is more beautiful than a rotting corpse.

But the last word goes to Archie. His curtain-speech is nothing if not ambiguous. The Bible rubs shoulders with

Beckett,★ and cynical undertones trouble the suave surface:

> Do not despair—many are happy much of the time;
> more eat than starve, more are healthy than sick, more
> curable than dying; not so many dying as dead; and one
> of the thieves was saved. Hell's bells and all's well—half
> the world is at peace with itself, and so is the other half;
> vast areas are unpolluted; millions of children grow up
> without suffering deprivation, and millions, while de-
> prived, grow up without suffering cruelties, and mil-
> lions, while deprived and cruelly treated, none the less
> grow up. No laughter is sad and many tears are joyful.
> At the graveside the undertaker doffs his hat and
> impregnates the prettiest mourner. Wham, bam, thank
> you Sam.

Has Archie's sinister scientism melted into the sort of benign
pragmatism that Professor Anderson in *Professional Foul* and
George Guthrie in *Night and Day* finally espouse? Or is this,
as Eric Salmon suggests, a 'casually sinister ending'? It is
hard to say, although certain parallels between this speech
and Malquist's heartless observations late in the novel about
the persecution of the Tibetans and related matters would
seem to tip the scales in Salmon's favour. Such ambiguity is
all very well in a realistic context but at one remove from
reality, which is where Stoppard works, here and elsewhere,
it starts to look suspiciously like muddle. It may be true, as
Archie is careful to point out at the end of Act II, that 'life
does not guarantee a denouement' but, as he confesses at the
same time, mystery novels do, and *Jumpers* is, I should have
thought, more a mystery play (though not in Lucina P.
Gabbard's sense of the term) than a slice of life.

★ The 'Sam' who is thanked at the end of the speech may be Samuel
Beckett. Certainly Hayman believes that Stoppard found a way of saying
thank-you to Beckett here. (The Sam could be Sam Clegthorpe, however,
and anyway 'Wham, bam, thank you Sam' is a proverbial exclamation.)
Stoppard himself, responding to Hayman's comment, talks of a parallelism
at the end of *Jumpers*. But a parallelism is not the same thing as a thank-you
and Stoppard may be referring to the Beckettian construction of Archie's
speech, which continually gives with one hand and takes away with the
other. Or perhaps the parallelism he has in mind is more specific: the
Augustinian observation that 'one of the thieves was saved' is quoted in
both *Godot* and *Murphy*, and in Stoppard's early story, 'Life, Times:
Fragments'.

Still, even if Archie's final stance remains a shade obscure, it seems reasonable to conclude with Salmon that the play comes down on the side of George and the angels. Morally, if not in fact, 'mystery' has triumphed over 'clockwork' once again.

7 Travesties
The Ultimate Unimportance of Art

It is a truth almost universally acknowledged that *Travesties* is about the relationship of art and politics. Stoppard himself said in 'Ambushes for the Audience' that the play—

> . . . asks whether an artist has to justify himself in political terms *at all* . . . whether the words 'revolutionary' and 'artist' are capable of being synonymous or whether they are mutually exclusive, or something in between.

Unfortunately, Stoppard stops short of an explicit account of the play's conclusions on these matters but his terminology here indicates that *Travesties* adheres to his customary structural pattern, which consists of a pair of polar opposites straddled by something in between. Margaret Gold takes up this hint and elaborates it:

> Joyce weighs in for the supreme value of art, and Lenin for politics as an absolute. Carr and Tzara exist in a situation where they attempt to mediate between those extremes, with Tzara standing for both art and politics, perhaps, and Carr standing for neither.

Joyce and Lenin are indeed depicted as polar opposites. There are just three inconsequential exceptions to the rule that Joyce appears only in the first act, and Lenin only in the second. The barrier that exists between Rosencrantz and Guildenstern, on the one hand, and the *Hamlet* cast, on the other, has here become absolute. And this analogy is an apt one since Lenin resembles Rosencrantz and Guildenstern both in his bumblingly inept logic, particularly as regards the function of art, and in his habit of speaking directly to the audience, while Joyce resembles the *Hamlet* cast in that he is presented as a very self-assured character in a play-within-the-play. Actually he is one degree further removed from reality than the *Hamlet* cast by virtue of the fact that this play-within-the-play emanates from the eccentric memory of Old Carr instead of being presented straight.

While employed in a small job at the British Consulate in Zürich in 1918, Henry Carr was nominated by James Joyce for the part of Algernon in a production of *The Importance of Being Earnest* which was being organized by one Claud Sykes. Carr excelled in the role, and Stoppard, who was unable to find out much about the historical Carr, imagined him glorying in his triumph over the next fifty-six years until his every memory of Zürich became entwined with the plot of Wilde's play. Thus, in Carr's memory, James Augusta Joyce (so registered at birth as the result of a clerical error—a happy accident for Stoppard) is conflated with Wilde's Aunt Augusta. Carr is provided with a sister whom Old Cecily, who is usually right, calls Sophia, but whom Old Carr thinks of as Gwendolen. She is given the requisite link with 'Augusta' Joyce in the form of a profound admiration for his work. Tristan Tzara is conflated with Wilde's Jack/Ernest, who was actually played by another Tristan—Tristan Rawson—in 1918. He falls in love with Gwendolen and has to placate 'Augusta' Joyce, as in the Wilde paradigm. But the form of this placation is the discovery not of a pedigree and a name—there is never any ambiguity about Tzara's first name so far as Gwendolen and Joyce are concerned—but of an admiration for Joyce's philosophy of art for art's sake. Since he inclines by nature towards a more revolutionary notion of art, this requirement sets up a tension in Tzara which establishes him as a typical Stoppardian straddler.

Wilde's Cecily becomes in Stoppard a young Zürich librarian. She has a professional attachment to Lenin (who might have become Miss Prism if Stoppard had wanted him inside the play-within-the-play*) comparable to Gwendolen's attachment to Joyce. And of course Carr, alias Algernon, takes a romantic interest in her comparable to Tzara's pursuit of Gwendolen. To win her love he has to assume another name (Tristan), as does his counterpart in Wilde, but much

---

* Young Carr briefly attempts to 'Prismize' Lenin in Act II when he imagines him to be some faithful governess. Cecily disabuses him. Stoppard discusses the matter in the first Hayman interview.

more important than this is Cecily's requirement that he applaud the ideas of Lenin. Since he is naturally conservative as regards both politics and art this creates a tension in him which qualifies him too as a straddler.

The first act focusses primarily on Joyce, Tzara and Gwendolen, though Carr too has an important part to play. At the very beginning, however, Cecily and the Lenins join Joyce, Tzara and Gwendolen for one of those introductory tableaux that are found so frequently in Stoppard. This one takes the same form as that in *Dirty Linen*. We get a lengthy sequence in which not a single sentence of standard English is spoken. Tzara recites nonsense poetry (though, as Tynan demonstrates, it makes sense in French); Joyce recites nonsense prose (derived from the 'Oxen of the Sun' episode of *Ulysses*); Gwendolen repeats what Joyce recites; Cecily says nothing but 'Ssssssh!'; and Lenin and Nadya talk in Russian. Their Russian will turn out to have a very real meaning when Cecily translates it in Act II but for the moment it is intended to sound just like the nonsense going on around them. Indeed, the frequency with which Nadya utters the syllable 'Da' (Russian for 'yes') provides an obvious link with Tzara's Dada-ism. A less obvious link, which I would never have noticed without Richard Ellmann's prompting, is with Molly Bloom's famous affirmative at the end of *Ulysses*.

It is not just the language which is absurd; such action as we see is likewise ridiculous. There are endless scraps of paper floating around the stage and getting into the wrong hands, and the way in which Cecily and Gwendolen unwittingly exchange folders is bound to seem comically stagey—if not quite as stagey as the moment when they discover their mistake at the end of the play.

Once an atmosphere of artificial nonsense has been built up, Old Carr is brought on to establish the precise frame in which this nonsense is to be contained. Stoppard suggests that Old Carr might play the piano—very badly—during the change of scene from the Library to Carr's Room. This provides an immediate link with *The Importance of Being Earnest*, which opens with a reference to some equally bad playing by Carr's counterpart, Algernon. But this fine detail is hardly necessary, for Old Carr soon makes it plain that the material we are about to view through his eyes will be put through a sieve labelled 'art' in general and *'The Importance of Being Earnest'* in particular.

The potential significance of *The Importance of Being Earnest* is indicated by the fact that Carr gets on to the subject of his 'personal triumph in the demanding role of Ernest, not Ernest, the other one' almost at once. His more general susceptibility to artistic licence is indicated obviously enough in a number of ways. Firstly, he makes a quite explicit attempt to present his memories as formal memoirs, and when he runs off the rails he is happy to assert blithely, 'that's the art of it'. Secondly, to introduce these memoirs he adopts a highly artificial style—or rather series of styles, oxymoron dominating the portrait of Joyce, poetic language that of Lenin and travel-brochure-ese (as in Arthur's monologue in *New-Found-Land*) that of Tzara and the Dada-ists. In each case the artifice is interrupted by Carr's own eccentric and bigotted voice. On the one hand this serves to stress the degree of distortion going on. On the other hand, however, it reminds us that Old Carr, as opposed to Young Carr and the other 'clockwork' figments of his doting mind, is a *real* character like the Lenins. We shall need to ponder his reality—and Old Cecily's—when we come to consider the dialogue between these two which ends the play. For the moment, however, it is the artifice of the dreams rather than the reality of the dreamer that is emphasized. This artifice is accentuated by his habit of relying on artificial aids to memory, particularly photographs. Joyce is visualized 'in a velvet smoking jacket of an unknown colour, photography being in those days a black and white affair'. This of course proves that Carr saw the smoking jacket only in photographs and therefore cannot have known the man very well. He is talking here about the post-Zürich Joyce so there is some justification for his ignorance. Carr is rather more open about his reliance on photographs to visualize Lenin, and we should realize long before the end of the play that Carr never saw Lenin in the flesh. Photography is not necessary as an aid in Tzara's case since Carr hardly seems capable of distinguishing between Tzara and a host of other artists from "tween the before-the-war-to-end-all-wars years and the between-the-wars years'. This part of the monologue is spent fooling around with a series of literary and sub-literary puns, which again indicate the extent to which art is triumphing over reality. Finally, we get an apostrophe to 'Switzerland, the still centre of the wheel of war', which contrives to make the very setting of the play seem utterly divorced from reality. (Stoppard adopted a similar attitude to Switzerland when he came to write the first scene of *The Real Thing* some ten years later.)

When at last the dialogue gets under way the artificial control imposed by Old Carr's memory continues to be evident. The scene with Bennett is modelled on Algernon's scene with Lane at the beginning of *The Importance of Being Earnest*, and there is a good deal of borrowing from other authors too—in Carr's big speech just before the second time-slip, for example. But the artifice is not confined to the surface of the text. Old Carr is not just embroidering past events; he is significantly distorting them, as Nabokov's senile or deranged narrators are wont to do (e.g. in *Despair)* and as Peter Shaffer's Salieri *fails* to do in *Amadeus* (which is one reason why that play is less satisfying than *Travesties*). At the end of the play Old Cecily cajoles Old Carr into revealing that the alleged master-servant relationship between himself and Bennett is a false one, since Bennett was in fact the British Consul in Zürich and Carr his underling. Here, then, is another artificial barrier between the audience and the true events of 1918. Yet another is provided by the celebrated time-slips when 'Old Carr's memory, which is not notably reliable . . . drops a scene' so that 'the story (like a toy train perhaps) . . . jumps the rails and has to be restarted at the point where it goes wild'. And if this device is accentuated, as Stoppard suggests it might be, by 'the sound of a cuckoo-clock, artificially amplified', then we are given, as in a number of Stoppard's other works, a literal demonstration of the 'clockwork' of these episodes.

Artifice continues to dominate as we witness the arrivals of Tzara, Joyce and Gwendolen, which are patterned on the entrances of Jack, Lady Bracknell and Gwendolen in the first act of *The Importance of Being Earnest*. Actually the arrival of these three characters is presented twice by Stoppard, first in a compressed and hilariously artificial form with Tzara/Jack depicted as 'a Rumanian nonsense' and Joyce initiating a whole scene couched in limericks, and then at greater length with all the characters speaking urbane, Wildean English. Of course, the very duplication of these entrances proves how artificial everything is at this point.

The first, compressed and absurd, run of this scene is Wildean only to the extent that a relationship is established between Gwendolen and Tzara/Jack/Ernest. The second run takes the parallel much further. Carr's interest in Cecily is aroused and he gets the opportunity to visit her as Tzara's younger brother, who has achieved a fictional existence as the result of a mix-up in the library where Tristan Tzara was named as Jack Tzara on his ticket. This ticket takes the place of the inscribed cigarette-box, which likewise bears the name of Jack, in *The Importance of Being Earnest*. Indeed, the second run of this scene parallels all the significant developments in Act I of Wilde's play. Joyce persuades Carr to appear in Sykes's production of *The Importance* just as Lady Bracknell persuades Algernon to help her plan her musical evening. Tzara, like Wilde's Jack, proposes to Gwendolen, and is interrupted in full flight by the return of Joyce, who utters Lady Bracknell's famous line: 'Rise, sir, from that semi-recumbent posture!' The importance that Wilde's Gwendolen attaches to the name Ernest is, as we have seen, converted into an insistence that Tzara should share her regard for Joyce's work. And Lady Bracknell's quizzing of Jack becomes a *tour de force* in which Joyce interrogates Tzara on the subject of Dada.

Stoppard's version of these events is remarkable—even more remarkable than Wilde's—for its artifice. There is a Malquistian emphasis on style. Thus Carr is more interested in the appearance of Algernon—his costumes and accessories—than in the substance of the part. The costumes do, in the event, affect Carr's financial 'substance', but that is a consideration which belongs with our analysis of the 'real' Old Carr rather than his projected younger self. Tzara's wooing of Gwendolen involves a welter of Shakespearean quotations. And Joyce's interrogation of Tzara is modelled on the catechism sequence in the 'Ithaca' section of *Ulysses*. For good measure it is also embroidered with some spectacular conjuring.

Amidst all this frippery the play's basic themes begin to emerge. Since the primary theme of Act I is the nature and function of art, the artificial context appears as a perfect medium for the message. But in fact the zany presentation serves ultimately to trivialize the ideas so that the endeavours of art are made to look much less substantial than the achievements of politics, which are viewed in a more sober, realistic perspective in Act II.

Art and politics are discussed at some length by Carr and Tzara between Joyce's first exit and his second entrance. Their debate is divided into two parts by another time-slip. The first part, though it touches on art, deals mainly with politics. Carr defends his participation in the war by citing the old-fashioned virtues of duty, patriotism and love of freedom. Tzara sees things differently:

> Wars are fought for oil wells and coaling stations; for control of the Dardanelles or the Suez Canal; for colonial pickings to buy cheap in and conquered markets to sell dear in. War is capitalism with the gloves off. . .

In short Tzara is in full agreement with Lenin on political matters. And Stoppard seems to endorse his views, for it is Carr who eventually loses his cool and has to be rescued by Old Carr's time-slip. And so the debate begins again and this time, after some trivial banter about Joyce, Gwendolen and Cecily, the focus shifts to art. Again Carr adopts a conservative line:

> Artists are members of a privileged class. Art is absurdly overrated by artists, which is understandable, but what is strange is that it is absurdly overrated by everyone else. . . . For every thousand people there's nine hundred doing the work, ninety doing well, nine doing good, and one lucky bastard who's the artist.

If the artist has any function at all, Carr maintains, it consists in the exercise of his special talent for creating more or less well the sort of objects which have been traditionally regarded as art. Tzara, on the other hand, adopts a radical view of art consonant with his radical view of politics. According to him the artist was once 'the priest-guardian of the magic that conjured the intelligence out of the appetites', but—

> Art created patrons and was corrupted. It began to celebrate the ambitions and acquisitions of the

paymaster . . . Without art man was a coffee-mill: but
with art, man—is a coffee-mill!

And so, as Tzara puts it later in the scene:

Now we need vandals and desecrators, simple-minded
demolition men to smash centuries of baroque subtlety,
to bring down the temple, and thus finally, to reconcile
the shame and the necessity of being an artist!

In this second part of the debate with Carr it is Tzara who
loses his cool and has to be rescued by the time-slip. By
analogy with the first part we may infer that Stoppard
favours Carr's views on this occasion. Tynan confirms this
reading, although it clearly offends against his radical beliefs,
and so do most audiences, who have even been known to
applaud Carr's portrait of the artist as a 'lucky bastard'.
Moreover, Carr's opinions are close to those of both Lenin,
who is a reactionary in art, as Tzara recognizes in Act II, and
Donner, the hero of *Artist Descending a Staircase*; Carr actually
quotes Donner *verbatim* in this episode.

Of our two straddlers, then, I reckon that Tzara is the
more convincing on the subject of politics and Carr the more
convincing on the subject of art. Joyce, who enters next,
seems to me to be wrong on both counts. He begins, as Tzara
and Carr did, with a political statement. He quotes 'Mr
Dooley' in order to demonstrate his complete indifference to
politics and the war. Then after the long catechism sequence
he turns his attention to art. In an impassioned monologue he
outlines his ideal of art for art's sake—art which enriches us
while leaving *'the world precisely as it finds it'*. Oddly
enough this speech was not in Stoppard's original draft; Peter
Wood, who directed the original production, made him add
it, and Stoppard told Hayman that he now regards it as 'the
most important speech in the play'.

An artist is the magician put among men to gratify—
capriciously—their urge for immortality. The temples
are built and brought down around him, continuously
and contiguously from Troy to the fields of Flanders. If
there is any meaning in any of it, it is what survives as
art . . .

Which is tantamount to saying with Wilde that 'Life imitates
Art far more than Art imitates Life'.

The speech is certainly impressive and it is given a strong position at the very end of the scene, just prior to Old Carr's framing monologue. But there are several factors working to undermine Joyce's eloquence. One is the context from which the speech arises. The hilarious catechism sequence, with its spectacular visual aids, has just ended, and Tzara has launched a furious assault on Joyce to the accompaniment of smashing crockery. So the audience has had both an earful and an eyeful before Joyce begins to speak. We are told that Joyce does not move during Tzara's tirade, and it may be that his very impassiveness would compel attention after this riot of activity. But it might not be very sympathetic attention, for Joyce's impassiveness is reminiscent of the chilling automaton-like behaviour of Albert, Archie, the Player and the other 'clockwork' villains of the Stoppard canon.

The speech's conclusion is even more damaging than its preamble. Joyce trivializes his argument by reverting to the idiom of Lady Bracknell—'I would strongly advise you to try and acquire some genius and if possible some subtlety before the season is quite over'—and he makes matters worse by departing with a final flourish of magic:

> JOYCE *produces a rabbit out of his hat, puts the hat on his head, and leaves, holding the rabbit.*

This piece of conjuring is ostensibly designed to add force to his verbal assault on the fashionable magic of Tzara and his kind. But at the same time it takes the mickey out of his own definition of the true artist as a 'magician put among men to gratify—capriciously—their urge for immortality'. Worse still, it may remind us of a much more sinister piece of conjuring at the end of the first act of *Jumpers*:

> ARCHIE *moves downstage, facing front, and like a magician about to demonstrate a trick, takes from his pocket a small square of material like a handkerchief, which he unfolds and unfolds and unfolds until it is a large plastic bag . . . The* FOUR JUMPERS *throw the body into the bag . . .*

At best, Joyce's speech is likely to appeal as a delightful irrelevance; at worst, it may carry a sinister suggestion of heartlessness. Carr and Tzara are much more fallible both in their reasoning and in their general behaviour, but this very fallibility proves that they are one step closer to reality and thus more humanly appealing. What, then, of Stoppard's insistence that this is the most important speech in the play? Well, this statement must be read in the light of some remarks that Stoppard made to Janet Watts while he was in the process of writing *Travesties*:

> When Auden said that his poetry didn't save one Jew from the gas chamber he'd said it all . . . I've never felt that art is important. That's been my secret guilt.*

So although Stoppard the artist may believe absolutely in Joyce's speech, Stoppard the man is, or was, capable of seeing art (Joyce's and his own) as part of the whole spectrum of human activity. And, viewed in this context, art becomes, as he told Watts, mere 'marginalia—the top tiny fraction of the whole edifice'.

Once Joyce has left the stage Stoppard does place him in this wider context by having Old Carr reminisce about the litigation which took place between them, and about Joyce's subsequent career and death. These down-to-earth details undercut the portrait of the intransigent artist that we have been given hitherto, although the author of *Ulysses* returns to haunt Carr at the very end of the act. And this widening of the focus continues in Act II, as Stoppard told Hayman:

> The second act is Lenin's act really . . . What was supposed to be happening was that we have this rather frivolous nonsense going on, and then the Lenin section comes in and says, 'Life is too important. We can't afford the luxury of this artificial frivolity, this nonsense going on in the arts'.

Originally Stoppard divorced the Lenins entirely from the rest of the play. He told Hayman that he 'stopped the play and had the actors coming down to read that entire passage [i.e. the whole Lenin section] from clipboards or lecterns'. Peter Wood objected that 'the whole thing is within the framework of Carr's memory except this bit'. Stoppard found this complaint unarguable and so he worked into the Lenin section some episodes involving Carr, Tzara and Cecily, not without misgivings; he later told Hayman that he still felt he was right in believing that 'the one thing I could

---

* By 1976 Stoppard was able to tell Steve Grant that he no longer felt guilty about being an artist.

not do was to integrate the Lenins into the *Importance* scheme'. In fact Stoppard need not have worried too much since with one or two exceptions the Lenins are still detached from the *Importance* scheme; the paths of Carr, Tzara and Cecily cross—but scarcely ever touch—those of the Lenins in Act II. The links between the two sets of characters, like those between Rosencrantz and Guildenstern and the players, are essentially factitious. To have set up real links would have meant violating the important point which Old Cecily makes in the epilogue:

> . . . you never got close to Vladimir Ilyich . . . I do remember Joyce . . . but that was the year after— 1918—and the train had long gone from the station! I waved a red hanky and cried long live the revolution as the carriage took him away in his bowler hat and yes, I said yes when you asked me, but he was the leader of millions by the time you did your Algernon . . .

Not only did Carr never know Lenin personally as he did Joyce and, according to Stoppard, Tzara, there was even a temporal dislocation between Lenin's departure from Zürich and the production of *The Importance of Being Earnest* that informs Carr's memories. Paul Johnson regards this glossing over of the facts as a flaw but it seems to me that Stoppard makes good dramatic use of the time discrepancy. Of course, there is, as we have seen, a Lenin who makes desultory appearances within Carr's memory. Carr and the artists he remembers make occasional references to Lenin, and at the beginning of Act I Lenin actually appears alongside them in what seems to be a scene from Carr's memory. But this is not the real Lenin; this is an artificial or 'clockwork' Lenin, comparable to the artificial Rosencrantz and Guildenstern created by the Tragedians and to the artificial Maddie created by the newspapers in *Dirty Linen*. When the real Lenin and Nadya come on in Act II they are redefined and clearly dissociated from this appearance in Act I. For the first words spoken by them in Act II constitute the conversation in Russian that we have already heard, but this time Cecily translates it into English. In other words, the audience suddenly discovers two characters who make sense, and they recognize that the couple who appeared to speak gibberish in Act I were 'clockwork' Lenins invented by Carr. (By the same token, the audience may go on to infer that *everything* in Act I was 'clockwork', if they have not already appreciated this.) Indeed, Cecily's lecture makes it sound as if the whole play is starting over again. When she tells of Lenin's arrival in Zürich she conscientiously repeats material which has been made abundantly clear in the first act:

> Here could be seen James Joyce, reshaping the novel into the permanent form of his own monument, the book the world now knows as *Ulysses!*—and here, too, the Dadaists were performing nightly at the Cabaret Voltaire in the Meierei Bar at Number One Spiegelgasse, led by a dark, boyish and obscure Rumanian poet . . .

And in a sense of course the play *is* starting over again in Act II; we are asked to look at things from a different perspective—the 'real' perspective of Lenin and Nadya.

The Lenins never talk in orthodox stage dialogue. Like Cecily in her lecture—another of Stoppard's characteristic introductory tableaux—they address the audience directly and undramatically, generally quoting either from his *Collected Writings* or from her *Memories of Lenin*. The non-dramatic mode of their discourse is accentuated when they begin to use visual aids to illustrate their points. Like Rosencrantz and Guildenstern, Moon and Birdboot, George Moore, Alexander Ivanov and others, they break through their roles to share the audience's reality.

Initially the Lenins are concerned with politics. They recount their reactions to the news of the 1917 revolution and the various plans which they devised for getting back to Russia. Then they turn to the subject of art, and quite suddenly Lenin (but not Nadya) finds himself within the play for the first time since the opening of Act I. He delivers a long speech from a high rostrum—'with the most dramatic change of effect from the general stage appearance preceding it'. And before he speaks the screen disappears so that all traces of the lecture ambiance which existed previously are removed. The lifting of the screen ought to reveal Old Carr if it was, as specified originally, lowered in front of him, and his appearance at this point would certainly assist the interpretation which I am about to advance. But Stoppard nowhere specifies that Carr should be present here although he does now indicate that Lenin's appearance should accord with Old Carr's initial description of him as balding, bearded and in the three-piece suit.

Lenin's harangue is ridiculous. Stoppard himself told Hayman,

> Lenin keeps convicting himself out of his own mouth. It's absurd. It's full of incredible syllogisms. All the publishing and libraries and bookshops and newspapers must be controlled by the Party. The press will be free. Anybody can write anything they like but anybody who uses the Party press to speak against the Party naturally won't be allowed to do it. And then you go back to the first proposition that everything's controlled by the Party, and you're going round in circles. It's sheer nonsense.

I should like to think that this ridiculous and dramatic speech emanates from Old Carr's memory. Not only is it the only Lenin speech of any significance to be set within the 'fourth wall'; it is also the only one dragged into the play from a remote period of Lenin's life (1905)—a period which Carr might legitimately know about—and the only one delivered in Nadya's absence. If we are not to read this speech into Old Carr's memory, then we must at least acknowledge that it is not the 'real' Lenin who delivers it but a public, 'clockwork' Lenin distinct from the private man whom we see with Nadya. As soon as this harangue is over Nadya returns, the lighting changes, and the subject of art is tackled once more, this time in the non-dramatic mode of discourse which the Lenins had employed before.

The ensuing duologue illustrates Lenin's ambivalence about art in a much more sympathetic way. Instead of the public man contradicting himself we see the private man agonizing, conceding that 'he was not a competent judge of poetical talent' and admitting mistakes. Lenin ends with a tortured speech of great emotional force. Its impact is accentuated by the fact that it is accompanied by a recording of the *Appassionata* sonata:

> I don't know of anything greater than the Appassionata. Amazing, superhuman music. It always makes me feel, perhaps naïvely, it makes me feel proud of the miracles that human beings can perform. But I can't listen to

music often. It affects my nerves, makes me want to say
nice stupid things and pat the heads of those people who
while living in this vile hell can create such beauty.
Nowadays we can't pat heads or we'll get our hands
bitten off. We've got to *hit* heads, hit them without
mercy, though ideally we're against doing violence to
people . . . Hm, one's duty is infernally hard . . .

As Stoppard admitted to Hayman, Lenin 'was in an impossible position. The ethics of necessity syndrome was operat-
ing'. Stoppard goes on to praise the human warmth of Frank
Windsor and Barbara Leigh-Hunt, who played Lenin and
Nadya in the original Royal Shakespeare Company production:

They're just blood heat, they're so human. When they
walk on [off?] the stage you don't really think that man
has contradicted himself throughout and condemned
himself out of his own mouth. You think he really has a
burden to carry, and Ashkenazy is doing his bit in the
loudspeaker, playing the Apassionata [*sic*]. The equation
is different, and even I'm seduced by it.

This quotation is a little vague but I should like to think that
Stoppard's references to the moment when the actors 'walk
on the stage' implicitly contrasts their combined appearances
'on the stage' with Lenin's inhuman solo from the high
rostrum, and that the phrase 'The equation is different' refers
again to the difference between Lenin on his own and Lenin
and Nadya together. It is, however, more likely that Stoppard is referring to the difference between the clinical presentation of the Lenins in his original draft and the warmer
more dramatic portrayal which Peter Wood persuaded him
to adopt.

Lenin disappears on this intense note. But Nadya is given
another speech to round off their part in the play. It too is
very moving—one of those compelling narrative diversions,
found often in Albee and in many other contemporary
American playwrights, that stop the drama dead in its tracks:

Once when Vladimir was in prison—in St Petersburg—
he wrote to me and asked that at certain times of day I
should go and stand on a particular square of pavement
on the Shpalernaya. When the prisoners were taken out

for exercise it was possible through one of the windows in the corridor to catch a momentary glimpse of this spot. I went for several days and stood a long while on the pavement there. But he never saw me. Something went wrong. I forget what.

It is the Lenins' response to life's 'mystery', sometimes funny, more often moving, that dominates Act II. But, as we have seen, Peter Wood persuaded Stoppard not to sever all links with Act I, and so he arranged—not altogether logically, I think—that his straddlers (Carr and Tzara) should intervene on a number of occasions. Thus the Lenins' meditations on art and politics are preceded by a debate between Cecily and Carr on the same topics. Cecily preaches Leninist doctrines rather mechanically, without getting into the kind of practical difficulties which later beset her mentor, and Carr responds with his habitual conservatism. The recurrence of the time-slip, coupled with the striking episode in which Cecily performs a strip-tease, proves that we are once again seeing things through Old Carr's memory.

There is a clear line of demarcation between this 'clockwork' and the 'mystery' of the Lenin sequences which follow. But there are also moments when Carr, Cecily and Tzara spy on, and even interact with, the Lenins. Carr listens attentively to the letter to Karpinsky, and Cecily follows suit almost at once. Tzara comments explicitly on the earlier letter to Yakov Ganetsky, and the Lenins, for their part, stop and stare at an interpolated 'clockwork' episode, which corresponds to the first encounter of Algernon/Ernest and Jack at Jack's house in Act II of *The Importance of Being Earnest*. I can see no way of accounting for this interaction; here, for once, Paul Johnson's complaints about Stoppard's misleading fictions seem to be valid. There is no way in which contact between Carr and the real Lenin can be justified, though one can sympathize with Stoppard's evident desire to maintain some vestiges of orthodox dramatic conflict. The problem is short-lived, however. For the rest of this sequence Carr and Tzara are clearly dissociated from the Lenins:

The corner of the stage now occupied by TZARA *and* CARR *is independent of the* LENINS. *It can no longer be said that the scene is taking place 'in the Library'.* CARR *and* TZARA *might be in a café; or anywhere.*

And the dissociation is not merely spatial; the speeches of Carr and Tzara are totally at odds with those of the Lenins. For example, while Carr maintains that 'the man to watch is Kerensky', Lenin insists that 'Kerensky is especially suspect'. The culmination of this dialogue on separate tracks is the juxtaposition of the sound of Lenin's train setting out for St Petersburg, on the one hand, and this determination from Carr, on the other: 'No, it is perfectly clear in my mind. He must be stopped . . . I shall telegraph the Minister in Berne'.

After this the dislocation of 'mystery' and 'clockwork' again becomes absolute. Carr and his cronies leave the stage and do not return until the Lenins have finally departed. Then the mood of the *Appassionata* degenerates into a music-hall rendition of 'Mr Gallagher and Mr Shean' and we get a final flurry of 'clockwork' in which the remaining sections of Wilde's plot are travestied at breathtaking speed. Clearly none of this is to be taken seriously. The sight of Carr and Tzara endorsing the ideas of Lenin and Joyce respectively is so preposterous that we are obviously far removed from reality.

So far, then, with one brief exception, the worlds of art and politics have been kept quite separate and it might seem that Tynan is right to insist that 'The hard polemic purpose of *Travesties* is to argue that art must be independent of politics'. But what looks on paper like a delicate balance between the two forces is disturbed on the stage by the fact that the Lenins enjoy a closer liaison with the audience than do the artists, who are bloodless figments of Old Carr's imagination. This imbalance becomes even more marked in the closing moments of the play. The travesty of *The Importance of Being Earnest* concludes with a dance for all concerned, which effects 'a complete dislocation of the play'. What follows is, given the precedent of *Jumpers*, probably best described as a coda. Old Carr reappears on stage, accompanied by a new character—Old Cecily. Their dialogue has the initial effect of spelling out still more emphatically the dislocation between art and politics. Old Cecily quickly establishes that Carr never saw Lenin and that he was

never the Consul.* These discoveries serve to confirm what
we should have grasped already: that the Lenin sequences in
Travesties are historically authentic whereas the Joyce/Tzara/
Gwendolen/Carr sequences are the artificial product of Old
Carr's erratic memory. But there is more to this passage than
a simple reinforcement of the art/politics dichotomy. Old
Cecily's determined attack upon her husband's memory
inevitably has the effect of devaluing the airy visions which
that memory has conjured up. True, Old Cecily provides,
for the *literati,* muted support for the endeavours of art early
in the coda when she describes her betrothal to Carr in words
which recall Molly Bloom's famous affirmative at the end of
Ulysses: '. . . and yes, I said yes when you asked me . . .' But
thereafter all her energies are devoted to sorting out the facts,
and eventually her determined realism rubs off on Carr
whose final speech ends not with the artificial bang, which
we might have expected, but with a realistic whimper. His
words echo those of Nadya's last speech, delivered earlier, as
well as the last words of *Dogg's Our Pet* and the first words of
Beckett's *The Unnameable*:

> I learned three things in Zürich during the war. I wrote
> them down. Firstly, you're either a revolutionary or
> you're not, and if you're not you might as well be an
> artist as anything else. Secondly, if you can't be an
> artist, you might as well be a revolutionary . . . I forget
> the third thing.

The build-up to that last sentence is much funnier than the
build-up to Nadya's 'I forget what', but the parallel still
serves to invest Old Carr with a tattered dignity, which is
akin to that of George Riley and George Moore.

It is really only now that we can fully appreciate the
engaging reality of Old Carr and distinguish it from the slick
'clockwork' of his dreams. But if we look back over the play
from this vantage-point we can see that poor, lovable,

---

* She rather spoils her no-nonsense image by maintaining that Tzara's
girlfriend was called Sophia and not Gwendolen; in fact her name was
Maya Chrusecz. Stoppard would seem to be guilty of jeopardizing
coherence for the sake of a pun on women's names and European capital
cities. Another important problem with Cecily is that she exists *outside Old
Carr's memory* as both Young Cecily (at the beginning of Act II) and Old
Cecily (at the end).

bumbling Old Carr was always in evidence behind the airy fantasies of Act I. Consider the time-slips, for example. As we have seen, they provide proof positive that what we are watching in Act I is an artifical construct emanating from Old Carr's mind. But when we ask ourselves what causes these time-slips we generally find that it is the pressure of some particularly vivid memory which Old Carr wishes to suppress. (Shades of 'Prufrock' again; indeed 'Prufrock' is quoted just before the first time-slip.) So paradoxically, while the device signals a high level of artifice or 'clockwork', it also indicates that reality, in the form of the dreamer's subconscious, is endeavouring to break through this facade. In fact, in their small way the time-slips give the lie to the common complaint that there is no real dramatic conflict in *Travesties*.

This realistic undercurrent in Act I, coupled with the more obvious appeal of the Lenins in Act II and the sympathetic portrait of bumbling Old Carr in the coda, serves ultimately to persuade the audience that life is more important than art. *Travesties* is not an anomalous withdrawal 'with style from the chaos'; like all the other plays it is a celebration of life's 'mystery'. The celebration is perhaps more muted than it was in *Jumpers*, and certainly much more muted than it becomes in *Professional Foul* and *Every Good Boy Deserves Favour*, but it is an authentic celebration nevertheless.

8 Dirty Linen *and* New-Found-Land
Sex Breaks the Language Barrier

Dirty Linen was written for Ed Berman's company, Inter-Action, and was performed by them at the Almost Free Theatre in April 1976. It quickly transferred to the Arts Theatre, where it became Stoppard's first big success outside the pale of the subsidized national companies. The commercial quality of the play may owe something to the fact that it was written very quickly. The verbal texture is consequently thinner and the farce broader than in the large-scale plays. To submit this lightweight, frothy piece to rigorous analysis would be to break a butterfly upon a wheel. Still, the point must be briefly made that *Dirty Linen* exhibits the same juxtaposition of 'mystery' and 'clockwork' as do the other plays.

As usual Stoppard provides a couple of condensed statements of his principal theme near the beginning of the play. Cocklebury-Smythe's distinction between real peers and artificial ones (Life Peers) anticipates the distinction between real and artificial relationships on which the play as a whole focusses. But a more important indication of things to come is provided by the opening exchange between Cocklebury-Smythe and McTeazle. Although their dress and accents proclaim them to be British, both men speak at first in a strange amalgam of French, Latin and Spanish. This artificial dialogue is eventually interrupted by a spontaneous ejaculation in good, earthy English from Cocklebury-Smythe: 'Bloody awkward though'. Immediately, however, he excuses his lapse with a topsy-turvy apology—'Pardon my French'—and reverts to foreign tags for a few moments more. This is merely the first of a series of clashes between an artificial, public, 'clockwork' idiom, on the one hand, and a realistic, spontaneous, private idiom, on the other. Before looking at the clashes, let us examine the two idioms separately. An example of the former is the Tennysonian Chairman's Report which the Committee debates in the first part of the play and which, if Cocklebury-Smythe is correct, has been foisted on Withenshaw, the Chairman, by the Prime Minister. Another example is the language used by the newspapers. Stoppard suggests that journalists are capable of a realistic idiom when they are off-duty, 'chasing after everything in a skirt', and even when they are on-duty, covering football matches. But when it comes to the matter of immorality among M.P.s they adopt a pompous, foreign-phrase-ridden idiom. Here, for example, is *The Times* on the subject:

> *Cherchez La Femme Fatale.* It needs no Gibbon come from the grave to spell out the danger to good government of a moral vacuum at the centre of power. Even so, Rome did not fall in a day, and *mutatis mutandis* it is not yet a case of *sauve qui peut for* the government. . . . Admittedly the silence hangs heavy in the House, no doubt on the principle of *qui s'excuse s'accuse,* but we expect the electorate to take in its stride *cum grano salis* stories that upwards of a hundred M.P.s are *in flagrante delicto,* still more that the *demi-mondaine* in most cases is a single and presumably exhausted Dubarry *de nos jours.*

The Guardian is equally pompous in tone and equally reliant on foreign phrases. Foreign phrases are lacking in *The Daily Mail's* coverage of the matter—Stoppard has to make some concessions to realism—but the pomposity is still evident.

The M.P.s themselves use a similar idiom for their public pronouncements. Foreign phrases are rare after the opening exchange between McTeazle and Cocklebury-Smythe, although the word 'quorum' crops up often enough to remind the audience of this feature of the pattern, and exchanges like the following (which is a variation on a formula first used early in *Enter a Free Man*) are so nonsensical that they virtually constitute a foreign language:

> COCKLEBURY-SMYTHE: It's rather more complicated than
> that—er—Arab oil and . . .
> CHAMBERLAIN: . . . the Unions.
> COCKLEBURY-SMYTHE: M.P.s don't have the power they
> used to have, you know.

> MCTEAZLE: Foreign exchange—the Bank of England.
> MRS EBURY: The multi-national companies.
> MCTEAZLE: Not to mention government by Cabinet.
> CHAMBERLAIN: Government by Cabal.
> MRS EBURY: Brussels.
> COCKLEBURY-SMYTHE: The Whips . . .

The absurdity of this catalogue is accentuated not only by Stoppard's direction that the speeches should overlap each other but also by the fact that it is a response to a perfectly sane and simple, if naively optimistic, remark by Maddie:

> Why don't they have a Select Committee to report on what M.P.s have been up to in their *working* hours— that's what people want to know.

Indeed throughout the play Maddie uses a plain, realistic idiom which comes straight from the heart (or thereabouts). Obvious symptoms of her directness are her habit of calling all her male acquaintances by the first names they use in bed rather than by the titles which they use during the day, and her habit of converting voting figures into football scores. (As in *Professional Foul* football becomes a kind of symbol for ordinary down-to-earth activities.)

The two idioms collide spectacularly and hilariously whenever there is intercourse (of one kind, at least) between Maddie and the M.P.s. Right at the beginning of the play McTeazle enquires pompously of Maddie, 'Do you use Gregg's or do you favour the Pitman method?'; she replies bluntly, 'I'm on the pill'. On this occasion there is no response from McTeazle; like so many of Stoppard's 'clock-work' characters he is directed to remain expressionless. On other occasions, however, there is evident tension between the M.P.s' bland public image and the private lust which Maddie inspires in them and which is latent in their very names—or in most of them; I confess to some uncertainty about the implications of Withenshaw and Mrs Ebury. Sometimes this tension is revealed involuntarily, as in this glorious speech of Cocklebury-Smythe's:

> McTeazle, why don't you go and see if you can raise those great tits—boobs—those boobies, absolute tits, don't you agree, Malcolm and Douglas . . ., why don't you have a quick poke, peek, in the Members' Bra—or

the cafeteria, they're probably guzzling coffee and Swedish panties, Danish . . .

More often the tension between public and private in the speech of the M.P.s is expressed voluntarily, private appeals to Maddie giving way to public statements of various kinds (italicized below) whenever a third person comes into earshot, as in the case of this speech by McTeazle:

> Maddie*ning the way one is kept waiting for* ours is a very tricky position, my dear. In normal times one can count on chaps being quite sympathetic to the sight of a Member of Parliament having dinner with a lovely young woman in some out-of-the-way nook—it could be a case of constituency business, they're not necessarily screw-*oo-ooge is, I think you'll find, not in 'David Copperfield' at all, still less in 'The Old Curiosity Sho'*-cking though it is, the sight of a Member of Parliament having some out-of-the-way nookie with a lovely young woman might well be a case of a genuine love match . . . (Stoppard's emphasis).

Attempts are made in the first part of the play to impose this tension between public and private on Maddie herself as, one by one, her lovers enjoin her to keep quiet about the scenes of their compromising encounters. She struggles desperately to 'Forget the Golden Carriage, the Watched Pot and the Coq d'Or . . . ' but on her open and ingenuous nature hypocrisy can never stick, and the injunctions to forget succeed only in 'achieving the opposite' of the effect intended.

Stoppard is on Maddie's side, of course. The politicians have to be taught to take down the artificial barriers which they have built around their natural instincts. And the newspapers, if not the public at large, have to be taught,

> . . . that it is the just and proper expectation of every Member of Parliament, no less than for every citizen of this country, that what they choose to do in their own time, and with whom, is . . . between them and their conscience . . . provided they do not transgress the rights of others or the law of the land . . .

Translated into stylistic terms this means that the formal, public idiom of the newspapers and of the committee members, while it might be appropriate in situations which involve 'the rights of others or the law of the land', is quite inappropriate to the entirely private relationships which are at issue in this play.

Once again, then, we find that Stoppard has juxtaposed the real and the abstract and has opted unequivocally for the former. And it is worth noting at this stage how this portrait of the abstract is embellished with references to various literary (and not so literary) works—novels by Dickens, poems by Tennyson and, of course, the newspapers. These references are really a sort of scaled-down equivalent to the plays-within-the-play in *Rosencrantz and Guildenstern Are Dead*, *The Real Inspector Hound* and *Travesties* and the music-within-the-play in *Every Good Boy Deserves Favour*, and they serve the same purpose of accentuating the artificiality of the attitudes with which they are associated. (Consider, for example, McTeazle's references to *David Copperfield* and *The Old Curiosity Shop* in the italicized section of the speech quoted above.)

But it is the M.P.s' responses to the pin-up photographs in the popular press that indicate most obviously the artificiality of their attitudes. Each time an M.P. comes upon one of these pictures Stoppard initiates a stage routine which is de-signed—rather like Rosencrantz and Guildenstern's con-frontations with their stage replicas—to sharpen the distinc-tion between Maddie's real, private sexuality and the bogus, public version of it. This is what happens:

> *This moment of the man reacting to the pin-up photograph, and the coincidental image of* MADDIE *in a pin-up pose is something which is to be repeated several times, so for brevity's sake it will be hereafter symbolized by the expletive 'Strewth!' It must be marked distinctly; a momentary freeze on stage, and probably a flash of light like a camera flash.* MADDIE *should look straight out at the audience for that moment.*

This routine occurs six times in the first part of *Dirty Linen*. On the first four occasions it is a single politician who says, 'Strewth!' and he is commenting on the newspaper pin-up. The audience, on the other hand, has its attention firmly fixed on the *real* pin-up—Maddie, in an ever-increasing state of undress. On the fifth occasion the presentation of the tableau is slightly different. Maddie herself displays one of the newspaper pin-ups to the Committee. But still the distinction between the artificial pin-up seen by the Committee and the real pin-up seen by the audience is preserved. This fifth tableau acts as a kind of bridging device between the earlier ones and the all-important final one, where the circumstances are significantly changed. Again it is Maddie who displays the newspaper pin-up from *The Sun* to the Committee but her reasons for doing so are much deeper and more personal than they were on the previous occasion. At first she was simply trying to make a point about newspapers; now she has become incensed at the artificial cant going on around the table, and she wants to expose its hypocrisy. More important, the pin-up in question features Maddie herself so that the distance which has so far been observed between the real pin-up and the artificial one in the newspaper is removed.

It is French who remarks on the identity of the two pin-ups, at the same time reducing Maddie to her bra and panties so that her actual appearance corresponds exactly to her image in *The Sun*. This is appropriate because French is the one member of the Committee who has not so far been seduced by Maddie and who has therefore remained free of the hypocrisy which taints everything said by the others. To date his sincerity has been misdirected; he has been assiduous in his search for evidence relating to misconduct by M.P.s and has thus vindicated Withenshaw's description of him as 'a sanctimonious busybody with an Energen roll where his balls ought to be'. Nevertheless, once the Energen roll has been rooted out by Maddie during the interval, his openness, redirected, will prove a decisive influence for the good. He is of course a catalytic figure in the sense defined by Birdboot in *The Real Inspector Hound*, but he is one of the few such characters in Stoppard whose function is not subverted.

French's initiative in naming Maddie causes the others to focus directly on her for the first time in the play; the collective 'Strewth!' on this occasion is directed at Maddie and not at the newspaper. The sixth tableau is therefore constructed in such a way as to indicate that a collective awakening, initiated by Maddie and French together, is at hand. Moreover, the fact that Maddie is now virtually naked suggests that the naked truth is about to emerge. But before this can happen the Division Bell rings, the cast of *Dirty*

Linen troops off and we find ourselves confronted by what the stage direction calls 'another play'.

Is *New-Found-Land* a wholly separate piece? It has certainly been performed and recorded separately, and the story of its genesis, told here by Hayman, would seem to confirm its autonomy:

> To celebrate his naturalization as a British subject and the 200th anniversary of the American Revolt, Ed Berman commissioned Stoppard to write the first in a series of new plays to be staged at the Almost Free Theatre under the title *The American Connection* . . . Having started on *Dirty Linen*, Stoppard found that it was developing into something which had no connection either with Ed Berman or with the United States, but which was too good to scrap. The solution was to write a shorter play, *New-Found-Land*, which could be interpolated, like an entr'acte, between the two halves of *Dirty Linen*.

Hayman proceeds to discuss *New-Found-Land* in isolation from *Dirty Linen*. He does acknowledge in passing that the two are 'seamed neatly together with small overlaps', but this seems to be a reference to the purely physical links between the plays—their use of the same setting and its associated sound-effects, and the way in which they literally overlap when the cast of *Dirty Linen* returns to the stage and brings the business of *New-Found-Land* to a summary conclusion.

There are, however, important thematic links as well. One that proves ultimately to be something of a red herring is the link between Withenshaw's casual observation that he 'once took a train journey right across America' and Arthur's long monologue on the same subject. A more meaningful link is that between the two Frenches—the M.P. in *Dirty Linen* and the First World War general. In his first long speech in *New-Found-Land* Bernard claims that Lloyd George once told him that 'French was a booby'. The word 'booby' has of course already been subjected to sexual innuendo in the early stages of *Dirty Linen*, and so the fact that it is now attached to French's name should tell us, if we have not already guessed, just what French and Maddie are up to in the ladies' cloakroom and while Bernard and Arthur are occupying the stage.* And, having recognized this, we are in a position to see that Bernard's entire monologue about winning £5 from Lloyd George is relevant to the themes of *Dirty Linen*. For the speech is a piece of romanticism which glosses over the fact that Bernard's mother was Lloyd George's mistress in much the same way that the politicians and the newspapers gloss over the reality of Maddie's affairs.

Arthur's monologue about America is similarly idealistic and again the idealism is directly relevant to *Dirty Linen*. Ostensibly the speech arises out of an eccentric American's application for British citizenship, which Bernard and Arthur are supposed to be considering. But at a deeper level what Arthur says is again relevant to the French/Maddie liaison by virtue of the quotation with which it opens: 'My America!— my new-found-land!' The line is of course lifted from Donne's 'Elegy XIX: To His Mistress Going to Bed', though it is perhaps worth remarking that it occurs also in Beckett's *Murphy*. Arthur's extrapolation of an image from a famous poem on this subject can be regarded as a sort of literary counterpart to those suggestive scenes of natural ebb-and-flow-and-ultimate-climax with which the cinema used to titillate us while the hero and heroine were at their business off-screen.

New-Found-Land—note the spelling, which links the play with Donne's poem—thus emerges as a kind of idealized dream-sequence, comparable to Ruth's dream, which occurs at the same point in *Night and Day*. The fact that Bernard goes to sleep once Arthur launches into his monologue reinforces this impression. So does Arthur's topsy-turvy geography. His journey through America can only be a journey of the mind; its landmarks are drawn from myth and literature rather than from reality.

The dreamy idealism of *New-Found-Land* is abruptly shat-

* There is a consistent development in the attitude to Maddie shown by the various members of the Committee. The first two to appear (Cockle-bury-Smythe and McTeazle) do not acknowledge her publicly at all; Chamberlain treats her 'with open crude lechery'; Withenshaw regales her with suggestive puns; and Mrs Ebury actually indulges in some physical contact. This development creates an expectation that the sixth member of the Committee (French) will take the ultimate liberty with Maddie—as indeed he does.

tered when the cast of *Dirty Linen* returns to the stage.
Bernard, eager to relate his Lloyd George story to a new
audience, produces his £5 note again, only to have it uncere-
moniously destroyed by Withenshaw, who takes it for one of
Maddie's *billets doux*. The Home Secretary undercuts
Arthur's romantic vision of America by coming to a completely arbitrary decision about the citizenship issue: 'One
more American can't make any difference'. This minor
triumph of realism is proleptic. When the Select Committee
resumes its deliberations, French, who has become a 'booby'
during the interval and can produce a pair of Maddie's
knickers to prove it, brings matters abruptly to a head by
proposing the adoption of a new Chairman's Report. This
new report, which has obviously been dictated to French by
Maddie (whereas the original one had been dictated to
Withenshaw by the Prime Minister) is couched in the direct,
private idiom which she has used throughout the play. Its
substance, as I have already noted, is that M.P.s are as free as
any other citizen to do what they like in their spare time.

Although French lapses nervously into foreign phrases
several times when introducing his proposal and even once
after its adoption ('Toujours l'amour'), it is clear that the
unanimous vote in its favour ('Arsenal 5—Newcastle nil')
represents an unequivocal triumph for reality over the sort of
abstract cant which was so prominent in the first part of the
play and in *New-Found-Land*. The dumb blonde has prevailed
over the clever dicks* and it is only fair that now, with the
pressure off her, so to speak, she should be allowed to
indulge in her one unprompted foreign phrase of the play:
'Finita La Commedia'. (Her earlier lapse into French is the
result of a misunderstanding; she takes Cocklebury-Smythe's
introduction of Mr French as a request that she should speak
in French, and so she responds, 'Enchantée.) As she delivers
her Italian epilogue Big Ben chimes the quarter-hour—the

---

* To Hayman Stoppard averred that '*Dirty Linen* was in my own mind
really a play about presenting a stereotype dumb blonde and dislocating the
assumptions about the stereotype'. Viewed in a wider perspective Maddie
might be seen as the first of Stoppard's instinctively-right-thinking
children, the precursor to Alastair (*Night and Day*), the two Sachas (*Every
Good Boy Deserves Favour* and *Professional Foul*) and Debbie (*The Real
Thing*).

fourth time it has struck in the course of the play, which, taken literally, would mean that the whole of *Dirty Linen-cum-New-Found-Land* should last a little over three-quarters of an hour—impossible. It is all too easy for critics to wax lyrical over the manifest intrusion of so meaty an abstraction as time into a work of literature, and I hope that I am not being over-ingenious when I suggest that the insistence on time passing in this play underlines the insistence on reality at other levels. In *If You're Glad I'll Be Frank* Gladys stresses the distinction between the artificial, mechanical clock and the reality of time:

> It's only the clock that goes tick tock
> and never the time that chimes.
> It's never the time that stops.

Similarly in *Travesties* Stoppard distinguishes between the 'cuckoo-clock artificially amplified' that signals Carr's time-slips and the 'naturalistic cuckoo-clock . . . seen to strike during the here-and-now scene of Old Carr's monologue'.

In *Dirty Linen* the chiming of Big Ben seems related, paradoxically enough, to Gladys's time rather than her clock, to the here-and-now rather than the artifice in *Travesties*. It is in the service of 'mystery' rather than 'clockwork'. Perhaps the point can be made more clearly by reference to another analogous statement about time, in Auden's poem, 'As I Walked Out One Evening'. (That Stoppard knows the poem intimately is suggested by the fact that in 'Ambushes for the Audience' he talks enthusiastically of 'Auden's glacier knocking in the cupboard'—an allusion to line 41.)

After Auden's lover has given vent to his Burnsian idealism about true love lasting 'Till China and Africa meet,/ And the river jumps over the mountain/And the salmon sing in the street'—sentiments echoed early in *The Real Inspector Hound*—the narrator steps in with this grim rejoinder:

> But all the clocks in the city
> Began to whirr and chime:
> 'O let not time deceive you,
> You cannot conquer time . . .'

The whirring and chiming of Big Ben in *Dirty Linen* make

the same point, which is indirectly related to the much more palatable point that the delightful reality of Maddie's sex-life should remain a private 'mystery', or series of mysteries, instead of being subjected to 'clockwork' public inquiries.

9 Every Good Boy Deserves Favour
Discordant Notes in an Orchestrated Society

Perhaps the most characteristic feature of Stoppard's art is his fondness for the play-within-the-play. The device appears in a number of different guises. In *Rosencrantz and Guildenstern Are Dead, The Real Inspector Hound, Travesties, Dogg's Hamlet* and *The Real Thing* it is presented straight. But in *Night and Day* it becomes a dream-sequence; in *Jumpers* it is reduced to some quotations from *Macbeth* together with a series of charades enacted by Archie and Dotty, with occasional assistance from George and Bones; in *After Magritte* it takes the form of a crazy flight of fancy (Foot's interpretation of events inside the Harris house and outside his own); and in *Professional Foul* it assumes a more realistic aspect as a portrait of academics at play in the conference-hall. In *A Separate Peace* the nearest equivalent to the play-within-the-play is a picture—the Magrittean mural which Brown substitutes for the real landscape outside. And in *Dirty Linen*, similarly, the pin-up photographs are presented as pictures-within-the-play, although there is also something closer to a play-within-the-play: Arthur's monologue in *New-Found-Land*.

Throughout all these metamorphoses the device goes on serving the same purpose: to create, at two removes from the real world inhabited by the audience, a repository for the artificial, 'clockwork' attitudes which Stoppard is always at pains to identify and discredit.

Stoppard wrote *Every Good Boy Deserves Favour* in collaboration with, and at the suggestion of, André Previn, as a 'play for actors and orchestra'. So the play-within-the-play has undergone yet another transformation and has emerged as an orchestra-within-the-play. Still the same purpose is served, however: all the characters associated with the orchestra are shown to have attitudes which are so mindlessly 'clockwork' that they may be deemed insane. One of the principals, Ivanov, is actually a confirmed lunatic. He believes that he is in control of a symphony orchestra, to which he contributes the triangle part. The play opens with a performance by this orchestra. But it is an imaginary performance:

> IVANOV *strikes the triangle, once. The orchestra starts miming a performance. He stands concentrating, listening to music which we cannot hear, and striking his triangle as and when the 'music' requires it . . .*

Once the point has been established, we are allowed to enter Ivanov's mind:

> *. . . very quietly, we begin to hear what* IVANOV *can hear, i.e. the orchestra becomes audible. So now his striking of the triangle begins to fit into the context which makes sense of it.*

This introductory tableau indicates that the orchestra is not a real phenomenon but a symptom of lunacy. From now on its playing always signifies madness, whether it be the private madness of Ivanov or the public madness of the Soviet system.

The play features three orthodox pillars of the Soviet state: the Teacher, the Doctor and the Colonel. The Teacher's entrances are always accompanied by music, usually that of her pupils' percussion band. When she defines the Soviet system as an orchestra whose members must play together she puts the audience in a position to construct an important syllogism: the orchestra-within-the-play symbolizes lunacy; the Soviet system is like an orchestra; therefore the Soviet system is crazy.

Previn's score makes the same point in a different way. It is basically a Shostakovich pastiche, and may thus be regarded as a symbol of Soviet orthodoxy. In a subtle way the equation of music with madness is made visually as well: the triangle part which Sacha is supposed to follow is written out in yellow, which is the colour associated with the dreaded Rad-Libs in *Jumpers*.

As well as music, the Teacher tries to instil in her pupils the elements of Euclidean geometry—an eminently 'clockwork' discipline. But both sets of rules are broken by young Sacha. He sabotages the Teacher's music by beating his triangle at random and his snare drum violently. And he defies the Teacher's attempts to instruct him in geometry by imposing a realistic interpretation on the concepts. His notion that 'A triangle is the shortest distance between three points' may allude to the way in which Sacha is torn between Soviet orthodoxy and his father's dissidence. When he goes on to proclaim that 'A circle is the longest distance to the same point' we may detect a wry comment on the circularity of Soviet judicial processes; and when he finally exclaims, 'A plane area bordered by high walls is a prison not a hospital' we recognize a direct attack on the Soviet habit of confining dissidents in mental institutions.

One such dissident is the play's protagonist, Sacha's father, Alexander. He has been transferred to the Third Civil Mental Hospital after a devastating spell of confinement in the Leningrad Special Psychiatric Hospital. Alexander's dissidence, like his son's, is expressed in terms of dissonance. He cannot hear Ivanov's orchestra, and when Ivanov questions him on the subject he declares categorically:

> I do not play an instrument. If I played an instrument I'd tell you what it was. But I do not play one. I have never played one. I do not know how to play one. I am not a musician.

To appreciate this play one must swallow all those cherished notions about 'the man that hath no music in himself' being 'fit for treasons, stratagems and spoils'; to Stoppard, whose musical expertise is not considerable, as he confessed to Joost Kuurman, the just are tone-deaf.

When the time comes for Alexander's account of how he became a dissident he addresses the audience directly, after the manner of Rosencrantz and Guildenstern, George Moore and the Lenins. This long understated speech is very moving. The one disturbing factor is the musical 'annotation'. The elegiac violins do help to create a pathetic mood but at the same time they destroy the over-riding logic which equates music with madness and dissonance with dissidence, and therefore with sanity. It might of course be argued that the music is appropriate here because Alexander is speaking of a time when he himself was more or less a conformist. Certainly once his story reaches the point of his first active

dissent the music is 'sabotaged'. But I rather suspect that
there was a small failure of communication between Stoppard and Previn. Stoppard intended the music to serve a
structural purpose but Previn could not resist using it in a
more incidental way to create atmosphere. (Two scenes
earlier Alexander's nightmare is likewise accompanied by
incidental music.) Still, although the orchestra supports
Alexander on these occasions, he never gives any support or
even acknowledgement to the orchestra. He is in fact the
only character in the play who ignores it altogether.

Alexander and Ivanov share a cell in the mental hospital
and in due course both are interviewed by the second
representative of the orthodox Soviet orchestra, the Doctor.
Ivanov is interviewed first. The Doctor tries hard to persuade
him that there is no orchestra, but not only can Ivanov and
the audience still hear it, the audience has seen the Doctor
himself emerge from the ranks of the on-stage orchestra and
move, with close orchestral accompaniment, to the acting-
area. He even has his violin on the desk before him as he
interviews Ivanov. The Doctor's hypocrisy is made fully
explicit during his second interview with Ivanov:

> IVANOV: I have no orchestra!
> [*Silence.* IVANOV *indicates the silence with a raised finger.*
> *He strikes his triangle again.*]
> DOCTOR: [*Suddenly*] Wait a minute!—what day is it?
> IVANOV: I have never *had* an orchestra!
> [*Silence. The* DOCTOR, *however, has become preoccupied*
> *and misses the significance of this.*]
> DOCTOR: *What day is it?* Tuesday?
> [IVANOV *strikes the triangle.*]
> IVANOV: I do not want an orchestra!
> [*Silence.*]
> DOCTOR: [*Horrified*] What time is it? I'm going to be late
> for the orchestra!
> [*The* DOCTOR *grabs his violin case and starts to leave.*
> IVANOV *strikes his triangle.*]
> IVANOV: *There is no orchestra!*
> DOCTOR: [*Leaving*] Of course there's a bloody orchestra!
> [*Music—one chord.* IVANOV *hears it and is mortified. More*
> *chords. The* DOCTOR *has left.*]
> IVANOV: [*Bewildered*] I have an orchestra.

When Alexander arrives for his first interview with the

Doctor, the Doctor is actually playing his violin, and the theme he is playing is a continuation of the music which accompanied the Teacher's expressions of orthodoxy in the previous scene. But the purpose of this interview and its sequel is not simply to repeat the clash between orthodoxy and dissidence at a metaphorical level but to translate it into explicit political terms. These important scenes delineate in some detail the barbaric and cynical treatment meted out to Soviet dissidents in what are euphemistically called mental hospitals. The climax of the first interview is a big speech based closely, as Stoppard acknowledges in his Introduction, on Victor Fainberg's article in 'Index on Censorship'.* Like Alexander's earlier account of how he became a dissident this important speech is virtually a soliloquy addressed directly to the audience.

The Doctor tries to persuade Alexander to stop his protests against the system so that he can be released from prison/ hospital. But Alexander will not cease. Therefore he cannot be released. And since he is on a hunger-strike (his second such protest) it seems likely that he will die, to the embarrassment of the authorities who 'don't like you to die unless you can die anonymously'. This logical impasse is resolved by a rather dubious piece of *legerdemain*. Quite late in the play we discover that Alexander's (and Sacha's) second name is Ivanov and that Ivanov's first name is Alexander. Confusion of identity thus becomes a possibility and, sure enough, when the Colonel arrives to interview the two hospital inmates at the end of the play, he puts the wrong set of questions to each and is able to release them both.

How is a director to handle this creaky device? Stoppard told Kuurman that he meant it to be clear that 'the Colonel understood what he was doing'—that he confused the two men deliberately because, like Victor Fainberg, Alexander 'was such an embarrassment that they were really dying to get rid of him'. Apparently this was not made clear in the first performances at the Festival Hall, and 'a lot of people thought that the Colonel had made a mistake'. The matter was rectified in the second London season at the Mermaid

* Vol. 4, no.2, published by Writers and Scholars International, 21 Russell Street, London WC2.

Theatre. In the only New Zealand production to date, presented by the Downstage Theatre Company with the New Zealand Symphony Orchestra, the director Philip Mann reverted to the idea of a mistake on the Colonel's part and embellished it effectively; the Colonel did a quick 'eeny-meeny-miney-mo' to sort out the two Ivanovs and, having identified them wrongly, rode roughshod over the Doctor's attempts (which are not in the published text, of course) to put him right. Thus our attention was drawn to the stupidity and pride of the Colonel and, by implication, of the system which he represents. This interpretation seems to me as effective as Stoppard's own in underscoring the 'clockwork' mentality of the Soviet state.

Of course, the freedom thus bestowed on Alexander and Ivanov is a nominal freedom devoid of substance. Ivanov will go on hearing his orchestra and, more important, Alexander will go on campaigning for civil rights and will no doubt find himself back in a mental hospital before long. The unhappiness of this ending is established above all by the music. The closing section of Previn's score is perhaps rather too long for the actors' comfort,* but it certainly succeeds in evoking an atmosphere of chilling menace. And on this occasion there is no tension between the affective quality of the music and the dramatic role of the orchestra. For the orchestra that produces these menacing sounds has by now drawn into its ranks all the characters who have defended Soviet orthodoxy. The Doctor is back at his desk among the violinists. The Teacher moves into the orchestra, though her role there is not specified. The Colonel does not stay until the end, but the organ music which accompanies his departure blends into the finale. For good measure Ivanov joins in with his triangle, thus finally cementing the link between his lunatic orchestra and the orchestra which symbolizes the Soviet system. Worse than all this, however, is the fact that young Sacha has fallen under the spell of the orchestra and is singing to its accompaniment the reassuring words (of which the sinister music and Alexander's protests make a mockery):

---

*Here as always I refer to the version for a full-scale symphony orchestra. There exists a reduced score for chamber orchestra, but I have never heard it.

'Papa, don't be crazy! . . . Everything can be all right!' That
it is really Sacha and not his father who is being crazy is
indicated by the fact that it was mad Ivanov, posing, not
inappropriately, as the Doctor, who converted Sacha to
orthodox beliefs (e.g. 'A line must be drawn!') and made him
promise to 'go back in the orchestra'.

Sacha's role is an intriguing one. He starts in one Stoppardian mould and ends in another. The former is the mould
from which Maddie in *Dirty Linen*, Sacha in *Professional Foul*
and Alastair in *Night and Day* were also fashioned. It produces young innocents with an instinctive sense of right and
wrong. The latter mould is the one which formed Frazer in
Albert's Bridge, the Tragedians in *Rosencrantz and Guildenstern
Are Dead* and Stoppard's other straddlers. These characters
are usually introduced to clarify the basic dialectic of the
plays, but Sacha assumes the role so late in the piece that he
has no real chance to perform this function. The important
thing in his case is simply the fall from innocence and purity
to experience and compromise. It casts a bleak shadow over
the play's conclusion.

Sacha's seduction by the orchestra leaves Alexander alone
in his dissonance/dissidence. He ignores the music, counter-
ing it with his peculiar form of spoken doggerel, which
includes the line, 'One and one is always two'—a diminution
of the formula borrowed by Dotty in *Jumpers* from Winston
Smith in Orwell's *1984*: 'Two and two are four'. At the end
Alexander moves away through the orchestra towards the
organ. Sacha runs ahead singing and tries to turn him back,
but Alexander refuses to be diverted from his righteous quest
for disharmony. What Stoppard says of Fainberg in his
Introduction is true also of Alexander: he is 'not a man to be
broken or silenced; an insistent, discordant note, one might
say, in an orchestrated society'.

10 Night and Day
An Uneasy Attempt at Realism

In *Dirty Linen* Stoppard subjected his own first profession of journalism to a somewhat casual, superficial scrutiny. *Night and Day* takes a harder, closer, more serious look at the same subject. The play is not oppressively earnest of course; the audience gets a good many laughs, most of them generated by the caustic, brittle wit of Ruth. But the laughter is never a symptom of gratuitous fun as it sometimes is in the earlier plays. In *Night and Day* the laughter presupposes thought; it arises from the cut-and-thrust of an intensive debate—or rather series of debates—involving Ruth, Wagner, Milne, Mageeba and, to a lesser extent, Carson and Guthrie. Moreover, the laughter fades towards the end as death and disillusionment invade the stage.

The new mood is accompanied—as it was in *Professional Foul*—by a change of mode. Apart from two dream-sequences and a handful of speeches in which 'Ruth' gives voice to the thoughts of Ruth, the play obeys the canons of realism. The technical high jinks which characterize the earlier plays, and which can easily distract audiences from the underlying themes, are lacking here. Stoppard anticipated this change in the second interview with Hayman, when he announced that he was 'sick of flashy mind-projections speaking in long, articulate witty sentences about the great abstractions' and that he intended to write for Michael Codron a West End play like Priestley's *The Linden Tree* or '*The Rattigan Version*'. (Codron did indeed present the first season of *Night and Day*. He had earlier put on *The Real Inspector Hound* and he has since done *The Real Thing*.) In fact, because of the prominence of intellectual debate in *Night and Day*, it was to Shaw rather than to Priestley or Rattigan that the critics turned for an analogy. In *The Sunday*

Telegraph on 12 November 1978, for example, Francis King wrote:

> The debate is full of Shavian intelligence, vivacity and wit. Shavian too is the author's greater involvement in the passion of conflicting ideas than in that of conflicting emotions . . .

The Shavian parallel is certainly apt in many respects. But there is at least one important difference between the two playwrights. In Shaw the ideas develop gradually and systematically, whereas in Stoppard they are presented fully-formed in discrete bursts. In fact Stoppard seems less interested in the ideas themselves than in the states of mind (idealistic or realistic: 'clockwork' or 'mysterious') to which they bear witness.

Because the contrast is instructive let us briefly review the Shavian method. Consider, for example, that most discursive of discussion-plays, *Heartbreak House*. Although the surface of the play is littered with inconsequential encounters and exchanges, which epitomize what Shaw calls in his Preface the 'utter enervation and futilization in that over-heated drawing-room atmosphere' of 'cultured, leisured Europe before the war', a coherent focus of meaning is provided by the systematic handling of Ellie Dunn's development. Her importance is indicated immediately by Captain Shotover's unwonted fuss about her reception. And then, having roused our interest in the girl, Shaw traces her development in three stages. These correspond not only to the three acts of the play but also, as Robert F. Whitman★ has recently reminded us, to the three phases of Hegelian dialectic: her romantic love for Marcus Darnley (thesis) gives place to a grimly selfish attachment to 'Boss' Mangan (antithesis), which is finally succeeded by a 'spiritual' bond with Captain Shotover (synthesis). This beautifully articulated plot is flanked by two equally shapely sub-plots in which Shotover's two daughters, Hesione and Ariadne, reduce Mangan and Randall respectively to heartbreak.

This sense of sustained, ordered development is lacking in *Night and Day*. There are five set-piece debates about journalism in the course of the play, but the links between them are

★ *Shaw and the Play of Ideas* (Ithaca and London, 1977), Chapter V.

extremely tenuous. The first pits Milne, aided for a moment by Guthrie, against Wagner. Wagner is a union man who advocates worker solidarity in the face of exploitation from above and competition from below. Milne, an anti-union man known to Wagner as 'the Grimsby scab', confronts him at this stage on purely pragmatic grounds; he argues that newspapers do not make vast profits for the bosses and that the quality of some journalism is such that many printers deserve to be paid more than journalists.

The second debate—a brief one—is between Ruth and Wagner a little later in Act I. Ruth, citing the coverage of her own divorce in the press, echoes Milne's complaint about the low standard of popular reporting. In the first Faber edition of the play Wagner's response is ambiguous, but in the second edition he openly concedes her point: 'Yeah—I agree with you. Newspapers have got more important things to do'. Thus one of the points at issue between Wagner and Milne seems to have been resolved in Milne's favour; only the question of the bosses' profiteering remains.

When Ruth and Milne come together for the third debate at the end of Act I, however, the terms of reference have changed radically. The question of profiteering is dropped altogether and by a confusing piece of sleight of hand Milne converts Wagner's insistence on worker solidarity from a means of ensuring good working conditions, which is how Wagner justified it, into a device for imposing on the press the views of a closed shop of journalists. This transition is not illogical of course but the casual manner in which it is made is likely to perplex an audience. Milne then proceeds to his main argument, which had not been mentioned during his initial debate with Wagner. 'A free press, free expression,' he maintains, is 'the last line of defence for all the other freedoms'—including the freedom of journalists to defy the official line taken by their union. This insistence on freedom leads Milne to defend 'junk journalism', which he and Ruth have both previously lambasted, as 'the evidence of a society that has got at least one thing right, that there should be nobody with the power to dictate where responsible journalism begins'.

The discussion of journalism in Act I is, as I hope I have demonstrated, not a little confusing. Things do not really improve in Act II, where there are just two set-piece debates: the first during the visit of President Mageeba to the Carsons' house, the second near the end of the play. In Faber's original published edition the first debate splits clearly into two parts: an argument between Ruth and Wagner, and what amounts to a monologue by Mageeba. By the second edition an attempt has been made to stitch these two parts together by transferring some of Ruth's early speeches, suitably modified, to Mageeba. Even so, the episode does not really constitute a clearly defined step in a developing argument about journalism.

The Ruth/Wagner argument in the first Faber edition begins with Wagner's accusation that 'young Milne has been bending your ear'. A semblance of continuity is thus established between Milne's ideas in Act I and Ruth's arguments here. But the link is really quite factitious. Milne came nowhere near formulating the case which Ruth now presents: that private control of newspapers is better than worker solidarity because a journalist sacked by a private boss can find work elsewhere—on a paper with a different point-of-view—whereas a journalist who crosses his colleagues cannot hope to find any other work. Wagner, who now for the first time concedes the point made by Milne at the end of Act I, that worker solidarity is designed to safeguard opinions as well as working conditions, retorts, in effect, that wealthy newspaper proprietors tend to have the same interests and that journalists must unite to protect their 'freedom to report facts that may not be congenial to, let us say, an English millionaire'. When Ruth observes that 'the whole country is littered with papers pushing every political line from Mao to Mosley and back again' and that this competition guarantees freedom, Wagner replies that this diversity of opinion is ideal rather than real since an extreme 'basement pamphleteer' cannot earn a living wage. Ruth's response is not entirely convincing: after an appeal to the law of the open market-place (which is surely open to the objection that the majority is always wrong—a line which one might have expected Ruth herself to take, given her expressed abhorrence of the popular press), she concludes lamely by seeming to concede Wagner's point that it takes a millionaire to run a paper and then expressing a pious confidence in the diversity of millionaires—a point which Wagner has already disputed.

In the second edition the mode of this discourse has changed but its content has not really been altered. Ruth is given a rhetorical edge over Wagner by the injection of a powerful ironic device into her speeches. She pretends throughout to be quoting her eight-year-old son, Alastair, so as to insinuate that what she is saying ought to be accessible to a child. The device is familiar from *Professional Foul* and *Every Good Boy Deserves Favour* but in this case one doubts its integrity since the substance of Ruth's arguments remains as tenuous as before. Moreover, two other factors peculiar to the second version make it harder than ever to place Ruth's ideas in the context of a continuing debate. One is the omission of the introductory reference to Milne. The other is the transference of most of Ruth's early speeches to Mageeba. It is actually specified in the stage directions that Ruth hadn't been listening to the early exchanges between Wagner and Mageeba. To be sure, she makes a strong comeback but the fact remains that the opening stage of this debate lacks any outward and visible link with its predecessor, between Ruth and Milne at the end of Act I. This change of cast is bound to suggest discontinuity in the ideas.

After Ruth has said her piece Mageeba enters the lists to expound his notion of a relatively free press—that is, 'a free press which is edited by one of my relatives'. The emergence of this doctrine of state control alongside the Ruth/Milne case for private ownership and Wagner's advocacy of worker solidarity should not of itself be confusing. Indeed, it looks for a moment rather like a Shavian synthesis, especially in the second version where Mageeba is given an earlier speech which seems to combine elements of both Ruth/Milne's thesis and Wagner's antithesis in such a way as to disconcert both these parties. 'There is nothing to be said for private ownership', he begins, to the satisfaction of Wagner. But then, to Wagner's chagrin, he goes on to say:

> The power of the proprietor is too limited to do any good. . . . A proprietor can only dismiss you from his *own* newspaper. The irresponsible journalist remains free to work elsewhere . . .

Worker solidarity is thus undercut in a way which would

please Ruth and Milne. Wagner, on the other hand, rightly
suspects that he is being outflanked. Ultimately, however,
the case for state control turns out to be a red herring—or
rather a convenient stick with which to beat Wagner (quite
literally). Once Mageeba leaves the scene the subject is never
raised again.

The final discussion of journalism occurs a little later.
Ruth, stirred by the news of Milne's death, pours out a
torrent of abuse against the profession. Her speeches are
powerful but they contain no new ideas. Indeed, there is
some evidence of a regression in her thought. Forgetting
Milne's defence of 'junk journalism' in Act I, which seemed
to convince her at the time, she pours scorn on the ephemeral
content of the popular press and for the third time in the play
we get a catalogue of lurid and ludicrous headlines.

Her principal antagonist on this occasion is George
Guthrie, a most interesting character whom Stoppard has
been holding in reserve for this climactic moment. Hitherto
he has shown himself to be a man of few words. He quickly
surrenders to Ruth once the exposition is over and the
discussion underway in Act I; 'I think I'll just sit and drink
my beer', he says, and while the others talk he simply goes to
sleep.

But by his deeds, if not by his words, Guthrie has achieved
considerable stature by the time he confronts Ruth again at
the end of the play. The arresting dream sequence at the very
beginning vividly establishes his presence, and thereafter the
audience is impressed by his friendly treatment of Alastair
(whom Wagner patronizes abominably), his quiet efficiency
as a photographer both inside the house and out in the
war-zone, and his shocked sense of outrage when he stum-
bles in to report the death of Milne in Act II. So when he does
find his tongue at the end of the play what he says carries a
good deal of weight. He rebuffs Ruth's attacks with these
plain words:

> People do awful things to each other. But it's worse in
> places where everybody is kept in the dark. It really is.
> Information is light. Information, in itself, about any-
> thing, is light. That's all you can say, really.

His views are obviously not unlike Milne's argument that 'a

free press, free expression [is] the last line of defence for all the other freedoms'. But there is a subtle and perhaps important difference. Milne seems primarily interested in opinions whereas Guthrie, as befits a photographer, emphasizes plain facts. Milne tends to lead us back to the business of ownership (whose opinions?) but Guthrie stands apart from all principles, issues and abstractions. He is, I believe, an archetypal Stoppardian hero, a man who refuses to try to reduce the world to 'clockwork' systems but simply immerses himself in life's 'mystery' and gets on with the job in hand. (The dream sequence with which the play begins suggests that Guthrie is not entirely confined to reality. However, his dream is of a much more realistic kind than Ruth's; indeed, it prefigures very accurately the ultimate fate of Milne.)

It is clearly time to abandon the Shavian approach to *Night and Day* and return to the orthodox Stoppardian juxtaposition of 'mystery' and 'clockwork'. The Shavian approach fails because of the lack of continuity—even consistency—in the ideas adventured in the various debates. Consistency exists, however, at one remove from the surface of the text. *Night and Day* is no exception to the general rule, spelled out in 'Ambushes for the Audience', that Stoppard's plays 'tend to bear on life in an oblique, distant, generalized way', to convey a 'universal perception' rather than a particular one. Of course, the realistic mode makes *Night and Day* look more particular than the others, and indeed I wonder if the particular vehicle and the 'universal' tenor are ultimately compatible. If audiences are required to step back and view the action in a distant, generalized way they need some fairly explicit signposts. In other plays we are directed unequivocally towards abstraction. Even *Professional Foul*, which is essentially realistic, has the *Colloquium Philosophicum* built into it to point the way. But *Night and Day* gives no such guidance. It is perhaps only by observing analogies with the other plays that we can make ourselves fully aware of its 'universal perception'. And the play which contains the closest analogies is *Jumpers*.

The villains of *Night and Day* are clearly Mageeba and Wagner. Like Archie, both are determined to impose a rigid pattern on men's thinking. Of the two Wagner is clearly the

more important and so it is he who must be regarded as the
Archie of the piece. He has none of Archie's style, of course,
but this has more to do with a difference in dramatic mode
than with any essential difference between the two characters. What they obviously share is a determination to make a
norm out of mankind's lowest common denominator; all
must bow to the opinions of the unimaginative majority. But
whereas Archie's determination never wavers, except
perhaps in that ambiguous final speech, Wagner eventually
receives his come-uppance. The newspaper for which he
writes, *The Sunday Globe*, goes on strike as a direct result of
his complaint about the printing of an article by Milne and so
Wagner has no outlet for his interview with Mageeba, which
would have been the biggest scoop of his life.

It would seem that Wagner learns something from this
set-back. The piece about Jake, which he telexes to the
Grimsby Messenger at the end, signifies a swallowing of pride.
Moreover, he refers no more to the politics of journalism but
gets down to the practical business of covering the war,
bravely and efficiently. Actually his professional competence
has never been in doubt. His early self-portrait as a fireman
who, unlike a foreign correspondent, files facts rather than
prose is convincing despite the echoes of Dickens's Mr
Gradgrind. Stoppard himself told Gollob and Roper that he
admired Wagner 'as a person because he takes his job
seriously and is good at it and isn't a hack'. But of course, as
Stoppard observes in the same breath, there are other matters
which limit Wagner's appeal; he cannot do justice to his
vocation while he maintains such a high political profile.

If Wagner is the Archie of *Night and Day*, there seem to be
two characters who resemble George Moore. One is
(George) Guthrie who, as we have seen, overcomes his
lethargy to deliver the important 'Information is light' speech
late in the play. The other is Jacob Milne, whose premature
death no doubt explains the prominence which Guthrie
suddenly achieves in these closing moments.

The resemblance between Milne and George Moore is
particularly striking. Both are attractive characters who are
more or less mouthpieces for Stoppard's own beliefs—'Milne
has my prejudice', said Stoppard to Gollob. But both also
exhibit a fair degree of naiveté that leads them to overstate

their cases. (In this respect Milne also resembles Paul Verrall, the idealistic young journalist in Garson Kanin's *Born Yesterday*, which Stoppard directed at Greenwich in 1973.) George overreaches in his attempts to prove the existence of God. And Milne's insistence that 'free expression is the last line of defence for all the other freedoms' is always in danger of being undermined by his strenuous distaste for some of the rubbish to which free expression gives rise.

Ruth's arguments often resemble Milne's, but there is an important difference: she lets her contempt for the popular press get out of hand until it swamps her professed enthusiasm for free expression. This distortion is understandable, of course, given the way Ruth was hounded by the press at the time of her marriage to Geoffrey Carson. She possesses a commodity which is rare in Stoppard: a naturalistic explanation for her conduct. Setting this isolated scrap of naturalism aside, however, we can see that Ruth is essentially a Stoppardian straddler. On the one hand she is attracted to Milne's liberalism, on the other to a form of censorship analogous, but by no means identical, to Wagner's. And like Dotty in *Jumpers*, Jane in *Lord Malquist and Mr Moon*, and indeed Billie in *Born Yesterday*, she feels the tension sexually as well; Milne and Wagner are the two men in her life. (Just why and when her husband dropped out of contention is never made clear.)

There are a number of obvious similarities between Ruth and Dotty. Right at the start of *Night and Day* 'Ruth' echoes Dotty's cries for help. Both women seem to be primarily nocturnal creatures, though Ruth lacks Dotty's specific obsession with the moon; both like to sing; both crave the affections of a reticent, idealistic man (George, Milne) while suffering the advances of a more assured, confident one (Archie, Wagner); and, last but not least, both roles were first played by the actress Diana Rigg. But Ruth's predicament is more confused than Dotty's, for reasons which I have already implied. Firstly, there is, or ought to be, a third man in Ruth's life: her husband Geoffrey. And, in the original version at least, she entertains thoughts of seducing Guthrie as well. The competing claims on Ruth's affections distract our attention from her relationships with Milne and Wagner, which are structurally more important. Secondly, these two relationships are in themselves rather confusing. Given the precedent of *Jumpers* we should expect Ruth's better side to be reflected in her relationship with Milne and her worse side in her relationship with Wagner. But in fact the equation is rather different. The affair with Wagner has one important factor in its favour: it actually happens. The affair with Milne, on the other hand, is no more than a piece of wish-fulfilment.

At the beginning of Act II there are a couple of subtle hints that what follows is only a dream. It is specified in the original but not the second version that Milne should be dressed as we first saw him, that is in his civvies rather than the military-style outfit in which he departed for Malakuangazi at the end of Act I. Since he is supposed to have just returned from this trip, the change of clothing introduces a degree of mystery which indicates that what follows may be only a dream. The second version accentuates the air of mystery by making Milne 'invisible in the darkness' at the beginning of Act II. It is as if he is conjured into existence by Ruth's thoughts. But for most of the audience the unreality of the episode is not apparent until Stoppard plays the now famous 'double-Ruth' trick at the end. Ruth's double makes what may well be the briefest appearance in stage history, coming from behind a sofa or tree, removing her clothes and walking naked from the stage while the real Ruth calmly chats to her husband, who has just entered.

So the affair with Milne is an unattainable ideal. What of the affair with Wagner? Ruth herself sees it as the ultimate degradation: by going off to bed with him a second time at the end of the play she fulfils her own definition of a tart. (In the second version 'Ruth' sings 'The Lady is a Tramp' to reinforce the point.) But if Wagner is, as I have suggested, a sadder but wiser character at the end of the play, the ultimate liaison between him and Ruth might be construed as an acceptance of reality by both characters. She has perforce abandoned the 'elevated, intellectual sort of thing' that she felt for Milne, and since she cannot contrive 'to be hammered out, disjointed, folded up and put away like linen in a drawer'—remember the hankering after clean linen shared by Gladys and John Brown—she accepts the best that life has to offer, which at the moment happens to be Wagner. For his part, Wagner forgets about his principles and turns his attention to people and facts—Milne, Ruth and the situation in Kambawe. Paradoxically, then, the liaison of 'Ruth' and Milne (the hero) accentuates Ruth's worse side, namely her hopeless idealism, while that of Ruth and Wagner (the villain) signifies a harsh but salutary return to earth.

This interpretation can be reinforced by reference to the play's title. In the original version it is made clear at the very beginning that the phrase 'night and day' signifies the everyday world. When Guthrie emerges groggily from his afternoon nap Ruth observes, 'You shouldn't sleep in the sun'; Guthrie says, 'It moved', and Ruth replies, 'It does that. It's called night and day'. Although this passage has been excised from the second version it remains fairly clear, thanks to speeches like Milne's account of journalists rushing around 'night and day' (late in Act I) that the world of 'night and day' is the real world—the flux which Milne and Guthrie champion and which Ruth and Wagner finally learn to tolerate.

As usual, however, Stoppard presents us with an alternative world, inhabited most notably by Ruth's *alter ego*, 'Ruth'. In his interview with Gollob and Roper he was quick to point out that he 'didn't intend her to be privileged because of . . . this internal voice which can speak "out" from behind the social mask'. It seems to me in fact that, far from being privileged, Ruth is actually discredited by the internal voice of 'Ruth'. 'Ruth' inhabits an artificial world of films, plays, music and painting. In the original version she sings Cole Porter's 'Night and Day' and 'I've Got You Under My Skin' and the Beatles' 'Help!', and transforms herself at various times into Elizabeth Taylor in *Elephant Walk*, Deborah Kerr in *King Solomon's Mines*, Tallulah (Bankhead, presumably) and an ill-defined character who bears the clichéd stage name of Cynthia. In the second version the first two songs are cut, though the sound of 'those damned drums' at the start of the scene still recalls the first line of 'Night and Day'. Instead, 'The Lady is a Tramp' is added, at the end, as are references to a play or film whose title she forgets and to the paintings of Whistler and Turner. And the artifice of the world of 'Ruth' is further accentuated by the omission of many of her more miscellaneous speeches. The 'Ruth' who remains after this pruning is almost exclusively intent on her past desire for

Wagner, her present desire for Milne and the artificial nature of the world into which these desires are projected.

As in Stoppard's other plays, these aesthetic preoccupations betoken a 'clockwork' state of mind, and at the beginning of Act II (the point at which the dream sequence in *Dirty Linen* also occurs) we get confirmation of this when 'Ruth' is placed inside a play-within-the-play. The world of this dream is, Milne tells us, 'a parallel world. No day or night, no responsibilities, no friction, almost no gravity'.

So, as always in Stoppard, the play presents us with two juxtaposed worlds: the workaday world of 'night and day' and a dream world of 'no day or night'. Although there is perhaps more sympathy than usual for the dreamer, we are surely meant to realize that her flights of fancy offer no valid escape from reality. Stoppard seems to have felt that this point was not obvious enough in the original version for he adds a most significant speech in which 'Ruth' confesses that her thoughts and dreams are just an endless regression leading nowhere:

> 'RUTH': On a packet of salt used in my grandmother's kitchen there was a label showing a girl holding a packet of salt with the label showing, and so on. It is said, with what authority I do not know, that this was the inspiration of Whistler's famous painting of my grandmother painting her self-portrait, the one he was painting. A different school holds that it was in fact the inspiration of Turner's painting of a packet of salt. During a storm at sea. Sorry. I was miles away. Come and sit down. I talk to myself in the middle of a conversation. In fact I talk to myself in the middle of an *imaginary* conversation, which is itself a refuge from some other conversation altogether, frequently imaginary. I hope you don't mind me telling you all this.

After this speech 'Ruth' all but disappears from the play, except for her singing of 'The Lady is a Tramp' at the end. The words of this song, and the deed which they reflect—the fact that Ruth is about to become a tramp herself by sleeping with Wagner a second time—are a clear indication that the idealized dream-world of 'Ruth' has crumbled into ruins. 'Night and day' have triumphed over the 'parallel world', and 'Ruth' has become Ruth, just as all the grandiose theorizing about journalism has collapsed, leaving us with a very matter-of-fact picture of two ordinary men going about the business of gathering news in the most efficient way possible.

11 The 'Dogg' Plays
Easy Does It

Writers who take the extreme step of inventing a new language usually want to highlight some particularly exaggerated trait in the characters who speak that language. Berlioz's demons in *La Damnation de Faust,* for example, are given a language (developed out of a hint in Swedenborg) whose prominent sibillants and harsh consonants evoke their serpentine and brutish natures. And, to take an example much closer to home, Ptydepe and Chorukov—the invented languages which feature in Vaclav Havel's play, *The Memorandum*—are arid, clinical constructs appropriate to what Tynan, quoting Vera Blackwell, calls 'the modern Frankenstein's monster: bureaucracy' from which they issue.

Tynan investigates the relationship of Stoppard and Havel (whom he calls Stoppard's *doppelgänger*) at some length and throws out a number of suggestions which should be examined closely some day by somebody with the requisite qualifications in both English and Czech. The idea that *Jumpers* was influenced by Havel's *Increased Difficulty of Concentration* certainly looks plausible. On the other hand, if Tynan is right about the similarities between *Travesties* and Havel's *Audience* and *Private View* then we must assume that Stoppard influenced Havel on this occasion, for *Audience* and *Private View* were written in 1975—a year later than *Travesties.* At any rate, it seems reasonable to assume that Stoppard knew about Havel's linguistic experiments before he set about devising Dogg. And by the time he came to write *Cahoot's Macbeth* he had also met Pavel Kohout, another Czech playwright with a penchant for investing bureaucratic characters with an invented, incomprehensible language. We have no record of his reactions to these Czech models but we do have his thoughts on a much more serious

and thorough-going piece of linguistic invention: Orghast.
This is the language devised by Ted Hughes for the play
Orghast, which Peter Brook's International Centre for Theat-
rical Research presented at Persepolis during the 1971 Shiraz
Festival.

Like Ptydepe, Chorukov and the languages invented by
Berlioz and Kohout, Orghast is meant to evoke character but
this time it is nothing less than the character of humanity as a
whole. As Stoppard explained, in a rather sceptical review of
Hughes's experiment published in *The Times Literary Supplement,* Orghast is built on the premise that 'the sound of the
human voice, as opposed to language, is capable of project-
ing very complicated mental states'—not just emotions but
'the greater complexity of names of objects, of action verbs,
of family relationships, of number and of simple sentences'.
Stoppard went on to note an analogy with music:

> Mr Hughes does not expect or intend it to work on an
> audience in the way that a foreign language might,
> dropping philological clues here and there to be picked
> up with varying success according to the varying capac-
> ity of its hearers to make use of them. Orghast aims to
> be a leveller of audiences by appealing not to semantic
> athleticism but to the instinctive recognition of a 'men-
> tal state' within a sound.

We have already had cause to note Stoppard's semantic
athleticism, his habit, at the beginning of *Travesties,* for
example, of dropping philological clues, and in *Every Good
Boy Deserves Favour* his antipathy to music. It would seem
then that he defines Orghast by way of a series of contrasts
with his own practices. It therefore comes as no surprise to
find that his verdict on Hughes's experiment is at best
lukewarm—'the question remains open'—and at worst dis-
tinctly cool: '*Orghast* . . . largely failed to transmit on an
instinctive level the meaning which had been put into it on an
intellectual level'. Nor is it surprising to find that Stoppard's
Dogg differs from Orghast, Ptydepe and their ilk in that it
ignores the instinctive level altogether and focusses entirely
on the intellectual level. In other words, Dogg is not a means

of evoking character;* it is simply a logical puzzle which the audience, and their representatives within the plays—Charlie in *Dogg's Our Pet*, Easy in *Dogg's Hamlet*—must solve on the basis of the philological clues that Stoppard provides. Hayman writes aptly of 'the action's clockwork mechanism'; there is no sub-text, no deeper resonance.

To discourage any quest for resonance Stoppard for the most part uses ordinary, concrete English words as the basis for the vocabulary of Dogg. And the decision as to which English words get which Dogg meanings is certainly not made on the basis of any kind of appropriateness. In fact the contrary is closer to the truth; insofar as any logic is discernible in the collocation of English words and Dogg meanings it is based on *in*appropriateness'. Thus 'Scabs, slobs, black yobs, yids, spicks, wops' becomes a form of address fit for a queen (or perhaps a 'wife of the Chairman of the Governors').

Dogg's Our Pet

The original Dogg play, *Dogg's Our Pet*, written in 1971, is little more than a linguistic joke, as Stoppard concedes in his Preface. The origins of the joke go back to Wittgenstein but the dramatic embellishment is typically Stoppardian. As usual the play is based upon a clear-cut juxtaposition of reality and artifice. Charlie, the protagonist, is a realist, who speaks everyday English like the audience; the rest of the cast speak only the artificial language, Dogg.

Charlie is engaged in the task of constructing a platform, steps and a wall out of planks, slabs, blocks, bricks and cubes. He has an assistant who remains off-stage and throws

* The fact that Dogg is named after and presided over by a headmaster who goes about in a mortar-board and gown may suggest that here, as in *Where Are They Now?*, which was written immediately before *Dogg's Our Pet*, Stoppard was intent on satirizing the archaic jargon and conduct of the English public school system. But it is more likely that Dogg is portrayed as a headmaster because of the pseudonym which Ed Berman uses when he writes for children: Prof R. L. Dogg (which becomes Dogg, R. L. in bibliographies and indices). Inter-Action's theatre company for children takes its name from this pseudonym: Dogg's Troupe. And 'Dogg's Our Pet' is an anagram of Dogg's Troupe.

the building materials to him from the wings. This assistant turns out to be a schoolboy Dogg-speaker called Brick. Since Brick 'knows in advance which pieces Charlie needs and in what order' it does not matter that he understands 'Here!' when Charlie calls 'Plank', 'Ready!' when Charlie calls 'Slab', 'Next!' when Charlie calls 'Block', and so on. Confusion does arise, however, when other Dogg-speakers come on the scene. At first Charlie's problems are slight, as when his second shout of 'Plank!' ('Here!' in Dogg) elicits a football from Baker (another schoolboy) instead of a plank from Brick. But when Dogg, the boys' headmaster, intervenes, Charlie's difficulties are magnified. His disagreements with Dogg are private and trivial to begin with but they take on a more serious public dimension when various blocks and slabs are put together by Charlie's assistants to form a wall which carries the message: DOGG POUT THERE ENDS. Dogg is outraged. He cuffs Charlie and knocks him through the wall, which collapses. The wall is rebuilt with different faces of the blocks exposed. This time it reads: SHOUT DOGG PERT NEED. Again Dogg is outraged and pushes Charlie through the wall, which is reassembled to read: DONT UPSET DOGG HERE.

At this point, the Lady, described as possibly the Queen 'or perhaps the wife of the Chairman of the Governors', enters to perform an ill-defined opening ceremony. She and Dogg are visibly shocked by the wall's latest message, and Charlie makes matters worse by bungling the presentation of a posy, which he acquired by accident when he called Dogg 'yob', the Dogg word for posy. This time, before Dogg can lay a hand on him, Charlie hurls himself through the wall, an action which Hayman defines as 'a variant on the old music-hall routine by which the Moon or Laurel character is suddenly one step ahead of the Boot or Hardy character, who has been meting out all the punishment'.

Charlie is indeed a Moon character, which means that he resembles not just the Moon of *Lord Malquist and Mr Moon* and Moon the critic in *The Real Inspector Hound* but also, since the name is generic in Stoppard, all those other bumbling victims, like Rosencrantz, Guildenstern and George Moore, who, even when subdued by the Boot characters, such as the Player, Archie and Dogg, enjoy the audience's full support.

Shortly after his third encounter with the wall, Charlie confirms his rapport with the audience in a very Stoppardian way: he climbs on to the platform and then addresses them directly, in the manner of Rosencrantz, Guildenstern, George Moore, Maddie and the rest. It is true that the Lady also addresses the audience directly, just before Charlie does, but she speaks in Dogg and therefore fails to communicate. Moreover, she speaks very formally, from notes, whereas Charlie speaks casually, from memory. And his memory is so unreliable that, like Old Carr at the end of *Travesties*, he has to end his speech by confessing that he has forgotten what the third point was. The content of Charlie's speech means more to the audience than it does to the other characters, only two of whom are on stage in any case, and who don't seem to be listening anyway to what he says:

> Firstly, just because it's been opened, there's no need to run amok kicking footballs through windows and writing on the walls. It's me who's got to keep this place looking new so let's start by leaving it as we find it.

We have seen the Lady perform an opening ceremony but we have not been given a clear indication as to just what it is that she was opening, though it would seem to have something to do with a school. However, the first audiences of *Dogg's Our Pet* knew that they were attending the inaugural season of a new London theatre, Inter-Action's Almost Free Theatre in Rupert Street. So Charlie's words would have had a more precise significance for them than they had for the characters in the play or for subsequent audiences. Thus the message as well as the medium of Charlie's speech cements his close relationship with the audience.

Dogg's Hamlet

When Stoppard decided to convert *Dogg's Our Pet* into a less occasional, more enduring piece he had to find a more enduring excuse for the erection of the wall and platform and the intervention of the Lady. And so the vague opening ceremony in *Dogg's Our Pet* becomes in *Dogg's Hamlet* a school prize-giving followed by a school play, for which Stoppard utilizes the *Fifteen-Minute Hamlet* which he first created for Inter-Action's Fun Art Bus in 1976. Stoppard uses the prize-giving ceremony to provide further evidence of the topsy-turvy world over which Dogg presides. Fox Major, who scoops the pool, prefers the table on which the prizes stand to the prizes themselves. And the *Fifteen-Minute Hamlet*, performed as it were in a foreign language by the Dogg-speaking schoolboys, is further evidence of what Jack Kroll (in a review for *Newsweek* on 24 September 1979) called the 'short-circuiting of human sensibility' in their world.

The earlier stages of the play are also filled out somewhat. As well as playing football, listening to the football results, handing out flags and helping with the platform, as they did in *Dogg's Our Pet*, the Dogg-speakers are now required to play around with a microphone, eat their lunch, sing a song and rehearse *Hamlet*. And right at the beginning Stoppard adds some business which, like the opening tableaux in the other plays, provides an arresting anticipation of the 'clock-work' nonsense to come. Before any character appears, the stage is invaded by a series of objects—three footballs in the Inter-Action edition and a football and a satchel in the Faber edition. Then when the characters do appear they are most eccentrically attired; the men are in schoolboys' clothing and the actor who is to play Ophelia wears a dress on top.

All these changes simply accentuate the 'clockwork' side of things. Meanwhile, in the 'real' world some rather more radical revisions are taking place. First, Charlie's name has been changed to Easy, and a new schoolboy (the one who wears the dress) has assumed the name of Charlie. These changes provide evidence of Stoppard's passion for orderly arrangement and in particular of his desire, expressed to Hayman, to avoid being 'arbitrary about naming characters'. In *Artist Descending a Staircase* he distributed the names on a geographical basis: Donner is German, Beauchamp is French, Martello is Italian and Sophie is Greek. In *Dogg's Hamlet* he works alphabetically; in order of appearance the characters are: Able (Abel in the Faber edition), Baker, Charlie, Dogg, Easy and Fox. These schemes provide an excellent indication of the contrived, unevocative nature of Stoppard's art.

The change in Charlie's name is much less important than the change in his role. Whereas Charlie remained at odds with the world of Dogg right to the end, Easy, after an even more stormy passage in the early stages, ultimately succumbs to the 'clockwork'. At first, as in *Dogg's Our Pet*, he is utterly mystified by the peculiar language and behaviour that surround him. Then, in a passage for which there is no precedent in *Dogg's Our Pet*, he gets angry as his attempt to build the platform is sabotaged, and he lands two stinging blows on Abel, who corresponds to the off-stage Brick in *Dogg's Our Pet*. These two assaults on Abel are answered by Dogg's two assaults on Easy, which take the same form as in the earlier play—Easy is knocked twice through the wall. And then, as in *Dogg's Our Pet*, Easy takes a third tumble through the wall on his own initiative.

In *Dogg's Hamlet* this third tumble is not so much the end of Easy's troubles as the beginning of a rapid initiation into the world of Dogg that has no counterpart in *Dogg's Our Pet*. (By the end of *Dogg's Our Pet*, Charlie seems to have mastered one word of Dogg: 'yob' (posy). But since he makes a mess of presenting the posy, handing it over after the opening-ceremony instead of before, we may assume that his mastery is far from complete.) As soon as he gets to his feet Easy makes his first faltering attempt to speak the lingo. He joins with Abel, Baker and Charlie in abusing Dogg. To begin with he curses in English: 'Stinkbag! Poxy crank! . . . Canting poncey creep! . . . Sadist! Fascist! . . .' But quite quickly, and almost imperceptibly, he lapses into the Dogg language. In the Inter-Action edition his next speech reads: 'Officious bastard! Six Pints! Lunatic!' But the Dogg phrase 'Six Pints' is cut from the Faber edition and we have to wait another three speeches for his first tentative stab at Dogg: 'Slab git, nit git', chants Baker, and Easy chimes in with 'Three bags full git!', which is still orthodox English (apart from the 'git') but it betrays an understanding of what Baker has just said. Thereafter it is more or less Dogg all the way for Easy. His transition from English to Dogg is a little more gradual in the earlier text but in both Easy speaks all Dogg and no English from the moment he announces the performance of *Hamlet*: 'Hamlet bedsocks Denmark. Yeti William Shakespeare'.

So the two worlds (Dogg's and Charlie's) that remained so resolutely apart in *Dogg's Our Pet* ultimately merge in *Dogg's*

Hamlet as Easy moves from 'mystery' to 'clockwork'. If *Dogg's Hamlet* were an autonomous piece it would constitute an exception to the rule that Stoppard champions 'mystery'. But of course it is not autonomous; it is just the first half of a play which is constructed on the same principle as *Travesties*:

> Right, we'll have a rollicking first act, and they'll all come back from their gin-and-tonics thinking 'Isn't it fun? What a lot of lovely jokes!'

Cahoot's Macbeth

Cahoot's Macbeth corresponds to the second act of *Travesties* in that it says, 'Life is too important. We can't afford the luxury of this artificial frivolity . . .!'

The seriousness of the play is perhaps not immediately apparent at a first viewing. It begins as *Dogg's Hamlet* ends, with a Shakespearean redaction. Nervous giggles can be expected from the audience for a moment or two as they search anxiously for more comedy but they should realize well before the Inspector calls, at the time of the knocking at the gate following Duncan's murder, that for once Stoppard is giving us Shakespeare straight rather than mechanized. Up to this point at least, *Cahoot's Macbeth*, though it is 'necessarily over-truncated', is every bit as serious as 'Kohout's elegant seventy-five minute version', which Stoppard discusses in his Preface to the Faber edition.

In order to emphasize that this *Macbeth* is *not* one of his characteristic plays-within-the-play, set at two removes from the world of the audience, Stoppard takes pains to highlight the intimate nature of the performance and to bind stage and audience closely together. The setting is a living room and the entrance at stage left is a makeshift one—not a door but a window with shutters. The stage is not a place apart but merely an extension of the space occupied by the audience. Factors like these help the audience to sense a real connection between their own world and the world of *Macbeth*. In Kohout's Prague performances this connection would have been much more apparent, for reasons which the Inspector outlines towards the middle of Stoppard's play:

> Shakespeare—or the Old Bill, as we call him in the
> force—is not a popular choice with my chief, owing to
> his popularity with the public, or, as we call it in the
> force, the filth. The fact is, when you get a universal and
> timeless writer like Shakespeare, there's a strong feeling
> that he could be spitting in the eyes of the beholder
> when he should be keeping his mind on Verona—
> hanging around the 'gents' . . . The chief says he'd
> rather you stood up and said, 'There is no freedom in
> this country' . . . what we don't like is a lot of people
> being cheeky and saying they are only Julius Caesar or
> Coriolanus or Macbeth . . .

An Anglo-Saxon audience is less likely to make an automatic
connection between *Macbeth* and their everyday lives but
they can hardly avoid suspending their disbelief when the
famous knocking at the gate from *Macbeth* Act II, Scene ii
coincides with the Inspector's arrival on the scene.

The knocking at the gate is the cue, in Stoppard as in
Shakespeare, for the exeunt of the Macbeths and so the
Inspector walks into 'an empty room'. He relishes the opportunity to hold the stage, turning on a virtuoso display of
'sarcastic politeness' as he cases the joint and indicates in an
overly heavy-handed way that the room is bugged. From the
first his speeches are characterized by that glib and vaguely
menacing tone which Stoppard, like Pinter, reserves for his
villains. In short, he turns on a performance which is much
more artificial than any we have seen from the actors
involved in *Macbeth*.

The Inspector is quickly confronted by the Hostess, who
provides a realistic foil for his artificial posturings. Her
speeches—like Maddie's in *Dirty Linen*—are brief and to the
point, and it is noteworthy that her initial approach to the
stage is made through the audience. As we have seen time
and time again a close association with the audience is used
by Stoppard to indicate a properly realistic attitude. Later we
find that the Hostess knows everybody in the audience
('They are all personal friends of mine') whereas the Inspector knows them only as names on an official dossier.

A healthy realism similar to the Hostess's is displayed by
the actors, Landovsky and Chramostova, when they step out

of character—something that the Player in *Rosencrantz and Guildenstern Are Dead* could never do—and return to the stage to confront the Inspector *in propriis personis*. The gap between their realism and his artifice is nicely demonstrated by Chramostova's terse reply, 'I'm not your darling', to the Inspector's mannered exclamation, 'Darling, you were marvellous'. The same gap is indicated by the Inspector's failure, as against the actors' skill, in distinguishing between roles on-stage and jobs in real life. Moreover, the Inspector has the habit, common among Stoppard's 'clockwork' characters, of using foreign phrases: 'Put your—placay manos—per capita . . . nix toiletto'. Like Ruth in *Night and Day* he likes to see life in terms of pictures and metaphors.

Even when *Macbeth* resumes, at the command of the Inspector, his flamboyant interjections still seem more of a performance than the performance itself. Throughout this central section, then, we have a characteristically Stoppardian juxtaposition of 'mystery' and 'clockwork'. However, the balance between these forces is disturbed by the arrival of a new character, or rather by the return of an old one: Easy, the protagonist of *Dogg's Hamlet*. Easy's command of the Dogg language has developed to such an extent that he now speaks nothing else. His sudden appearance amid the performance of *Macbeth* naturally causes some bewilderment on stage, and it is a nice touch of Stoppard's to have him walk unwittingly into the part of the mysterious Third Murderer. His subsequent reincarnations as the ghost of Banquo, the first apparition (in the Inter-Action edition only) and the 'two or three . . . that bring . . . word/Macduff is fled to England' (*Macbeth* Act IV, Scene i) are scarcely less bewildering—the last one actually stops the show for a while—but they are certainly less menacing. And when Easy is shown to be in cahoots with Cahoot, who turns out to be a fluent Dogg-speaker, we realize that he is after all on the side of the angels.

In fact, Easy provides the means by which the actors express their defiance of the system in the closing pages of Stoppard's text. Firstly, Easy's transmission of the Dogg language to the rest of the *Macbeth* cast allows the actors to conclude their depiction of tyrannicide with impunity. Macduff actually goes so far as to direct his Dogg-version of 'Turn, hell-hound, turn' ('Spiral, tricycle, spiral!') directly at the uncomprehending Inspector, who unwittingly replies, 'Okay!'—'Slab!'. Secondly, the 'wood' (planks, slabs, blocks and cubes, as in *Dogg's Hamlet*, but with a pun on Shakespeare's Birnam Wood) which Easy has brought on the back of his 'two-ton artichoke' enables the actors to build a platform★ so that the play's climax can be acted out, quite literally, above the heads of the Inspector and his cronies.

Thus the artificial language, Dogg, finally becomes the medium for 'affirming art, life and freedom', as Kroll put it in his *Newsweek* review. It is of course most unlike Stoppard to condone artifice in this way, and the fact that Easy reverts suddenly to English in his last three speeches (just as he lapsed into Dogg at the end of *Dogg's Hamlet*) suggests that Stoppard may have felt uneasy about the paradoxical conjunction of 'mystery' and 'clockwork' prior to this. But there are viable explanations for the paradox. First, we should consider the possibility that the play is quasi-autobiographical. In his Preface to the Faber edition Stoppard tells of his meeting with Kohout and Landovsky in Prague, of a visit to a Prague theatre in Landovsky's company and of subsequent friendly letters, written in slightly faltering English, from Kohout. '*Cahoot's Macbeth* was inspired by these events', he maintains, although he goes on to insist that 'Cahoot is not Kohout . . .'

Let us assume for a minute, however, that Cahoot *is* Kohout. Then the English used by all the characters up to the arrival of Easy must correspond to Czech. The foreign language (Dogg), which Easy introduces and which Cahoot, and he alone to begin with, understands, might very well correspond to English and Easy might therefore be Stoppard's self-portrait. The suggestion is not as unkind to Stoppard as it may seem at first. While it is true that Easy is—like Chaucer's Chaucer in *The Canterbury Tales*—gauche and inarticulate as a character, even when he is speaking English, his role is a vitally important one; without his intervention Cahoot's production of *Macbeth* could hardly have run its course. So if Easy is Stoppard the moral of the play would seem to be the almost immodest one that the

★ A 'battlement' is referred to in a stage direction just prior to the unloading of Easy's 'wood'. It is not clear how or when this arrives on stage.

Czech dissidents depend for their survival on the support of Western sympathizers like Stoppard. However, this auto-biographical interpretation would hardly occur to an audience which had neither read the Preface nor heard of Stoppard's dealings with Kohout. Such an audience would be more likely to conclude that the dissident actors' ultimate recourse to Dogg is ironical. Direct dealing will get them nowhere, as the Inspector makes clear early in the piece:

> The chief says he'd rather you stood up and said, 'There is no freedom in this country', then there's nothing underhand and we all know where we stand. You get your lads together and we get our lads together and when it's all over, one of us is in power and you're in gaol.

Their only hope is to baffle the authorities by the indirectness of their expression, and the use of Dogg becomes a last resort when the authorities are employing jargon which is as Dogg-like as this:

> Scabs! Stinking slobs - crooks. You're nicked, Jock. Punks make me puke. Kick back, I'll break necks, smack chops, put yobs in padlocks and fix facts. Clamp down on poncy gits like a ton of bricks.

The gibberish of the concluding pages should thus be viewed as a necessary evil; its only justification is that it 'out-Herods Herod'. The play concludes therefore on an ironic note as does its predecessor, *Every Good Boy Deserves Favour*, in which a noble end (Alexander's release) is achieved by a totally inadequate means (mistaken identity).

12 The Real Thing
The Real Stoppard?

At first sight *The Real Thing* looks like an autobiographical play: Stoppard's '*Long Night's Journey into Day*' or '*A Voyage Round My Two Wives*'. The main character, Henry, is a playwright whose life and work are in many respects similar to Stoppard's. In fact, Stoppard plays a trick on his audience at the start that ensures that he and Henry are, at least for a short time, indistinguishable. Not until Scene II do we discover that Scene I, which looked very Stoppardian—like a lower-key *Jumpers* in fact (with cards replacing acrobats)— was in fact the beginning of a play by Henry called 'House of Cards'.

Although the distinction between them is thereafter clear, remarkable similarities continue to emerge—in their attitudes to their work, for example. In Scene V Henry argues vehemently that craftsmanship matters more than content in the making of plays:

> I don't think writers are sacred, but words are. They deserve respect. If you get the right ones in the right order, you can nudge the world a little or make a poem which children will speak for you when you're dead . . . But when they get their corners knocked off, they're no good any more. . . . It's rubbish . . . it's *balls*.

Besides Coleridge, this speech echoes Stoppard himself. In 'Ambushes for the Audience', for example, he maintains that brains are more important than balls.

In many more incidental respects Henry's art resembles Stoppard's—in his fondness for long, intricate and seemingly irrelevant speeches, such as Max's homily against digital watches in Scene I; his inability, if Charlotte is to be believed, to portray convincing women; and his tendency to work at one remove from reality. Personally as well as professionally the two men are closely akin. Both enjoy cricket and fishing; both undergo divorce before finding security in a second marriage (and the play is dedicated to Miriam, Stoppard's second wife); neither has much taste in music; and in the inaugural production, though not in the published text, the snatch from the radio programme 'Desert Island Discs' early in Scene III revealed that Henry, like Stoppard, gave up a career in journalism to write full-time for the stage.

Another apparent similarity arises from the fact that Henry is goaded into a semblance of political commitment when Annie persuades him to rewrite Brodie's play for television. But here the parallel becomes more tenuous, for the political activism which has characterized Stoppard's life and work since 1977, whatever it may have owed to the promptings of Miriam, has been more whole-hearted than Henry's. And it has certainly proved more durable. To put it another way, the objects of Stoppard's political attentions—Havel, Kohout, Bukovsky and the rest—have always been more worthy and substantial figures than Brodie, the man of straw with whom Henry is persuaded to involve himself.

This discrepancy between Henry and Stoppard is enough to prove that *The Real Thing* is not simply an autobiographical ramble. A certain autobiographical input is undeniable and it casts an interesting and unwonted shadow over the play's conclusion, as I shall show in due course. But like Stoppard's other works, this one is primarily concerned with ideas. It analyses two important problems and comes to clear-cut decisions about both of them. One of the problems is Annie's rather than Henry's. From the start she is deeply involved in the 'Justice for Brodie Committee'. Brodie is a young soldier who joined a march to protest against the siting of American missiles on English soil. In the course of the march he set fire to the wreath to the Unknown Soldier on the Cenotaph and resisted arrest. He ended up with a six-year jail sentence. Annie's first husband, Max, expresses huge admiration for Brodie in Scene II:

> Imagine it. The guts of it, the sheer moral courage. An ordinary soldier using his weekend pass to demonstrate against their bloody missiles.

Already Annie's attitude is rather more ambivalent; when her commitment to Brodie threatens to get in the way of her love for Henry she has no hesitation in deciding in favour of Henry. Nevertheless, she continues to work on Brodie's behalf, and in order to keep his name before the public she decides to get him to write a television play about his experiences. Stoppard *habitués* will immediately see this as an ominous move: once Brodie gets inside a play-within-the-play he is bound to seem an unreal, 'clockwork' character. A little embellishment in Peter Wood's production made this point very neatly. Scene XI was set in the television studio during the filming of Brodie's play, and Billy, the actor playing Brodie, was made to 'dry' and to excuse himself with a protest against the unreality of having Brodie in a first-class carriage speaking first-class English.

The script produced by Brodie is gauche and unmarketable but Henry is persuaded to rewrite it, much against his better judgement, and the play is eventually screened. Amid the attendant publicity Brodie is released from jail. Brodie eventually makes an appearance, in the thirteenth and final scene of the play. He is quick to deny Annie any opportunity for self-congratulation, and insists that his release had nothing to do with the play or with Annie or with the 'Justice for Brodie Committee':

> I'm out because the missiles I was marching against are using up the money they need for a prison to put me in.

And within minutes every trace of idealism has been removed from both Brodie's original escapade and Annie's loyalty to his cause. Annie reveals that Brodie's motives were not public and altruistic but private and selfish, and that her loyalty was a matter not of abstract principle but of personal guilt:

> He was helpless, like a three-legged calf, nervous as anything. A boy on the train. Chatting me up. Nice. He'd been in some trouble at the camp, some row, I forget, he was going absent without leave. He didn't know anything about a march . . . By the time we got to Liverpool Street he would have followed me into the Ku Klux Klan . . . not an idea in his head except to impress me. What else could I do? He was my recruit.

Brodie confirms her account and Annie summarily concludes their relationship by smashing a bowl of dip in his face.

The terms of Annie's rejection of Brodie are worth studying. Essentially they amount to a reiteration of Henry's point from Scene II: that 'Public postures have the configuration of private derangement'. And another though less elegant way of putting this would be to say that human behaviour is determined by the 'mystery' of each individual's private situation rather than by abstract, 'clockwork' principles.

In a very different and more complex context Henry also has to learn to eschew 'clockwork' in favour of 'mystery'. In Scene I we see the (temporary) break-down of a marriage as depicted by Henry in his play, 'House of Cards'. Neither of the partners gets very worked up about their predicament. Some cool, calculated detective work by the husband (played by Max) has led him to suspect that his wife (played by Charlotte) has a lover whom she contrives to visit by pretending to take business trips abroad. The play begins with the scene in which the husband confronts the wife with his suspicions. There is some cerebral badinage on both sides, after which she makes a dignified exit and he remains sufficiently collected to laugh aloud at the present which she claims to have brought him from Switzerland—'a miniature Alp in a glass bowl'.

Even before Charlotte does her hatchet-job on 'House of Cards' in Scene II, it should be clear from a number of characteristic pointers that Scene I is a piece of Stoppardian 'clockwork'. Apart from the unreal calm of the characters there is the tell-tale disquisition on clocks (or rather digital watches), the artificial nature of the wife's gift and its provenance—Switzerland, which, besides being the home of clocks, is seen, at least in *Travesties*, as a kind of artificial haven from the pressures of reality: 'the still centre of the wheel of war', as Henry Carr puts it. And of course the whole scene is part of a play-within-the-play, which is a sure token of its artificiality.

The next three scenes confirm this artificiality in very different ways. In Scene II Charlotte inveighs against Henry's play on the grounds of its unreality:

That's the difference between plays and real life—
thinking time. . . . 'Must say I take my hat off to you,

> coming home with Rembrandt place mats for your
> mother.' You don't really think that if Henry caught me
> out with a lover, he'd sit around being witty about place
> mats? Like hell he would. He'd come apart like a
> pick-a-sticks . . .

And in Scene III Max corroborates her point by coming apart
in just this manner after discovering his wife Annie's adultery
with Henry. (One is reminded of the story told by the Player
in *Rosencrantz and Guildenstern Are Dead* about the very
undramatic death of the actor whom he had 'hanged in the
middle of a play'.)

The stage direction at the head of Scene III requires that the
disposition of the furniture and doors be immediately reminiscent of that at the beginning of Scene I. The inaugural
production failed to meet this requirement (and several
others like it) but clearly the reminiscence is intended to
underline a contrast rather than a similarity; Scene III depicts
a real marriage breakdown whereas Scene I was a 'clockwork' fantasy.

It is not just the husbands' reactions that are contrasted; the
ways in which the respective adulteries are discovered are
also very different. The husband of Scene I finds a nice clean
passport in a drawer, and infers that his wife has not gone
abroad as she claimed to have done; Max finds a handkerchief
soiled with blood and other bodily fluids between the front
seats of his car.

In Scene IV we finally find Henry conceding that he
doesn't know how to write about love:

> I try to write it properly, and it just comes out
> embarrassing. It's either childish or it's rude. And the
> rude bits are absolutely juvenile. I can't use any of it.
> . . . Perhaps I should write it completely artificial.
> Blank verse. Poetic imagery . . .

Apparently Henry never does succeed in making his love
scenes, or indeed his plays overall, more life-like. Brodie
complains in Scene XIII that Henry's rewrite of his television
play was clever but that he liked the earlier version better;
and there is little sign of realism in the science fiction play
from which Annie gives us a sample in Scene V. Moreover,
as Scenes IV and V make clear, Henry fails to write the play
which he promised Annie as a present when they first came

together and which was presumably intended to be a realistic portrait of their love.

The nature of Henry's art ceases to be of central importance from Scene IV onwards, however. Indeed, art in general quickly becomes a minor issue, for Annie demonstrates that it is not so much the words on the page as the sub-text that matters, whether in a naturalistic piece like Strindberg's *Miss Julie* (Scene IV) or in the 'blank verse' and 'poetic imagery' of Ford's *'Tis Pity She's a Whore* (Scene VIII). (Incidentally, Ford's play is neither Jacobean, as Henry thinks, nor Elizabethan, as Annie insists, but Caroline. This error remained—in Scene V—in Peter Wood's production.)

When Annie tells Henry, in Scene IV, that he will have to learn to deal with sub-text she is really issuing a challenge to his personality rather than to his craftsmanship. And from this point on Henry's personality becomes the chief centre of interest in what might be called the main plot. Before the end of Scene IV, after which comes the interval and a gap of two years in the play's time scheme, it is evident that Henry himself is in many ways as clinical and unemotional as his plays, which now take their accustomed Stoppardian place as a metaphor for a state of mind (Henry's) rather than as items of interest *per se*. This metaphorical connection is neatly effected when we discover, late in Scene IV, that Henry wears the sort of digital-watch-complete-with-alarm that was the target of so much ridicule in the featured scene from 'House of Cards'.

Henry's emotional sterility is indicated by his refusal to acknowledge the slightest jealousy of either Brodie, whom Annie continues to visit regularly, or Gerald, who plays Jean to Annie's Julie in the Strindberg—according to Annie the only jealousy of which Henry is capable is jealousy 'of the idea of the writer'. He also maintains a cool, professional response at the sight of Miranda Jessop stripping on television, and remains similarly detached when making love to Annie while she is 'totally zonked' under the influence of a 'Mog'. At the end of Scene IV we find him expatiating complacently on the insularity of passion:

> I love it. I love the way it blurs the distinction between
> all the people who aren't one's lover. Only two kinds of
> presence in the world. There's you and there's them.

Even those unaware of Stoppard's habitual distrust of such
clean and absolute distinctions must suspect that this is a case
of pride going before a fall. And, sure enough, though Annie
responds, 'I love you so' to this speech, within seconds she is
riffling through his papers, apparently seeking evidence that
he is not as sublimely faithful as he claims to be. (At least, I
take this to be her motive; the business is rather obscure,
although Stoppard obviously intends it to be very significant.) She finds nothing. Instead, in the second half of
the play, she takes the initiative which forces Henry into
the acknowledgement that life is more complex, more
mysterious than he had suspected.

In Scenes VI and VIII we see Annie teetering on the brink
of an affair with Billy, who plays Giovanni to her Annabella
in a Glasgow season of '*Tis Pity She's a Whore*. By the time
she returns to London Henry has realized that something is
up and so, as in Scenes I and III (and Stoppard's stage
direction reminds us of the parallels), we get a confrontation
between an aggrieved husband and an apparently errant wife.

Several important features distinguish this confrontation
from the previous two. Firstly, Henry, despite a thorough
search, comes up with no incriminating evidence against
Annie—nothing to compare with Max's handkerchief or the
forgotten passport in Scene I. Secondly, the adultery is
unequivocally denied on this occasion, and when Henry puts
the supplementary question, 'Did you want to?', Annie
loftily rebukes him for invading her privacy. She then leaves
him with a piece of advice which must surely come straight
from the author's mouth: 'You have to find a part of yourself
where I'm not important or you won't be worth loving'.

This doctrine is of course anathema to Henry but he
struggles manfully to accept it, and in Scene XII we find him
paying lip-service at least to Annie's freedom. He allows her
to take an incoming call from Billy in the bedroom and when
she reappears, instead of fulminating, he considerately
phones the television studios with a cooked-up excuse for her
lateness. (In Peter Wood's production this episode was
modified considerably and Henry was made to seem much
more upset by Billy's call.) But he then undoes all his good
work with this heart-felt outburst: 'The trouble is, I can't *find*
a part of myself where you're not important'.

Stoppard doesn't really explain how this tension is resolved. In the short term Annie simply asks for time to
straighten out her loyalties, and Henry must accede to her
request since enough time elapses between Scenes XII and
XIII for Brodie's play to be recorded and edited, if not
transmitted. (The video that the characters watch in Scene
XIII may be an advance copy which predates the public
transmission of the play.) Then, in Scene XIII, Annie dismis-
ses Brodie from her life, and Billy too, we assume, since
Billy and Brodie are almost a composite personality: the
private and public sides respectively of Annie's extra-marital
activities, as it were—they have the same first name; they
both make up to Annie in a railway-carriage; and Billy plays
Brodie in Brodie's play. Annie presumably guesses that the
mysterious telephone call at the end of the scene comes from
Billy. So when Henry says into the phone, 'Did you want to
speak to Annie?' and she says, loudly enough for the caller to
hear, 'No', she is effectively signalling the end of the affair.
(In fact the call is from Max.)

   With Billy and Brodie out of the way Annie and Henry can
live happily ever after. But on what terms? Has Annie agreed
to enter the ivory tower of love defined by Henry in Scene IV
or has Henry conceded her request for certain freedoms? It is
impossible to tell from the ending itself but the whole drift of
Act II has been towards the latter alternative.

   There are two characters besides Annie and Henry who
contribute signally to this drift: Charlotte in Scene VII and
Debbie in Scene IX. (These two scenes were rearranged
somewhat in Peter Wood's production: Charlotte was introduced along with Debbie in Scene IX, and a number of
consequential changes were made. Presumably Peter Wood
felt the need to break up the rather tedious series of duets of
which Act II consists.) Charlotte reveals to Henry that their
marriage, while it lasted, was much messier (more 'mysterious') than he had imagined. She had had no fewer than nine
lovers. When he objects, 'I thought we'd made a commitment', she retorts scornfully:

> There are no commitments, only bargains. And they
> have to be made again every day. You think making a
> commitment is *it*. Finish. You think it sets like a

> concrete platform, and it'll take any strain you want to
> put on it . . . you're an idiot. *Were* an idiot.

And Debbie—an older version of the instinctively reliable
child whom we have encountered in *Professional Foul*, *Every
Good Boy Deserves Favour* and *Night and Day*—makes a
related point when she argues that infidelity is not simply a
question of 'having it off':

> We had this fellow come round from the Council to
> look at the fire escape. He spent ten minutes looking at
> the fire escape and an hour and a half betraying his wife.
> Little jokes about her ways, her relatives, her cooking,
> who she fancied on T.V. It was his way of flirting.

Henry responds with a long idealistic speech about the special
knowledge that sets lovers apart from the rest of mankind.
But Debbie is ready with the epigram that Henry echoes in
Scene XII: 'Exclusive rights isn't love, it's colonization'.

The confrontation with Debbie also undermines Henry's
rigid theories about education. His elitist insistence on 'Latin
and ponies' has, it transpires, done nothing to preserve
Debbie's virginity or to purify her grammar. The former she
lost to the groom, closely followed by the Latin master,
while on the latter score she shows herself to be an advocate
of the new oracy rather than the old literacy; when Henry
unleashes one of his polished epigrams she wearily responds,
'Don't write it, Fa. Just say it'.

Another incidental speech which contributes to the play's
drift away from closed systems towards the flux of reality is
Annie's response to Billy's criticism of the class system in
Scene VI:

> There's no system. People group together when they've
> got something in common. Sometimes it's religion and
> sometimes it's, I don't know, breeding budgies or being
> at Eton. Big and small groups overlapping. You can't
> blame them. It's a cultural thing; it's not *classes* or *system*.

So there can be little doubt that the play as a whole comes
down on the side of 'mystery' and repudiates 'clockwork' in
its two given forms: Henry's theories about love and Annie's
about politics. And yet inevitably the autobiographical ghost
comes back to haunt such an absolute conclusion. When
Henry turns up the recording of 'I'm a Believer' in the

closing seconds of the play we are reminded that the taste for low-grade pop music which he shares with his creator persists unabated, despite a couple of brief flirtations with the classics in the course of Act II. So the play ends with a strong reminder of the kinship between Henry and Stoppard.

Many in the audience will be unaware of this and the other parallels but most must surely see that Henry has been portrayed throughout with much more sympathy than Stoppard's other 'clockwork' characters—The Player, Archie, Joyce and Malquist (*pace* Tynan) and the rest. What is going on, I think, is not so much the simple fudging that we get at the end of *Enter a Free Man* and *A Separate Peace* but a real ambivalence which amounts in the end to a rueful recognition on Stoppard's part that his ends and means are, and indeed always have been, in conflict with each other. Rather like Wilde prior to *The Importance of Being Earnest*, he has hitherto tried to wed a genius for epigram and word-play with a serious moral purpose—to write farces which prove the existence of God, as he said of *Jumpers*. And because clever word-play sits more easily on villains than on heroes (as Shakespeare found in *Othello*), Stoppard has so far spent his career in the discrediting of his greatest talent. Many people have been so beguiled by the word-play that they have simply ignored the moral purpose, of course.

This aesthetic masochism comes into focus more clearly than ever before in *The Real Thing*, and it may be that Stoppard now has an important decision to make about his future work: whether to pursue wit at the expense of morality, as he did, except in a couple of brief passages, in *On the Razzle* and as Wilde did in *The Importance of Being Earnest*, or to pursue the morality and minimize the wit.

The Real Thing itself would seem to constitute a step in the latter direction. Charlotte, Henry and Debbie provide some of the old verbal crackle but much of the language is slick and trendy rather than genuinely clever. Similarly, although some of the craftsmanship is as pleasing as ever, all this is as tinsel on the surface of a play that plods its way, especially in Act II, through a succession of scenes which are both unduly static and unduly similar in construction. In the published text every scene in Act II except the last consists of a debate between two characters. Stoppard, mindful no doubt of the old accusation that his plays 'don't really make clear state-ments', has pursued his themes so relentlessly on this occa-sion that he has produced a rather dull play. It is to be hoped that he can rediscover the old formula for leavening the moral 'mystery' with some engaging 'clockwork', but if the two must be divorced I would prefer to have the 'clock-work'.

13 Conclusion
Plays, Novels and Masques

Stoppard's career as a writer really took off in August 1966. In that month *Rosencrantz and Guildenstern Are Dead* was premièred on the fringe of the Edinburgh Festival, and *Lord Malquist and Mr Moon* was published in London by Anthony Blond. Stoppard told Janet Watts, no doubt with his tongue as far into his cheek as it ever has time to get, that 'there was no doubt in my mind whatsoever that the novel would make my reputation, and the play would be of little consequence either way'.

The enormous magnitude of his mistake is now history and although *Lord Malquist and Mr Moon* has found a few discerning admirers, there is no doubt in my mind that the majority has not erred in preferring Stoppard the dramatist. Some idea of his limitations as a novelist can be gained by comparing these two passages, the first an extract from *Lord Malquist and Mr Moon*, the second a roughly parallel piece from Thomas Pynchon's acclaimed novel, *V*:*

> He looked at himself in the mirror and his compassion for his image was reflected back into himself but it did not comfort him. When he leaned forward between the hinged mirror-leaves he caught the reflection of his reflection and the reflection of that, and of that, and he saw himself multiplied and diminished between the mirrors, himself aghast in the exact centre of a line that stretched to the edges of a flat earth. He closed his eyes and got up and fell over the dressing-stool. He went back to the bedroom.

> Rachel was looking into the mirror at an angle of 45°, and so had a view of the [clock] face turned toward the

* New York, 1964.

room and the face on the other side, reflected in the mirror; here were time and reverse-time, co-existing, cancelling one another exactly out. Were there many such reference points, scattered through the world, perhaps only at nodes like this room which housed a transient population of the imperfect, the dissatisfied; did real time plus virtual or mirror-time equal zero and thus serve some half-understood moral purpose? Or was it only the mirror world that counted; only a promise of a kind that the inward bow of a nose-bridge or a promontory of extra cartilage at the chin meant a reversal of ill fortune such that the world of the altered would thenceforth run on mirror-time; work and love by mirror-light and be only, till death stopped the heart's ticking (metronome's music) quietly as light ceases to vibrate, an imp's dance under the century's own chandeliers . . .*

It is not difficult to see that the Stoppard passage is flatter, more specific in its import than the Pynchon. Stoppard's long central sentence may look complex and evocative at first glance but in fact its syntax works quite mechanically to underline the infinite regress of reflections presented by the two mirrors. It is really no more evocative than the bald statements made by the next two sentences. The whole paragraph has been *organized* very efficiently to express Moon's precise actions and impressions. Everything is stated; nothing lurks beneath the surface.

The Pynchon works very differently. We are immersed much more deeply in the character's stream of consciousness, and Rachel's confused sense of what the mirror-image signifies is conveyed not just by the explicit reference to the 'half-understood moral purpose' of the tableau but also by the evocative imagery—'an imp's dance under the century's own chandeliers'—and by the Woolfian rhythms of the passage. This is not so much organized as *organic* writing. As a passage for reading, marking, learning and inwardly digesting, the Pynchon is certainly superior. The more one dwells on it, the more one is rewarded with subtle insights and

---

* Early in *Lord Malquist and Mr Moon* Stoppard refers to the 'V' of Jane's throat. Later he describes 'the rolled V' of Lady Malquist's robe. Could these be veiled allusions to Pynchon's novel?

innuendoes. The Stoppard, on the other hand, involves the reader at a purely cognitive level. Closer scrutiny yields no gain. And this flatness in the telling makes for a rather dull novel, even though the events described are in themselves exciting. On this evidence Stoppard is unlikely to take his place in the great tradition of English novelists who set down in richly textured prose the findings of their earnest sensibilities. Stoppard does indeed lay claim to both texture and sensibility, but, to Mark Amory at least, he defined the words in ways which would be quite foreign to F. R Leavis and I. A. Richards and other Practical and New Critics:

> There is a secret in art, isn't there? And the secret consists of what the artist has secretly and privately done. You will tumble some [secrets and allusions] and not others. The whole process of putting them in . . . gives art that texture which sensibility tells one is valuable.

Both texture and sensibility have here become quantifiable concepts; texture varies according to the number of secrets a work contains, and sensibility can be measured by the number of secrets which are discovered. This is far from the qualitative mode of assessment that Leavis and the rest prefer. Indeed, it is closer to the scientific approach to literature advocated by C. P. Snow, whom Leavis attacked with such vituperation in a speech subsequently reprinted in *Nor Shall My Sword: Discourses on Pluralism, Compassion and Social Hope* (London, 1972). But then Leavis's methods, and those of Practical and New Criticism generally, were never really intended for the appreciation of drama. A theatre audience cannot linger over the text in search of subtler shades of meaning. Of course, if the play has been published some lingering can be done in the study prior to the performance but even this can prove more of a hindrance than a help if, for example, the director is particularly innovative, or, as often happens in Stoppard's case, the published text has been revised for the performance.

What is true of the drama is true of all kinds of public utterance. Anyone who has been subjected to a public reading of the poetry of John Donne will know that what appeals in the study is often unintelligible from a lectern. Those easy, colloquial openings may sound theatrical but they disguise an underlying complexity to which a single continuous reading cannot possibly do justice. It is arguable, I suppose, that a very expert performance will produce the right sort of effect by subliminal rather than by conscious means. Indeed, Katharine Worth has recently argued, in *The Irish Drama of Europe from Yeats to Beckett* (London, 1978), that the mainstream of twentieth-century drama, which she traces from Maeterlinck to Beckett, works this way. However, Worth seems to me to underestimate the appeal to the mind in O'Casey and, to a lesser extent, in Pinter and Beckett, and even if she is right, her 'mainstream' remains a very narrow one. So it seems safe to assert that for the vast majority of works written for public utterance the appropriate critical criteria are quite distinct from—indeed almost opposite to—those commonly employed to evaluate works intended for private scrutiny.

Whereas subtlety, ambiguity and complexity are admirable qualities in a novel or a lyric poem, the drama thrives on simplicity. And I would suggest that the bigger the audience is, the greater the simplicity has to be—hence melodrama. First of all, the *language* needs to be simple enough for the audience to get the sense immediately. This does not necessarily involve making every word plain and unambiguous, though this would seem to be the aim in the plays of Shaw, for example. Subtleties and complexities are tolerable as long as the overall drift is clear. In this speech from *Othello* (Act IV, Scene ii) the rapid succession of images appears tangled and contorted, justifiably so, since Othello is in a tangled state of mind; but the emphatic syntax, with its careful highlighting of the 'ifs' and 'buts', makes the basic drift abundantly clear:

> Had it pleased heaven
> To try me with affliction; had they rained
> All kind of sores and shames on my bare head,
> Steeped me in poverty to the very lips,
> Given to captivity me and my utmost hopes,
> I should have found in some place of my soul
> A drop of patience; but, alas, to make me
> A fixed figure for the time of scorn
> To point his slow unmoving finger at!
> Yet could I bear that too; well, very well;

> But there where I have garnered up my heart,
> Where either I must live or bear no life,
> The fountain from the which my current runs,
> Or else dries up—to be discarded thence!
> Or keep it as a cistern for foul toads
> To knot and gender in! Turn thy complexion there,
> Patience, thou young and rose-lipped cherubin,
> Ay, there, look grim as hell!

In Stoppard's dialogue confusions and contortions are even more abundant, and although he also tries to inject emphatic structuring devices such as the syllogism to clear a way through the linguistic and logical thickets, there will be few in the audience who do not lose their way from time to time. However, in Stoppard's case (and arguably even in Shakespeare's) it is often unnecessary to pursue the more tortured trains of thought very closely. It is worth keeping up if one can, of course, since the *non sequiturs* of George Moore, Rosencrantz and Guildenstern, Lenin and the rest are consistently hilarious. But the important thing is simply to recognize that they spend much of their time talking nonsense; in the last analysis the details of that nonsense are not crucially important. In other words, for all the intricacy of Stoppard's language, and for all his protestations about writing 'away into a tunnel' and simply adding 'one line to another line', it is clear that he tends to think in terms of large chunks of dialogue or monologue rather than, or perhaps as well as, in terms of the individual word or line. He has an advanced sense of structure, pattern, architecture—call it what we will. It is no accident that architects keep popping up in *The Real Thing*. And in his critical comments too we find a lively awareness of structure. In the first Hayman interview, for example, he praises Beckett's 'architecture', and draws attention to the similar design of *Jumpers* and *Travesties*:

> You start with a prologue which is slightly strange. Then you have an interminable monologue which is rather funny. Then you have scenes. Then you end up with another monologue. And you have unexpected bits of music and dance, and at the same time people are playing ping-pong with various intellectual arguments.

Stoppard's habit of foreshadowing his themes in virtually

self-contained tableaux attached to the front of the plays also indicates a strong sense of overall design. And a rather different factor which points in the same direction is his tendency to repeat himself, not only in the plays but also in interviews. (It would seem that, despite his reputation for exuberance and spontaneity, he does not always live for the moment, but is inclined to stand back a little from life in order to recognize contrasts and parallels.)

An accentuated awareness of design is of course a prime requisite of the dramatist—and of the musician, who composes a purer kind of aural art. In music the commonest pattern is probably sonata form; in drama it is undoubtedly the well-made play, a formula that goes back as far as Greek New Comedy and is still to be found today in plays where plot is paramount. Stoppard is more interested in ideas than in plot. One immediately thinks of Shaw, who used Hegelian dialectic as a formula on which to construct plays of ideas. But, as I have argued in Chapter 10, Stoppard is interested less in the way ideas evolve than in the relationships between systems of thought which are already fully formed. So his plays tend to be built upon a series of juxtapositions to which, I suppose, the closest analogy is the Jacobean court masque—a form which also dealt with contrasting ideas.

In the masque, simplicity of structure was taken to an extreme. Typically, the forces of evil were presented in the first half of the play (the anti-masque), and then, to quote Ben Jonson's *Masque of Queens*, 'the whole face of the scene altered, scarce suffering the memory of such a thing' and the forces of good were brought on stage for the masque proper. Stoppard generally handles his juxtapositions much less crudely but *Travesties* in particular has been accused by Tynan of lacking any 'internal dynamic', any 'narrative thrust that impels the characters, whether farcically or tragically or in any intermediate mode, toward a credible state of crisis, anxiety, or desperation'. *Travesties* is perhaps an extreme case but all Stoppard's plays resemble masques insofar as they present a fairly simplified confrontation between 'mighty opposites'.

Moreover, the masque analogy helps to explain another feature of Stoppard's dramaturgy that has attracted considerable comment, most of it adverse: the insubstantial nature of his characters. The most frequent complaint—which, oddly enough, has also been made about Joseph Conrad, another literary acquisition from Eastern Europe—is that Stoppard can't create convincing women. 'His female characters are somewhere between playmates and amanuenses. He simply doesn't understand them'. This is Derek Marlowe's comment, quoted by Tynan. Not unnaturally, Stoppard rejects the accusation. The terms in which he rejects it, however, are at first sight somewhat surprising: 'If Derek had said that I don't understand *people*, it would have made more sense'. This appears to be a very damaging piece of self-criticism but what Stoppard really means is that he is not interested in naturalistic or 'truth-telling writing', which, he has often said, 'tends to go off like fruit'; he prefers to stand at one remove from life and look at it 'in an oblique, distant, generalized way'. 'That's what art is best at', he argues in 'Ambushes for the Audience'. 'The object is the universal perception'.

The characters who contribute to this universal perception are, as he conceded to Hayman, 'two-dimensional dream people' just as the characters in masques were simply personified abstractions. There is of course one important exception to this rule that Stoppard's characters are two-dimensional: just as the masquers stepped from the stage and joined with the audience in a dance at the end of a masque, so Stoppard's equivalents to these forces of good occasionally step forward to commune directly with the audience. At these moments the plays can generate genuine emotion—a quality which they are generally felt to lack. (The fact that it is nearly always a male character who establishes this rapport with the audience may explain why Stoppard's men seem more convincing than his women, although this is a chicken-and-egg situation.) For the most part, however, the characters are deliberately two-dimensional. The few plays in which we do find 'people as real . . . as the people in *Coronation Street*' (Hayman) are clearly aberrations and, with the exception of *Professional Foul*, unsuccessful aberrations too; it transpires that their characters are 'only real because I've seen them in other people's plays'. Though this was said, to Hayman, of *Enter a Free Man*, it applies almost equally well to *Night and Day*, where, for example, Wagner is a stereotyped Australian, Milne a stereotyped 'boy scout in an Austin Reed outfit', Mageeba a descendant of the General Rosas encountered by Charles Darwin and Carson a complete non-entity. (Carson advises Wagner to be careful if Mageeba laughs. Likewise, Darwin observed of Rosas in his *Notebook*: 'laughing bad sign'. The notion that laughter betokens incipient violence in Blacks has now become something of a cliché.)

The simplicity of the design and the characterization in Stoppard's plays compensates the audience for the close attention which it is bound to give to the elaborate action and the intricate language. In the masque the audience was similarly compensated for the close attention which it was bound to give to the elaborate spectacle, designed by Inigo Jones, and the intricate music, composed by Alfonso Ferrabosco and others.

The analogy may appear unflattering to Stoppard. After all, the masque occupies an obscure and often denigrated niche in the history of the drama—although Peter Brook did something to revive its ethos with his 1969 production of *A Midsummer Night's Dream*. But in the last analysis its clear-cut structure is not too far removed from, say, the precision of Shakespeare's architecture which Mark Rose has expounded so lucidly in *Shakespearean Design* (Cambridge, Mass., 1972). And its cardboard characterization simply takes to an extreme a tendency to be found in any comedy of manners— indeed perhaps in any effective play, for, as Eric Bentley has written (in *The Life of the Drama*—New York, 1965), 'a *character* is not a *role* unless it can be put across in a few acted scenes. Any idea for a character which cannot be put across at that velocity and by that method is unsuited to dramatic art'. (Bentley's chapter, 'In Praise of Types', is worth comparing with Stoppard's observations about stereotypes in the second Hayman interview.)

If the masque analogy still seems unworthy of Stoppard, then perhaps opera, whose origins are of course bound up with those of the masque, would serve almost as well. Again we generally find surface complexity (the subtleties of the music) balanced by simplicity of characterization and design. But in poetry, the novel, and other literary forms designed for scrutiny in the study (including 'closet drama' if that is not a contradiction in terms) things are altogether different. No compensation is needed for the superficial complexities since the reader may be assumed to have as much leisure as necessary to sort them out. It is therefore disappointing to find that in *Lord Malquist and Mr Moon* there is no more depth to the plot or the characterization than there is in the plays. The book is really just a string of logical puzzles which ultimately become tedious by virtue of their sameness and their lack of resonance. There is no essential difference between the weird conjunction of blackness, Irishness and Jewishness found in O'Hara and the unsettling (at least for Moon) combination of abandoned behaviour and professed chastity found in Jane, and neither O'Hara's eccentricity nor Jane's involves the reader in any way since both are viewed entirely from the outside. We never sense how it might feel to be a black Irish Jew (if that is what O'Hara really is) or a promiscuous young virgin (if that is what Jane really is). Moon is the only character in the book whose consciousness we enter and whose perplexity we share, but his predicament does not develop significantly and, as I have already tried to show, it tends to be stated rather than evoked.

On the stage these problems would disappear. The simple framework would provide a welcome handhold for audiences bewildered by the non-stop bombardment of zany speech and spectacle. Furthermore, the characters would assume some semblance of vitality when bodied forth by living actors: Diana Rigg would inevitably play Jane, and Michael Hordern—suitably rejuvenated—would be Moon.

At the risk of concluding with a truism, then, I submit that Stoppard is a superb dramatist but no novelist, and that his peculiar recipe for the drama consists of a complex and brilliant facade supported by architecture which is masque-like in its simplicity.

Appendix I
Pure Stoppard: Minor Works

A number of Stoppard's plays for radio and television have (at the time of writing) not yet been printed. These include: *The Dissolution of Dominic Boot* (radio, 1964), *M is for Moon Among Other Things* (radio, 1964), *Teeth* (television, 1966), *Neutral Ground* (television, 1968), *The Engagement* (television, 1970) and the *The Dog It Was That Died* (radio, 1982). None of these is considered here. Interested parties should consult Randolph Ryan for plot summaries and production details, and Hayman for criticism. Hayman also discusses an apprentice piece for the stage, *The Gamblers* (1965). An early play for television, *This Way Out With Samuel Boot* (1964), remains unperformed as well as unpublished. (Tynan discusses it at some length.) And *The Boundary* (1975), written for television in collaboration with Clive Exton, is reviewed by Hunter. To date nobody seems to have paid any attention to the five episodes which Stoppard wrote for the long-running BBC radio soap opera, *The Dales*, in 1964.

One further category of plays is ignored here. Several of Stoppard's works have undergone a change of medium since they were first published. Thus, for example, *If You're Glad I'll Be Frank*, *Albert's Bridge* and *A Separate Peace* have all been adapted for the stage; *Professional Foul* and *A Separate Peace* have been adapted for radio, and the Library of Congress boasts a film-script of *Rosencrantz and Guildenstern Are Dead*. In all cases I have ignored the adapted version.

This leaves seven works for treatment in this chapter: three short stories, three plays for radio and one, *A Separate Peace*, for television.

'Reunion'; 'Life, Times: Fragments'; 'The Story'

Of the three short stories printed in *Introduction 2* 'The Story' is the most conventional—and the least instructive for our purposes. It tells of the tragic consequences which ensue when a private misdemeanour by a public-schoolmaster is given exposure in the national press. The focus on journalism anticipates *Dirty Linen* and *Night and Day*, and the clash between public and private, which is heightened by some play on the meaning of the word 'favour', can be seen as a primitive anticipation of the full-scale conflict between 'mystery' and 'clockwork' in Stoppard's later work. The automatic responses of the press corps are especially close to the automatous behaviour of characters like Archie in *Jumpers* and the Player in *Rosencrantz and Guildenstern Are Dead*. But the continuous narrative and the realistic mode together ensure that this underlying structure is never as obtrusive as it is in the subsequent works.

'Life, Times: Fragments' is one step closer to the norm by virtue of the oscillation between autobiographical narration, which documents the 'life', and the 'eye of God' technique, which chronicles the 'times'. The story presents a portrait of a failed writer. As we should expect, the autobiographical sections provide an intimate portrait of his confusion and mounting despair, while the passages told in the third person reveal the tougher 'clockwork' self which he shows to the world. The way 'He laughed and stopped laughing as two distinct actions' clearly anticipates a later 'clockwork' character—the Player, in *Rosencrantz and Guildenstern Are Dead*, who 'laughs briefly and in a second has never laughed in his life'.

Besides looking forward to the juxtaposition of 'mystery' and 'clockwork' in the later works, the alternation of 'I' and 'he' in 'Life, Times: Fragments' looks back to the tension between 'I' and 'you' in T. S. Eliot's 'Love Song of J. Alfred Prufrock'. Stoppard's expressed admiration for this poem (e.g. in the first Hayman interview) suggests that the resemblance is not just accidental, and his third story in *Introduction 2*, 'Reunion', provides proof positive of a link. A man and a woman, closeted in a kitchen, skirt around the 'overwhelming question' of love in much the same way as 'one' and 'I' do in 'Prufrock'. Prufrock's 'you' longs to squeeze 'the universe into a ball/To roll it toward' the 'overwhelming question'. Stoppard's man believes that—

> There is a certain word . . . which if shouted at the right pitch and in a silence worthy of it, would nudge the universe into gear. . . . All the things which just miss will just click right, and the mind that heaves and pops like boiling porridge will level off, secretly . . . His world will have shuddered into a great and marvellous calm in which books will be written and flowers picked and loves contemplated.

Unfortunately, 'No one knows what the word is' and it is 'above syllogisms'. The woman suggests 'Fire!' but the man objects that it 'may not be English at all', and proposes a series of nonce-words: 'Pafflid . . . brilge, culp, matrap, drinnop, quelp, trid, crik . . .'

This extrapolation of Eliot's image contains the germ of various reactions to the 'mystery' of life in Stoppard's later works: Rosencrantz's cry of 'Fire!', for example, and Guildenstern's repudiation of syllogisms earlier in that play, and the extravagant coinage of nonce-words in the *Dogg* plays. But above all it is the predicament of Moon in *Lord Malquist and Mr Moon* that is prefigured here. The man's 'word' anticipates Moon's bomb, which is also designed to 'nudge the universe into gear'. Moon's plan fails when his bomb turns out to be a giant balloon. The man in 'Reunion' fails for reasons which are, in terms of imagery at least, closely related. The woman rejects his advances, a point which Hayman seems to have missed:

> . . . and the hollow ballooned, shaking emptily, his body disconnecting and the sea coming up fast, beyond relief from ritual counting or public obscenities, where only murder would stop it now, and it took a long time, stairs and streets later, before he got a hold on it again, without, as always, having murdered anybody.

If You're Glad I'll Be Frank

There is a strong family likeness between Gladys, the central character of this delightful little play, and the heroes of the next two plays in the canon of Stoppard's published works. Like Albert of *Albert's Bridge* and John Brown in *A Separate Peace*, Gladys seems always to have been baffled by the incomprehensible flux, the 'mystery' of life. All three seek security within cloisters—academic cloisters in Albert's case, religious ones in Gladys's and Brown's. And all three suffer an initial rebuff. Gladys explains that she—

> . . . was going to be a nun, but they wouldn't have me because I didn't believe . . . It was the serenity I was after, that and the clean linen . . .

She must have stumbled into marriage at some point, but then she got the chance of a literally 'clockwork' existence, as the Post Office's 'Speaking Clock'. By the time the play opens, however, she has begun to tire of this mechanical existence. A rescuer is at hand; her long-lost husband, Frank, a bus-driver whose life is likewise ruled by a rigid timetable, telephones the Speaking Clock and recognizes Gladys's voice. He decides to save her. At first he tries to do this while keeping his own 'clockwork' intact; he gets ahead of schedule so that he can stop the bus for a minute or so at the Post Office and try to locate Gladys there. He soon finds that he needs more time, however, and so he throws caution to the winds and abandons his timetable—and his bus, and presumably his job.

Gladys clearly wants to be saved; she is starting to crack under the strain, thinking thoughts which are hilariously at odds with what she is saying. When she countenances an obscene outburst to put 'the fear of God into their alarm-setting, egg-timing, train-catching, coffee-breaking faith in an uncomprehended clockwork' we are reminded of Guildenstern with his dagger, Moon with his bomb and the narrator of 'Reunion' with his 'word'.

But the lords of the Post Office, who are so 'clockwork' that their entrances coincide with the chimes of Big Ben, close ranks to get Gladys back on the rails and to frustrate Frank's efforts to free her. Frank is told that the Speaking Clock is simply a recording, an automaton. So Gladys is left in her 'clockwork' world. It is clear, however, that if she could escape she would. So by implication, if not in fact, the play champions life's 'mystery' and castigates the 'clock-work' which the Post Office represents.

A Separate Peace

The central concerns of *If You're Glad I'll Be Frank* are reviewed in Stoppard's second play for television, *A Separate Peace*. Only the manner of presentation has changed, from zany expressionism to straightforward realism. Hayman explains why:

> Television is less conducive than radio to originality in writing because less depends on the words, and *A Separate Peace* is a less unconventional play than *If You're Glad I'll Be Frank* . . .

Like Gladys and Albert, and the heroes of Beckett's early fiction, for which Stoppard expressed his admiration to Hayman, John Brown always coveted a cloistered life. He tried to become a monk but failed for the same reason that prevented Gladys from becoming a nun: 'they wouldn't have me because I didn't believe'. He found peace for a time during the war in a prison camp, where 'life was regulated, in a box of earth and wire and sky'. Now, many years on, he endeavours to rediscover that 'separate peace' in the Beech-wood Nursing Home. To the bewilderment of the hospital staff he has no ailments; he comes, like Gladys to her convent, simply for 'the privacy . . . and the clean linen'.

> A hospital is a very dependable place. Anything could be going on outside . . . Fire, flood and misery of all kinds, across the world or over the hill, it can all go on, but this is a private ward; I'm paying for it . . . There's one thing that's always impressed me about hospitals—they've all got their own generators. In case of power cuts. And water tanks. I mean, a hospital can carry on, set loose from the world. The meals come in on trays, on the dot—the dust never settles before it's wiped—clean laundry at the appointed time—the matron does her round and temperatures are taken; pulses too, taken in pure conditions, not affected by anything outside.

In short, as Brown remarks upon first entering his private ward, the whole place works like clockwork. And he does

everything in his power to underscore this artificial routine.
He even goes so far as to decorate the walls of his room with
a mural that rivals the landscape outside. This mural, which
Hayman likens to Magritte's *La Condition Humaine*, was
obviously contrived specifically for television and it would
be most effective in that medium. It strikes me as the one
truly imaginative detail in an otherwise flat and uninspired
play.

The chief spokesman for life's 'mystery' is a sympathetic
young nurse, Maggie Coates. Her finest hour comes at the
conclusion of Brown's long eulogy of hospitals, quoted
above. He ends with the claim that in a hospital, 'You need
never know anything, it doesn't touch you'. This dialogue
ensues:

> MAGGIE: That's not true, Brownie.
> BROWN: I know it's not.
> MAGGIE: Then you shouldn't try and make it true.
> BROWN: I know I shouldn't.
> [*Pause.*]

Elsewhere, however, Maggie is a less effective antagonist,
mainly because Stoppard has also cast her as a spy, employed
by the hospital authorities to find out Brown's identity and
background. She eventually succeeds; Brown's family and
friends are summoned and he is forced to concede that they
have won: his 'separate peace' is shattered.

This may sound like a laudable victory of 'mystery' over
'clockwork' but the moral is not as clear-cut as it usually is in
Stoppard. The hospital authorities, represented by the Doctor, Matron and two nurses, are too lightly sketched to serve
as worthy proponents of 'mystery', and Maggie is compromised by her double-dealing. Brown attracts more sympathy than any of them. Moreover, he never explicitly
renounces his 'clockwork', for at the end of the play he
evades his looming family by discharging himself from
hospital in the night, with Maggie's reluctant connivance,
and goes off not to face the world (as Victor Cahn assumes)
but to seek his 'separate peace' elsewhere.

Here, as in *Enter a Free Man*, a balance is struck between
the competing claims of 'mystery' and 'clockwork'. In this
case the unwonted indecision may have been dictated by the
fact that the play 'was written specifically to go with a

half-hour film . . . about international chess masters and grand-masters for the Chess Congress at Hastings in about 1965'. What was needed, Stoppard explained in 'Ambushes for the Audience', was 'some kind of play which was about exclusion, about disappearing into oneself, about finding a substitute for reality'—a play 'which at least suggested what we were saying about chess-players'. To have criticized John Brown would have meant criticizing the chess-players by analogy.

Where Are They Now?

Although *Where Are They Now?* (1970) was written later than *Albert's Bridge* (1967) it takes us back to the simple, unstraddled juxtaposition of 'mystery' and 'clockwork' that is to be found in Stoppard's earliest plays.

'Harpo' Gale is a realist who suffered agonies in the 'clockwork' system of his public school—a system which has changed little, incidentally, as the scenes involving young Marks and Bellamy prove. Gale was principally afflicted by the French master, Jenkins. (Here as elsewhere—the opening tableaux of *Travesties* and *Dirty Linen*, for example—foreign languages are associated with 'clockwork'.) Thirty years on he returns to an old boys' dinner which is every bit as 'clockwork' as the school system itself. So 'clockwork' is the event in fact that an imposter from another school is able to sit through the whole evening without realizing that he is at the wrong dinner.

Gale's express purpose in attending is 'to see if I'd got [Jenkins] right—if he had any other existence which might explain him'. Jenkins, however, has died a few days before the dinner, so Gale is forced to conclude that the Jenkins he remembers was the only Jenkins. And when the headmaster calls for a moment's silence as a tribute to the dead man, Gale refuses to comply. Instead, he treats the assembled company to an uncompromising portrait of the insensitive brute that he knew. (This long soliloquy corresponds to the speeches in which the heroes of the stage plays address the audience directly.)

To be sure, at the last moment a small complication is

injected into this rigid design. The play ends with a flashback to a day in Gale's school life, which shows that he was far from miserable. It was not all brutal 'clockwork'. But it is hard to believe that this is meant to constitute a significant undermining of Gale's attitudes. The rest of the play has provided so much evidence in his favour that one small question-mark, even when placed right at the end, cannot make much difference. Certainly in John Tydeman's production for the BBC the episode had little impact. It looks as though Stoppard, aware that the play had become excessively masque-like, made a desperate last-minute attempt to impose some subtlety from the outside.

Artist Descending a Staircase

In the next radio play, *Artist Descending a Staircase*, the subtlety does seem to well up from within. It is much the most sophisticated work that Stoppard has produced for radio. And—more to the point here—it is perhaps the most sympathetic depiction of real flesh and blood that he has given us in any medium. Donner, Sophie and even Martello are approached with a degree of affection which verges at times on sentimentality. But beneath this unwonted humanity lurks the same old juxtaposition of 'mystery' and 'clockwork' that we have seen in all the other works.

Donner, Martello and Beauchamp are *avant garde* artists who have lived and worked together since before the First World War. Since 1922 their home has been 'a single large attic studio approached by a staircase'—a milieu which suggests the rarefied atmosphere of Albert's bridge and perhaps even more the lonely garret inhabited by Beckett's Murphy. But although they live and work together, belong to the same movement, exhibit together and even, in the early days, dress alike, it soon becomes clear that they are quite different in temperament. The most 'clockwork' of the three is Beauchamp, whom, by analogy with Stoppard's own description of Archie in *Jumpers*, we may label the villain. Beauchamp's art is rigorously abstract; Donner defines it as 'the mechanical expression of a small intellectual idea'. He begins by taping games of ping-pong and chess, and ends by attempting to tape silence. His nature is likewise cold and ruthless. It allows him to abandon Sophie, and this in turn leads to her suicide.

Martello's art is less outrageously abstract. It is epitomized by the 'construction' described in the third sequence of the play—a sort of surreal image of the dead Sophie, built out of materials suggested by *The Song of Solomon*. Martello is consistently thoughtful and courteous. It is he who introduces Sophie to the artists' world, and when she expresses a preference for naturalistic art he gives a pleasant and plausible defence of their more experimental approach. Moreover, he has the humanity to confess at the end of his career that he has 'achieved nothing but mental acrobatics'. Beauchamp betrays no such doubts about his work.

Donner is something of a maverick by comparison with the other two artists—a 'mystery'-man, so to speak. Beauchamp recalls that Donner once 'told Tarzan [i.e. Tristan Tzara] he was too conservative', and yet of the three he is the one most in tune with Sophie's insistence that the artist should 'paint beauty . . . and the subtlest beauty is in nature'. Donner goes on to produce some weird and wonderful pieces, including edible art and sculptures in sugar, but in the end he comes back to the norm defined by Sophie: 'painting what the eye sees'. His last work is a painting of 'a naked woman sitting about a garden with a unicorn eating the roses'. As Beauchamp objects, this is not completely naturalistic, but in fact the unicorn, a common Stoppardian symbol for life's 'mystery', does not conflict with Sophie's ideal. To her it was legitimate for the artist to improve on nature, as she herself could:

> If I hear hoofbeats, I can put a unicorn in the garden and
> no one can open my eyes against it and say it isn't true.

Both Donner and Sophie, in fact, are realists. Both exhibit a practical, matter-of-fact streak which Beauchamp and Martello lack. Sophie, though blind, can tell the difference between a landau and a brewer's dray, though she is unpretentious enough to admit that she wouldn't know the difference between Indian and Singhalese tea. Similarly, Donner is the only one of the three artists who can distinguish between German and French soldiers, and he is also the only one willing to admit that the reality of their holiday in France has not quite matched their expectations. Moreover, even Donner's wildest artistic experiments are realistic in some sense; by making his art edible he at least ensured its appeal 'to a man with an empty belly'.

The audience's sympathy for Donner and Sophie is deepened by the late revelation of a tragic misunderstanding connected with Sophie's death. She committed suicide at the prospect of being left alone with Donner after her abandonment by Beauchamp. But it is eventually revealed that it was in fact Donner that she loved in the first place and that her failing vision caused her to confuse him with Beauchamp.

Donner's death, if less tragic, is more significant in a thematic sense. The cause of his death is a fall down the attic staircase. Neither Beauchamp nor Martello witnessed the fall, but Beauchamp had left a tape-recorder going in the studio (in an effort to record the sound of silence) so that the sounds of Donner's last moments are preserved. The tape (to which Martello and Beauchamp are listening as the play begins) appears to indicate that Donner was interrupted in the course of a nap by an intruder. Donner, on waking, called out a friendly 'Ah, there you are'—only to be rewarded by a blow, which sent him to his death. Since Martello and Beauchamp are the only people to whom Donner was likely to make such a greeting they begin (and end) the play by accusing each other of his murder. But by means of a flashback Stoppard reveals that what Martello and Beauchamp take to be the sound of Donner's snoring was in fact the sound of a fly buzzing round the studio, that the footsteps were Donner's own, that Donner's words were addressed to the fly and that the blow was directed at the fly by Donner himself. In lunging at the fly Donner lost his balance and fell to his death down the stairs.

The conclusion to be drawn is not just Beauchamp's glib verdict, which is truer than he realizes, that: 'As flies to wanton boys are we to the Gods: they kill us for their sport'. A more significant point is that Beauchamp's 'clockwork' equipment and 'clockwork' logic have failed altogether to penetrate the 'mystery' of Donner's death, and indeed the 'mystery' of Donner's personality.

Appendix II
Applied Stoppard: The Adaptations

When the editors of *Theatre Quarterly* tried to pin down the essence of Stoppard's art in 'Ambushes for the Audience', he protested:

> I'm a professional writer—I'm for hire . . . I've written all kinds of stuff, everything from seventy episodes of a serial translated into Arabic for Bush House, to a one-off spy thing for Granada.

His 70-part serial, *A Student's Diary*, is certainly the most spectacular example of Stoppard's willingness to have a go at anything. But the plays exhibit considerable diversity too. *Jumpers* and *Travesties* are big, spectacular pieces which exploit to the full the generous resources of Britain's subsidized theatres. *After Magritte*, *Dirty Linen* and the *Dogg* plays, on the other hand, were designed to Ed Berman's sparer specifications. And *Night and Day* and *The Real Thing*, with their small casts, their realism and their relatively undemanding effects, were obviously tailored to the requirements of the commercial West End theatres. Each is, as Stoppard put it in his second interview with Hayman, 'a [Michael] Codron-type play'.

Beneath this diversity, however, there lies an essential sameness. And it is surprising how often this is true also of Stoppard's wide range of adaptations. Stoppard the adaptor tends to choose works in which reality and some kind of dream-world or play-within-the-play are juxtaposed. Occasionally, though, his raw material resists the rigorously binary formula which he favours, and in these cases, especially *Tango* and *Undiscovered Country*, the tension between the original and the Stoppardian overlay throws Stoppard's preoccupations into useful relief.

The adaptations are of two main kinds. First, there are translations of plays by foreign playwrights: Mrozek, Lorca, Schnitzler and Nestroy. I call them translations simply for convenience. In fact, French is the only foreign language Stoppard knows well, and so in all these cases he has had to depend on literal translations supplied by others: Nicholas Bethell and an unnamed friend, Katie Kendall, Neville and Stephen Plaice, and John Harrison respectively. Stoppard's activity has been to turn these versions into something 'actable', as he put it in the Preface to *Undiscovered Country*.

The second category of adaptations consists of screenplays based on others' (English) fiction. Because these have never been published as texts they will be considered only briefly in the concluding pages of this chapter. (Stoppard's adaptation for television of Jerome K. Jerome's *Three Men in a Boat* (1975) is not dealt with here.) The translation of Lorca's *House of Bernarda Alba* is also given scant attention, since it remains unpublished. My main business is with Mrozek's *Tango*, Schnitzler's *Undiscovered Country (Das weite Land)* and Nestroy's *On the Razzle (Einen Jux will er sich machen)*.

Tango

The Mrozek translation stands apart from Stoppard's others by virtue of its early date. He was virtually unknown as a writer and therefore particularly amenable to bizarre and breathless commissions when, in 1965, the Royal Shakespeare Company ran into trouble with the translation of *Tango* which had been provided by Nicholas Bethell. In a private letter, written seventeen years on, Stoppard recalled the affair thus:

> It was only about a fortnight before rehearsals were due to begin that the director, Trevor Nunn, called in extra help (me) to make the dialogue more speakable. Bethell's advantage was that he could read Polish and mine was supposed to be that I could write dialogue.

At this early stage in his career Stoppard seems to have been more reluctant to depart significantly from his original than he has subsequently become. His translation was, as he remarked in the same letter, 'made as faithful as possible . . .

too faithful in fact. The play obviously didn't work as well in English as it had worked in the original'. It is nevertheless remarkable how often characteristics of the mature Stoppard are prefigured here. Either 'the temptation to add a flick here and there became irresistible' (as it did in *Undiscovered Country*) or else the influence of Mrozek on Stoppard is greater than anybody has yet surmised. Some of the parallels are quite superficial. For example, the set design anticipates that of *Jumpers*, except for the fact that we cannot see into the room which opens off the corridor, stage-right. Instead we see into a room at the back—Eleonora's bedroom—to which there is no equivalent in *Jumpers*. The bizarre props which litter this set, especially the bowler-hat, look forward to *After Magritte*. And the dialogue is full of Stoppardian touches; for instance, Stomil's defence of the artistic revolution resembles Tzara's in *Travesties*, while Arthur's responses tend to be like Carr's. But these analogies between Stomil and Tzara, on the one hand, and Arthur and Carr, on the other, prompt the more important observation that the basic structure of Mrozek's play resembles the familiar Stoppardian juxtaposition.

Tango is set in a post-revolutionary society. Early in the play Stomil explains what this means:

> Revolution!—with one jump into the modern age! Free at last from the old art and the old life!—man goes forward, on his own two feet, topples the old gods and climbs up on the pedestal—the chains broken, the fetters smashed!—Revolution and expansion—they're our watchwords! Down with the old forms, crack convention wide open and long live the new life—dynamic, creative, free!—beyond form!—oh yes—beyond form!

In this society, as in the world presided over by Archie's Rad-Libs in *Jumpers*, 'morality and aesthetics have had their day'; principles are out and opinions are in. One set of characters—Stomil, his wife Eleonora and his mother Eugenia—revels in this new-found freedom, and advertizes its progressiveness by adopting a vulgar commoner, Eddie, as its mascot. Another set—Stomil's son Arthur and Eugenia's brother Eugene—longs for the pre-revolutionary certainties, protesting, in terms which anticipate *Artist Descending a Staircase*, that 'this isn't a game of intellectual ping-pong—

this is life'. A third set—Arthur's cousin Ala, and, in aberrant moments in Acts II and III, Stomil and Eleonora— vacillates between the attitudes of the other two.

Obviously this disposition of forces approximates to Stop- pard's habitual formula involving 'clockwork', 'mystery' and a straddler. And there are a number of details which reinforce this parallel. For example, the 'clockwork' characters are first seen playing a game of cards which is not unlike what Clive James calls the 'Farjeonesque game of bridge' played by the actors in *The Real Inspector Hound*. The charades enacted by Archie and Dotty in *Jumpers* provide a somewhat looser analogy. And the ambiguous relationship between Dotty and Archie which causes George so much anguish is foreshad- owed in Act II of *Tango* when Stomil, momentarily roused to jealousy by Arthur's insinuations, breaks into his wife's bedroom only to find that she and Eddie are engaged in nothing more incriminating than a game of cards.

But ultimately the resemblance between Stoppard and Mrozek is only skin-deep. For a start there is a crucial and obvious difference between Archie's efficient, plastic-coated pragmatism and Stomil's slovenly self-indulgence. It is true that Stomil's lazy laissez-faire attitudes ultimately permit the rise of a tyrant (Eddie) who is every bit as sinister as Archie, but Eddie's seizure of power is merely a final *coup de théâtre*; the bulk of the play focusses not on him but on the fatal weakness of the bourgeois liberalism which gives him his opportunity.

On the other hand, Mrozek's Arthur is no George Moore. In fact, there are several occasions when he looks much more like a Stoppardian villain. Right at the beginning, for in- stance, when we learn that he is studying philosophy and it is suggested that he might go into a monastery, we think at once of Albert in *Albert's Bridge*. Despite this unpromising beginning, Arthur manages to generate some sympathy for his stand against the new radicalism. But there are continual reminders of his 'clockwork' austerity. In Act II, for exam- ple, Stomil suddenly bursts out with this accusation:

> You're just a dirty little formalist. You don't give a
> damn about me or your mother. They can all drop dead
> so long as the form is preserved . . .

And ultimately we find Arthur behaving mechanically and conceding that 'the old conventions won't bring back reality'. He then casts about for another idea on which to base a philosophy of life and, having rejected God, sport and common sense, he concludes that 'the only possible thing is power!' But Eddie preempts his bid to build a tyranny on this premise. He clubs Arthur down, with a brutality which is quite foreign to Stoppard, except perhaps for the moment in *Night and Day* when Mageeba strikes Wagner, and inaugurates his own regime with a sinister *danse macabre*—the tango of the title. Arthur dies in a daze, his last coherent words a protestation of love for Ala. Suddenly he has become human again, and his plight should generate the sort of sympathy that we feel for Guildenstern, George Moore and their ilk.

Overall, then, Arthur turns out to be a much more complex character than any of Stoppard's. He attracts us one minute and repels us the next; he gives voice to a philosophy which looks like the humanism of George Moore but which ultimately signifies nothing. He is, in short, a realistic character whose death, Mrozek insists, must 'appear entirely realistic', rather than a mere mouthpiece for a fixed set of ideas. And the same point could be made about Stomil and a number of other characters.

To say this is not to deny that the play has an obvious and important allegorical dimension. It is clear, for example, that Arthur is conceived as a representative of the spirit of counter-revolution, that Stomil represents the well-meaning liberalism of the middle-classes which brings on the revolution, and that Eddie represents the unprincipled opportunism which seizes power out of the vacuum created by the revolution. But as works like *Everyman, The Faerie Queene, Pilgrim's Progress* and the novels of William Golding remind us, allegorical characters can be depicted realistically. Mrozek's characters are thoroughly human. Indeed, it is ultimately a very human point that he wishes to make about them: that Stomil and Arthur, so different on the surface, are very much alike beneath the skin. Both are hollow men who lack the integrity to give substance to their respective ideologies. Arthur speaks for Stomil as well as himself when he complains, 'Reason was my sin—and abstraction, reason's lecherous daughter'. Stomil himself has a similar speech when his moment of *anagnorisis* comes:

> I always thought that we were ruled not by people but by ideas—and that violence was the animal in us taking its revenge. But now I see it's only Eddie.

Ideas and ideologies ultimately dissolve into character in Mrozek's work. He is interested in the common frailty of Stomil and Arthur (and its consequence: Eddie's seizure of power) rather than in their conflicting ideologies *per se*. In Stoppard, however, ideas inevitably take precedence over character. He works at one remove from life, viewing it obliquely and from a distance. As a result his characters become mouthpieces for certain fixed points of view rather than palpable human beings. As Derek Marlowe said to Tynan:

> . . . the grand events, the highs and lows of human behaviour, [Tom] sees with a sort of aloof, omniscient amusement. The world doesn't impinge on his work, and you'd think after reading his plays that no emotional experience had ever impinged on his world.

This is an overstatement. The predicaments of Stoppard's protagonists—Rosencrantz and Guildenstern, George Moore, Lenin and Nadya, Alexander Ivanov and the rest—do generate some emotional impact. But the way in which Mrozek's subject-matter keeps bursting out of its Stoppardian straitjacket indicates that there is some truth in Marlowe's diagnosis.

The House of Bernarda Alba

After *Tango* Stoppard concentrated on his own plays (including *Rosencrantz and Guildenstern Are Dead* and *Jumpers*) for seven years, and it was not until 1973 that he turned his hand to translation once again. This time it was Garcia Lorca's classic, *The House of Bernarda Alba*. It was a curious choice since, as Stoppard himself observed to Michael Leech, 'to adapt Lorca you need to be a poet, a playwright, and fluent in Spanish—and I'm only one of those things!'

Katie Kendall, a student of Spanish at Bristol University, helped him through the language barrier. But even though

The House of Bernarda Alba is the least poetic of Lorca's tragedies, Stoppard must have had great difficulty with the idiom, which is so unlike his own cerebral one. And there are two other problems that must have caused him some bother: the play has an all-female cast, and it fairly smoulders with repressed sexuality.

The Stoppard translation was received cordially enough in 1973 but it has been revived only once (in San Francisco) and it remains unpublished. In fact it seems now to be altogether inaccessible. (Stoppard's agents, Frazer and Dunlop Ltd., do not acknowledge possession of a copy.) So it is reasonable to surmise that in Stoppard's mind at least the problems posed by Lorca were not successfully surmounted.

Contrasts can be as useful as parallels when one is endeavouring to characterize an author's work. Mrozek's *Tango* represents a partial contrast to the Stoppardian norm; Lorca and Stoppard, on the other hand, strike me as being polar opposites in almost every respect.

Undiscovered Country

After *The House of Bernarda Alba* it was another six years before Stoppard tried translation again. This time the commission came from the National Theatre and the text in question was an Austrian classic, *Das weite Land* (*The Vast Country*) by Arthur Schnitzler. The choice was a fortunate one and *Undiscovered Country* has proved a success both in production and in print.

The title of Schnitzler's play comes from an important speech delivered by Dr von Aigner in the third act. Asked by Friedrich Hofreiter why he constantly deceived his wife despite his love for her he replies:

> Has it not occurred to you what kind of complicated creatures human beings essentially are? There's room for so much in us at the same time! Love and betrayal . . . fidelity and infidelity . . . adoration of one woman and yearning for another or others. We try to create order in ourselves, as much as possible, but this order is always only artificial . . . whatever is natural is chaos. Yes, my dear Hofreiter, the soul . . . is a vast country,

as a poet once described it . . . it could also have been a
hotel manager.

The poet in question is probably Fontane, who, in *Effie
Briest*, allows Effie's father to evade awkward questions by
parroting the phrase, 'Das ist ein weites Feld' ('That is a vast
area'). In his search for a set of cultural references that would
be more appropriate for an English audience, Stoppard
substituted Shakespeare for Fontane. 'Undiscovered country'
comes from Hamlet's best-known soliloquy, where, however, it refers to the next world rather than the soul.
Ingenious as the substitution is, it puts a rather different
complexion on von Aigner's speech and ultimately on the
play as a whole. A vast country can be explored but an
undiscovered one cannot. And the crucial difference between
Undiscovered Country and *Das weite Land* is that Schnitzler,
spurred on no doubt by his association with Freud (who once
referred to Schnitzler as his *doppelgänger*), probes his characters' psyches much more deeply than Stoppard does.

Both playwrights delight in exposing the games that
people play—what Michael Billington in his *Guardian* review
of 21 June 1979 called 'the polite sexual excuse-me' which
shields the real pressures of life. But when these pressures do
break through the 'clockwork' facade Stoppard is more
reluctant than Schnitzler to analyse them, so that what Mauer
calls 'the mysterious connection between things' remains
more of a mystery than it does in the original.

Consider again the speech of von Aigner's quoted above.
As well as turning the soul's 'vast country' into an 'undiscovered country', Stoppard translates the opening sentence
thus: 'Haven't you ever thought what a strange uncharted
country is human behaviour?' That word 'uncharted' points
unmistakably to Stoppard's reluctance to probe the human
condition. There are several other illustrations of this same
tendency in the Stoppard. At the end of Act I, for instance, a
speech in which Friedrich protests that 'Life is a complicated
arrangement. . . . But interesting . . . very interesting' is
simply omitted. So is a passage in Act IV in which Friedrich
muses on the complexity of women. More important than
the omission of speeches about complexity, however, is the
omission of the complexities themselves. All of the major

characters in the play are simplified to some extent by
Stoppard. Take Genia, for example. Late in Act I she has a
long debate with Friedrich about the implications of the
suicide of their friend Korsakow. Genia reveals that Korsakow killed himself because she rejected his advances, and
Friedrich asks whether she regrets having driven him to his
death. In Stoppard a forthright reply from Genia ends the
discussion: 'I'm sorry he's dead. But what should I reproach
myself for?—my faithfulness?' This simple statement re-
places a long and complex passage in which Friedrich probes
Genia's motives and eventually draws from her the cryptic
statement that she refrained from adultery because 'I would
not have been able to. God knows why. I would not have
been able to'. Clearly Schnitzler's Genia is a complex crea-
ture, swayed by passions of which she is barely conscious and
which she certainly does not understand. Stoppard's Genia,
on the other hand, is simply a faithful wife.

A little earlier in Act I Stoppard simplifies Genia again. At
the beginning of the same conversation with Friedrich, Genia
announces that she wants to visit their son Joey (Percy in
Schnitzler) in England, where he is at a public school. In
Schnitzler it soon becomes clear that what Genia has in mind
is a permanent separation from Friedrich. Stoppard glosses
over this implication, presumably because it seems to conflict
with the fidelity which prevented her from becoming Korsakow's mistress.

Having set Genia up as a constant wife in the opening
scenes, Stoppard must subject his audience to a rude shock
when he comes to depict her adultery with Otto von Aigner
in Act IV. It is as if Genia has been entirely transformed—
from constancy to adultery, from ingenuousness to role-
playing, from 'mystery' to 'clockwork'. Stoppard actually
aggravates the transition by making her slightly more callous
in the later scenes (e.g. her farewell to Otto) than she is in
Schnitzler. The transition from innocence to experience is
much less abrupt in the original because we have seen from
the first that Genia is affected by mysterious and apparently
contradictory passions which may lead her almost anywhere.
Schnitzler's portrait of Genia is naturalistic; Stoppard's is
stylized.

Friedrich too is simplified by Stoppard, but unlike Genia,

who is made more innocent in the early scenes, he is blackened. Three examples must suffice. Late in Act I Stoppard omits a longish exchange between Friedrich and Genia, which includes Friedrich's admission that he 'felt sorry for [Korsakow] in a way I seldom feel sorry for someone. . .' Without this passage Friedrich's attitude to Korsakow seems entirely callous. Similarly, in Act II Stoppard cuts several speeches between Erna and Dr Mauer, including Mauer's account of the terrible effect that the much earlier death of Doctor Bernhaupt had on Friedrich. Again the result is to accentuate the callous side of Friedrich. Thirdly, in Act IV Stoppard omits Friedrich's confession to Mauer that he left Lake Vols in order to escape from himself. Without this speech we get the impression that Friedrich's departure from Lake Vols was prompted simply by his concern that his affair with Erna should not be found out. There is no other suggestion in the text that Friedrich is in any way dissatisfied with his philanderings.

Even in Schnitzler's original, Friedrich is certainly not a nice character but he does exhibit traces of humanity beneath his frenetic role-playing. In Stoppard, however, he becomes totally absorbed in the 'foolish games . . . that love affairs are'. And Stoppard accentuates his 'clockwork' nature by imposing on him a number of the tricks that characterize Archie and his other villains. Friedrich likes to use foreign phrases but even more telling is his taste for slick comments and Wildean epigrams. An example of the latter is his response to Mauer's bitter remark in Act IV that Friedrich is beginning to amuse him:

> Well, that's something. Since certainty is unattainable, entertainment value is the only justification for conversation.

Another example is his remark to Genia much earlier in the play: 'In an ideal world more and more people would see less and less of each other'. In this case especially, comparison with Schnitzler's original shows how thoroughly Friedrich has been Archie-ized by Stoppard. In the Schnitzler, Friedrich says, 'I think that overall human relationships should be based more on yearning than on habit'. Again Stoppard is responsible for the impudent greeting which Friedrich tosses

to his wife as he makes his first entrance in Act I: 'Good
evening, Genia. How are you? Do you want to come to
America?' Schnitzler allows the invitation to arise naturally
out of the ensuing dialogue. Finally, Stoppard is responsible
for the mechanical way in which Friedrich handles Paul
Kreindl's interruption of his interrogation of Genia late in
Act I; 'it's six of one and . . .' he is saying when Paul enters,
and when Paul leaves, shortly after, Friedrich resumes without hesitation, 'and half a dozen of the other'. Schnitzler has
Friedrich repeat his last line—'I'll put it another way'—to get
the interrogation going again.

So the extra 'flicks' which Stoppard admits to having
added often have the effect of simplifying the characters until
they correspond to one or other of the two types that he likes
to juxtapose. That this simplification was undertaken quite
deliberately is indicated by an important change in the
speech, late in Act IV, in which Mauer comes as close as any
of the characters to summing up the theme of the play.
Provoked by Genia's assertion that life is no more than a
series of foolish games, he protests, in Stoppard's version:

> I assure you Genia, I would have nothing at all against a
> world in which love really was in fact nothing but a
> delightful game . . . But in that case . . . let it be played
> honestly . . . But this hole-in-the-corner posturing,
> this bogus civility between people made wretched
> by jealousy, cowardice, lust—I find all that sad and
> horrible. . .

For Stoppard the civility is bogus, a mere facade, obscuring
the jealousy, cowardice and lust that exist beneath the
surface. Schnitzler, on the other hand, has Mauer talk less
absolutely of an 'alternation of modesty and impudence, of
cowardly jealousy and feigned indifference, of burning passion and empty lust'. The moral judgment implied by
Stoppard's word 'bogus' is lacking here; for Schnitzler the
modesty, impudence, passion and lust are equally real, and
the jealousy and indifference equally despicable. He cannot
reduce the complexities of the human psyche to the simple
scheme which Stoppard prefers.

This desire for simplicity is indicated again by a speech
which Stoppard adds to the conversation between Mauer and
Genia early in the play. Mauer observes of Mrs von Aigner, a

celebrated actress who left her philandering husband, 'Perhaps, after all those years in the theatre, real life took her by surprise'. This juxtaposition of art and life is quite alien to Schnitzler for whom constant oscillation between sincerity and role-playing is the norm.

Mrs von Aigner is in fact something of an embarrassment for Stoppard in that, although an actress by profession, she eschews role-playing in real life. In order to circumvent this problem Stoppard seems to suggest, in Mauer's speech about her quoted above, for example, that she has retired from acting. The fact that he calls her Mrs von Aigner instead of Mrs Meinhold, which is the name—her stage-name, presumably—that Schnitzler uses for her, reinforces this impression. And it is interesting that the kinds of plays in which she used to appear have been altered by Stoppard. Schnitzler refers to them as tragedies and comedies; Stoppard calls them melodramas and farces. This change illustrates very nicely the way in which Stoppard uses art—and drama, in particular—to epitomize unreal, 'clockwork' behaviour.

Stoppard's simplification of Schnitzler's original is not limited to the characterization. The very atmosphere is simplified too. The death motif which haunts *Das weite Land* is severely curtailed in *Undiscovered Country*, for example by the omission of two passages involving death and ghosts on either side of von Aigner's 'undiscovered country' speech. And the opening stage direction, with its careful evocation of the Hofreiters' sanctuary-like garden, ominously drenched with rain, has been reduced to a few bald phrases.

Another factor that affects the atmosphere is Stoppard's habit of transposing material in order to break up long and significant confrontations. A good example occurs at the end of Act IV. Natter has been spreading malicious rumours implicating Friedrich in the death of Korsakow. Friedrich confronts him, obviously intending to force the matter to a duel, but Natter will not be drawn and finally discomforts Friedrich completely by hinting that he knows of Genia's liaison with Otto. The result of this revelation is, of course, the duel between Otto and Friedrich which constitutes the play's climax. Stoppard shortens the scene between Friedrich and Natter, and cools its tone somewhat. More important than these modifications, however, is the interpolation of a trivial though ironical episode in which Paul appears from the tennis court to arrange a game between Friedrich and Otto. Schnitzler places this episode at the end of the confrontation between Friedrich and Natter; Stoppard moves it to a point midway through the confrontation—just before Natter's crucial hint about Genia and Otto, in fact. So in Schnitzler the tension mounts throughout the scene between Friedrich and Natter, and the audience gets no comic relief until the end; in Stoppard, on the other hand, seriousness and silliness alternate during the scene, with the result that we are kept removed from Friedrich's predicament and can see it as just another example of his perennial posturing.

It seems reasonable to conclude that Stoppard's adaptations of the original were prompted by a desire to substitute for Schnitzler's organic evocation of human complexity an organized demonstration of the 'mystery' of life and the inadequacy (if not iniquity) of all 'clockwork' systems which seek to impose order on this chaos.

Of course, there are also many more innocent changes which simply remove material of little consequence to a London audience in the late 1970's. Three characters, one of whom (Doktor Meyer) serves as a focus for Schnitzler's habitual satire of the denizens of northern Germany, are omitted from Act III. And much information about matters such as Friedrich's business and von Aigner's career is also cut. But cumulatively even these changes perhaps affect the nature of the play somewhat. Schnitzler creates the impression of a whole society as a background to and an influence upon the actions and attitudes of his principals. By omitting much of the evidence for this background Stoppard converts the world of the play into something *sui generis*. A subtle piece of Chekhovian naturalism has become a rather clinical thesis-play in Stoppard's customary mould.

On the Razzle

This translation is very different in kind from Stoppard's previous efforts. In his programme note for the original production at the National Theatre Stoppard himself drew attention to this difference:

> So this text is not really a translation of Nestroy's play
> in the strictest sense. My method might be compared to
> cross-country hiking with map and compass, where one
> takes a bearing on the next landmark and picks one's
> own way towards it: a method which would not have
> done when a few years ago I was turning Schnitzler's
> *Das weite Land* into *Undiscovered Country* . . . In the case
> of *Undiscovered Country*, the Ibsenesque undercurrents of
> the play made it important to establish as precisely as
> possible what every phrase meant, root out the allu-
> sions, find the niceties of etiquette, and so on, and
> generally to aim for equivalence . . . But with *On the
> Razzle* I abandoned quite early on the onus of con-
> veying Nestroy intact into English.

So a true translation was not his aim in this case. As we shall
see, he even added a few details to Nestroy's plot, although
in this respect he took fewer liberties than an earlier adaptor
of the play, Thornton Wilder. Wilder's first version was
called *The Merchant of Yonkers*. It reproduced Nestroy's plot
fairly exactly but was not a great success. Only when he
invented a new character, Dolly Levi, the matchmaker, did
he hit the jackpot. And *The Matchmaker* hit an even bigger
jackpot when it was turned into the musical *Hello Dolly*.

Although *On the Razzle* is not true to the letter of *Einen
Jux,* Stoppard has endeavoured to reproduce its spirit. Nestroy aimed 'to please, to entertain, to get people laughing'
(according to the National Theatre Programme) and Stoppard has tried to do the same. Accordingly the play epitomizes the popular conception of Stoppard's art. It is, to quote
Mrs Blumenblatt, 'a blazing cuckoo-clock' of comic devices,
especially linguistic ones: puns, malapropisms, spoonerisms,
reiterated catch-phrases and bawdy *doubles entendres.*

Stoppard's linguistic virtuosity poses some problems, of
course. Michael Billington observed in his review for *The
Guardian* (10 September 1981), that it is difficult to retain 'the
momentum of farce while stuffing the text with verbal
pyrotechnics', and several critics felt that some potentially
funny episodes, including the restaurant scene and the garden
scene, fell flat because of the cloying effect of all the verbiage.
But there were only a few solemn exceptions to the view that

the play as a whole was, as one radio-reviewer put it, 'a real
Razzle Dazzle'.

Stoppard's aim was not just to make the tale as comic an
entertainment as possible, however; in his introduction to the
printed text (which, as usual, differs considerably from the
version actually performed at the National Theatre) he
acknowledges an interest in 'the almost mythic tale of two
country mice escaping to town for a day of illicit freedom,
adventure, mishap and narrow escapes from discovery'.
Something other than pure froth is implied here, and indeed
there are a couple of moments in the play when we sense
something substantial beneath the clockwork facade. The
moments in question are the exchanges between Christopher
and Weinberl which frame their razzle in town. The first of
these exchanges arises out of their employer's decision to
promote them—Christopher from apprentice to chief sales
assistant and Weinberl from chief sales assistant to a part-
nership in the firm. The two men express their delight in a
very Stoppardian dialogue on separate tracks until Christopher suddenly realizes that his promotion leaves him worse
off than he was before:

> You're a partner and I'm the entire staff. I'll have two
> lord-high masters instead of one, three counting the
> widow, and the weight of my authority will be felt by
> the housekeeper's cat.

He launches into a torrent of lamentation which is comically
stylized to begin with—'Whither the striving and how the
abiding for a poor boy in the grocery trade?'—but which
eventually becomes quite affecting despite the prevalence of
cliché:

> Oh, Mr Weinberl, I have come into my kingdom and I
> see that it is the locked room from which you celebrate
> your escape! And if I have to wait until I am as old as
> you, *that's longer than I've been alive*!

Weinberl follows Christopher's elegiac lead with a speech
which, unlike Christopher's, is reasonably close to Nestroy's
original until the final sentence. In the Nestroy this sentence
translates thus: 'I must—I must achieve the experiences of a
rapscallion at any cost'. Stoppard's version is deeper, more
'mythic': 'I've got to acquire a past before it's too late!'

Christopher's response is to propose they go on the razzle in Vienna. Weinberl hesitates momentarily but then indicates his support for the plan by declaring, 'We'll stop the clocks'. This turns out to be a malapropism for 'cook the books' but for the initiates, Weinberl's slip of the tongue is a clear signal that we are about to leave the 'clockwork' existence of the grocery shop for the exciting 'mystery' of the real world. And indeed the ensuing razzle does enrich the lives of Christopher and Weinberl very markedly. After the *scène à faire* Stoppard adds a coda for which there is no precedent in Nestroy. Back in the shop and alone, Christopher and Weinberl relive the high points of their adventure in the city. But almost immediately their mood evaporates; Weinberl sighs and Christopher takes up his broom and both feel their situation to be every bit as depressing as it was before. Then a small ragamuffin appears at the door, enquiring about a job. He is summarily engaged as an apprentice and so at last Christopher has someone to look down on and Weinberl has someone to show off to. This apprentice boy, who has no counterpart in Nestroy, is clearly for Stoppard a kind of *deus ex machina* whose function is to reward Christopher and Weinberl for their initiative. He provides evidence that the pair have really come up in the world. And when he also prompts Christopher to confess that his experience in Vienna had been wonderful, the audience is left with the impression that the new-found stature of Christopher and Weinberl is a direct consequence of their razzle. Thus the episode as a whole suggests that the 'past' that they have acquired in Vienna is more than a string of empty memories. It is a foundation for a better future—a liberating encounter with the 'mystery' of life.

Screenplays: The Romantic Englishwoman; The Human Factor; Despair

Stoppard has failed to achieve Pinter's reputation as a writer for the screen. None of the three films with which he has been associated has been received with much enthusiasm by the critics, and only *The Romantic Englishwoman* (1975) has had any commercial success. There seems little point, then, in reviewing them at any length here, although I have been unable to resist the temptation to use the screenplay for *Despair* (1977) as a platform from which to explore some parallels between Stoppard and Nabokov.

Stoppard's first venture into film was his adaptation of Thomas Wiseman's novel, *The Romantic Englishwoman*, for Joseph Losey, the director with whom Pinter has worked so successfully. Wiseman's book was already very Stoppardian in design. It tells of a novelist, Lewis Fielding, who uses his bourgeois, materialistic wife as the basis for a fictional character and then finds the story coming true when she runs off with a young poet. Stoppard turned the novelist into a screen-writer and backed up his 'clockwork' fantasies with some clips from his film-within-the-film. He also made the poet rather more attractive than he is in the novel, so that, although Fielding and his wife finally revert to their 'clockwork' existence (symbolized by the abundance of mirrors in their house), we are left with a predilection for the poet's 'mystery' (symbolized by his empty bag and blank notebooks).

Graham Greene's *The Human Factor* is about rigid systems—The Foreign Office, Communism, apartheid—and the human factors that sabotage their operations. This tension may sound Stoppardian but Greene's depiction of it is much more subtle, more realistic than the kind of juxtaposition that Stoppard prefers. And since Stoppard, nervous perhaps of Greene's huge reputation, stayed very close to the original text when adapting the book for Otto Preminger, the film (1980) shows few signs of his controlling hand. (But Greene seems to have left his mark on Stoppard; the names Boris and Maurice in the Faber edition of *Cahoot's Macbeth* were probably lifted from *The Human Factor*.)

Despair is a much more suitable case for treatment. Stoppard has made no secret of his admiration for Nabokov, and the most cursory reading of *Despair* will reveal a host of motifs which seem to have rubbed off on Stoppard at various points of his career. Like so many of Stoppard's characters, Nabokov's Hermann is obsessed by word-play—and by mirrors. He shares Malquist's sartorial preoccupations, and his idea of publishing 'expensive volumes *de luxe* dealing exhaustively with sexual relations as revealed in literature, art, science' recalls Malquist's study of *Hamlet* as a source of book titles. He even anticipates Dotty's fondness for rhyming 'moon' and 'June'. But above all Hermann resembles Henry Carr and *Despair* resembles *Travesties*. There are continual reminders that the novel is under the control of Hermann's 'devious memory', which 'has its own whims and rules'. In *The Times* of 8 June 1974 (page 9) Peter Wood compared the narrative technique in *Travesties* with that of Nabokov's *Pale Fire*. To me it seems that *Despair* offers an even closer parallel. Consider, for example, the way in which the book opens. After two highly self-conscious paragraphs in which he congratulates himself on his aesthetic prowess, Hermann settles down to describe his background. He portrays his mother as 'a pure Russian . . . from an old princely stock' who loved to 'recline in her rocking chair, fanning herself, munching chocolate' on hot summer days. He then sketches his own history from 1914 to 1930, noting, among other things, that he 'read exactly one thousand and eighteen books . . . kept count of them'. This paragraph ends in mid-sentence and he returns to the subject of his mother:

> A slight digression: that bit about my mother was a deliberate lie. In reality she was a woman of the people . . . I could, of course, have crossed it out, but I purposely leave it there as a sample of one of my essential traits: my light-hearted, inspired lying.

All this is very Carr-like. The lying, the digressions, the sentence-fragments, even little turns of phrase such as the omission of the pronoun in 'kept count of them'—these characteristics, and others, reappear in *Travesties*. But what matters most in both the novel and the play is the way in which the narrator reduces his experience to an elegant 'clockwork' formula.

We have seen how Carr escapes into a dream-world peopled by Wildean distortions of Joyce, Tzara and others until Old Cecily brings him back to reality at the end of the play. Hermann too ignores reality, including the affair which his wife Lydia and her cousin Ardalion are carrying on under his nose, and creates an alternative existence which is seen variously as a play-, a painting-, a story- and a film-within-the-novel. When Hermann meets Felix, a man whom he regards as his double, he gets the idea of swapping identities so that he can step into this alternative existence. Felix is dressed up as Hermann and then murdered, and Hermann begins a new life as Felix. (Since Felix was a rootless vagrant Hermann achieves complete freedom in his new identity.) What spoils the plan is the fact that Felix was not Hermann's double at all; the idea that he was is one of a host of delusions which arise from Hermann's schizophrenia (the word occurs in the film but not in the novel). Nobody is fooled by the ruse and Hermann is eventually caught and, we assume, brought to justice.

Stoppard could hardly have found a more suitable story and he went about his task with evident relish, embellishing the clash between 'mystery' and 'clockwork' in some characteristic ways. For example, Stoppard converts Felix from a tramp into a circus performer and has Hermann approach him through a hall of mirrors. This accentuates the idea that Hermann's relationship with his double is a 'clockwork' one, a play-within-the-film, as it were. And to reinforce this idea mirrors continue to appear in the scenes involving Hermann, just as they do in the 'clockwork' episodes of *The Romantic Englishwoman*. The same point is made earlier when, in a scene invented by Stoppard, Hermann gets the idea of exploiting a double from a cops-and-robbers film. On the other hand, the reality from which Hermann seeks to retreat is also elaborated, mainly through the injection of a few scenes depicting Nazi atrocities, one of which coincides with Hermann's writing of the fateful letter of assignation to Felix—a nice juxtaposition. No doubt the director, Rainer Werner Fassbinder, a fervent hater of Nazism, also had a hand in these additions to Nabokov's text. By numerous other means as well, Stoppard and Fassbinder reinforce the split between Hermann's fantasy-world and the reality which surrounds him. But, ingenious as the devices often are, it cannot be said that the film is a complete success. Indeed, Stoppard readily confessed to Hardin his dissatisfaction with the finished product. Its most obvious limitation, of course, is that it cannot delay the revelation that Felix is not Hermann's double. That Hermann is deluded in finding a resemblance is evident as soon as Felix appears—the more evident in that Hermann is played by Dirk Bogarde. The loss of this element of surprise from the plot imposes enormous demands on the characterization—demands that Stoppard, Fassbinder and Bogarde could not fulfil.

Almost inevitably, then, Nabokov's novel is more satisfying than Stoppard's screenplay. But this discrepancy can be attributed entirely to the difference of medium; it clearly has nothing to do with any fundamental incompatibility between the two men such as we saw in the case of Stoppard and Mrozek. I have already noted a number of particular respects in which the works of Stoppard and Nabokov are similar. It remains to make the more general point that both are rather abstract writers, more interested in manipulating language and ideas than in conjuring up an authentic sense of time, place or character. 'No rough edges on Tom. None of those awkward local references. There never were', said Peter Nichols to Tynan, implying, it would seem, that Stoppard carefully tailors his plays for an international market. But there seems to be a deeper reason for the lack of local references, for they are wanting in the interviews as well. And it is interesting how little Stoppard reveals, in both the interviews and the plays (with the partial exception of *The Real Thing*), about himself and his family. Pressed by Tynan on the subject of his father's death he replied, 'we've never delved into it'. And, although his children get a mention from time to time, references to his mother, his step-father, his brother, his first wife and even his second are extremely rare. This reticence may owe something to the fact that Stoppard, like Nabokov, is an *emigré*. Tynan certainly thinks so and he quotes one of Stoppard's directors as saying, 'You have to be foreign to write English with that kind of hypnotized brilliance'. But Stoppard himself, though he used to toy with this idea occasionally, has recently come to doubt it. Kerensky quotes him as saying:

> At one time I thought perhaps I enjoyed playing with the English language because I came to it late; I used to compare myself to Nabokov and say it was like suddenly finding oneself on top of a mountain and looking down, instead of laboriously climbing up as most people do when they learn a language from childhood. But then I discovered that Nabokov had spoken English from childhood and anyway I myself had never been literate in any other language. English was the working

language at my schools in India. I think I'd probably have been interested in language just the same, if I'd been a Czechoslovak writer instead of a British one.

In the light of this testimony Tynan's emphasis on Stoppard's *emigré* status begins to look somewhat simplistic. And, since Stoppard is fluent only in English (and often stigmatizes his characters for their use of foreign phrases) he hardly qualifies as an 'extraterritorial'—the label that George Steiner uses for rootless, multilingual writers like Beckett, Borges and Nabokov in his book, *Extraterritorial: Papers on Literature and the Language Revolution* (New York, 1971). It is interesting, however, how high certain extraterritorials, such as Beckett, Nabokov, Wilde and Flann O'Brien, rank in Stoppard's estimation. Clearly the extraterritorial club is one in which he feels at home even though he lacks the official entrance requirement.

Bibliography

Works by Stoppard

A full bibliographical analysis of the Stoppard canon is urgently needed. Directors and critics alike are often unaware that most of the major plays exist in significantly different versions. In the final chapter of *From Writer to Reader: Studies in Editorial Method* Philip Gaskell has shown how the version of *Travesties* which Stoppard composed in the study was modified in the course of rehearsals and performances. *Travesties* was published a little while after the play opened in London, and so Stoppard was able to incorporate some of these modifications in the published text. Consequently *Travesties*—almost alone among the major plays—has remained unrevised in print.

Usually Faber and Faber Ltd. publishes a first edition to coincide with the opening of the London season. Inevitably this reproduces the unrevised text and it is immediately rendered obsolete by the changes made during rehearsals. A second edition is therefore required to bring the printed text more or less into line with the performed text. Where a French's Acting Edition exists it will often indicate further revisions. Conversely, the Inter-Action edition of *Dogg's Hamlet, Cahoot's Macbeth* contains an earlier, though more accurate, text than its Faber counterpart. The (American) Grove Press editions are generally based on the revised Faber texts, but two—*Jumpers* and *Rosencrantz and Guildenstern Are Dead*—have been through the same revising mill.

The following list is an attempt to summarize the different editions in English published to date. In compiling it I have had considerable assistance from Samuel French Ltd., Grove Press Inc., Tom Stoppard himself and Faber and Faber Ltd. (especially Frank Pike and Brian Dickson). This assistance is gratefully acknowledged, but, alas, it does not mean that the list is authoritative. The files of Faber and Faber Ltd. are not complete enough to record every new development, and some of their publicity is unfortunately ambiguous. The oft-repeated claim that *Rosencrantz and Guildenstern Are Dead* went into a second edition in 1968, for example, refers to the change from a paper-covered edition to a paperbound one and not to the change in the text, which took place the year before (I assume in December, but possibly in August). These problems have no doubt been compounded by errors of my own.

The following abbreviations have been used in the list:
>FF = Faber and Faber Ltd.
>FL = Samuel French Ltd. (London)
>FNY = Samuel French Ltd. (New York)
>GP = Grove Press Inc.

I have attempted to provide the date of every distinct edition, although this has proved impossible in the case of the Samuel French editions, which carry no dates. A figure in brackets after a date signifies the number of subsequent impressions or reprintings of the edition in question. The word 'Revised' after a date signifies that the edition in question incorporates significant changes to the text of the previous edition *from the same publishing house*. Where the word 'Revised' does not accompany the date of a second or subsequent edition it may be assumed that the changes introduced are of a technical nature, such as different pagination (in the 1978 FF *Rosencrantz*) or a different binding (in the 1968 FF *Rosencrantz*).

(1) Major Original Works and Minor Works Published Separately

After Magritte
>FF: Paper 1971 (3)
>FL
>GP—see under *'The Real Inspector Hound'* and *'After Magritte'*

Albert's Bridge
>FF: Paper 1970
>FL
>Also in *Plays and Players* XV (October 1967), pp. 21–30.

'Albert's Bridge' and *'If You're Glad I'll Be Frank'*
>FF: Case 1969; Paper 1969

'Albert's Bridge and *Other Plays* [Includes *If You're Glad I'll Be Frank, Artist Descending a Staircase, Where Are They Now?* and *A Separate Peace* as well as *Albert's Bridge*]
    GP: Case 1977; Paper 1977
'Artist Descending a Staircase' and *'Where Are They Now?'*
    FF: Case 1973; Paper 1973 (2)
    GP—see under *'Albert's Bridge'* and *Other Plays*
'Dirty Linen' and *'New-Found-Land'*
    FF: Paper 1976 (3)
    FL
    GP: Case 1976; Paper 1976 (2)
Dogg's Hamlet, Cahoot's Macbeth
    FF: Case 1980; Paper 1980
    Inter-Action (London): Paper 1979
Enter a Free Man
    FF: Case 1968; Paper 1968 (5)
    FNY
    GP: Paper 1972 (2)
'Every Good Boy Deserves Favour: A Play for Actors and Orchestra' and *'Professional Foul: A Play for Television'*
    FF: Case 1978; Paper 1978 (3)
    GP: Case 1978; Paper 1978 (1)
The Fifteen Minute Hamlet
    FL
If You're Glad I'll Be Frank
    FF: Paper 1976—see also under *'Albert's Bridge'* and *'If You're Glad I'll Be Frank'*
    FL
    FNY
    GP—see under *'Albert's Bridge'* and *Other Plays*
    Also in James Redmond and Hallam Tennyson (edd.), *Contemporary One-Act Plays* (London: Heinemann, 1976), pp. 71–102.
Jumpers
    FF: Case 1972; Paper 1972 (1), 1973 Revised (3)
    GP: Case 1972, 1981 Revised; Paper 1973 Revised (4)
Lord Malquist and Mr Moon
    Anthony Blond (London), 1966
    Balantine (New York), 1969
    FF: Case 1974; Paper 1980
    GP: Paper 1975
    Knopf (New York), 1968
    Panther (London), 1968

Night and Day
    FF: Case 1978; Paper 1978, 1979 Revised (1)
    FL
    FNY
    GP: Case 1979; Paper 1979 (1)

On the Razzle: Adapted from 'Einen Jux will er sich machen' by
Johann Nestroy
    FF: Paper 1981, 1982 Revised

The Real Inspector Hound
    FF: Case 1968 (1); Paper 1970 Revised (5)
    FL
    FNY
    GP: Paper 1969

'The Real Inspector Hound' and *'After Magritte'*
    GP: Paper 1975 (4)

The Real Thing
    FF: Paper 1982

Rosencrantz and Guildenstern Are Dead
    FF: Case 1967 (1); Paper 1967 (2), 1967 (December) Revised,
        1968 (5), 1978 (1)
    FL
    FNY
    GP: Case 1967, 1978 Revised; Paper 1967, 1968 Revised (22)
    Also in *Evergreen Review* XII (March 1968), pp. 47–72 and
        (selections) in Otis L. Guernsey Jr (ed.), *The Best Plays of
        1967–1968* (New York: Dodd Mead, 1968), pp. 171–91.

A Separate Peace
    FL
    GP—see under *'Albert's Bridge'* and *Other Plays*
    Also in Alan Durband (ed.), *Playbill Two* (London:
    Hutchinson, 1969), pp. 105–38.

Travesties
    FF: Case 1975 (1); Paper 1975 (4)
    GP: Case 1975; Paper 1975 (5)
    Also (selections) in Otis L. Guernsey Jr (ed.), *The Best Plays of
    1975–1976* (New York: Dodd Mead, 1976), pp. 149–67.

Where Are They Now?
    FF:—see under *'Artist Descending a Staircase'* and *'Where Are
        They Now'*
    GP—see under *'Albert's Bridge'* and *Other Plays*

(2) Translations

Mrozek, Slawomir. *Tango* (translated by Nicholas Bethell, adapted by Tom Stoppard). London: Cape, 1968. Reprinted in *Three East European Plays* (Harmondsworth: Penguin, 1970), pp. 93–182.

Nestroy, Johann—see under *On the Razzle* in Section (1) above.

Schnitzler, Arthur. *Undiscovered Country: 'Das weite Land' in an English Version by Tom Stoppard.*
FF: Paper 1980.

(3) Minor Works in Anthologies, Journals etc.

(i) *Plays and Dramatic Fragments*

'Dogg's Our Pet'. In Ed. Berman (ed.), *Ten of the Best: British Short Plays* (London: Inter-Action, 1979), pp. 79–94.

'Leftover from *Travesties*'. *Adam* XXXII (1980), pp. 11–12.

'*Professional Foul*: Scenes from a Television Play'. *Encounter* L (February 1978), pp. 18–24.

(ii) *Stories*

'Life, Times: Fragments'. In *Introduction 2: Stories by New Writers* (FF, 1964), pp. 126–30.

'Reunion'. In *ibid.*, pp. 121–25.

'The Story'. In *ibid.*, pp. 131–36. Reprinted in *Evergreen Review* XII (July 1968), pp. 53–55.

(iii) *Articles*

[I have declined to trace Stoppard's early efforts as a journalist—in the *Western Daily Press* (1954–58), the *Bristol Evening World* (1958–60), various newspapers (1960–62) and *Scene* (1963).]

'But for the Middle Classes'. *Times Literary Supplement* (3 June 1977), p. 677.

'A Case of Vice Triumphant'. *Plays and Players* XIV (March 1967), pp. 16–19.

'Childbirth'. *Vogue* CXXVIII (May 1971), p. 54.

'The Definite Maybe'. *Author* LXXVIII (1967), pp. 18–20.

'Dirty Linen in Prague'. *New York Times* (11 February 1977), Section I, p. 27.

'The Face at the Window'. *Sunday Times* (27 February 1977), p. 33.

'I'm not Keen on Experiments'. *New York Times* (8 March 1970), Section II, p. 17.

'In Praise of Pedantry'. *Punch* (14 July 1971), pp. 62–63.

'Just Impossible'. *Plays and Players* XIV (January 1967), pp. 28–29.

'Looking-Glass World'. *New Statesman* (28 October 1977), pp. 571–72.

'Nothing in Mind'. *London Magazine* XVII (February 1978), pp. 65–68.

'Playwrights and Professors'. *Times Literary Supplement* (13 October 1972), p. 1219.

'Prague: The Story of the Chartists'. *New York Review of Books* (4 August 1977), pp. 11–15.

'Prague's Wall of Silence'. *Times* (18 November 1981), p. 10.

Review of *Orghast* by Ted Hughes. *Times Literary Supplement* (1 October 1971), p. 1174.

Review of *A Supplement to the Oxford English Dictionary, Volume 1, A-G. Punch* (13 December 1972), pp. 893-94.

'Something to Declare'. *Sunday Times* (25 February 1968), p. 47.

'Tom Stoppard on the K.G.B.'s Olympic Trials'. *Sunday Times* (6 April 1980), p. 16.

'A Very Satirical Thing Happened to Me on the Way to the Theatre Tonight'. *Encore* X (March–April 1963), pp. 33–36.

'Wildlife Observed. The Galapagos: Paradise and Purgatory'. *Observer Magazine* (29 November 1981), pp. 38–51.

'Yes. We Have No Banana'. *Guardian* (10 December 1971), p. 10.

Letters to: *The Times* (7 February 1977, p. 15; 11 August 1977, p. 13; 17 October 1977, p. 13; 3 November 1980, p. 13).
         The Sunday Times (15 June 1980, p. 12).
         The Daily Telegraph (17 March 1979, p. 20).

Criticism (including interviews)

The most comprehensive bibliography of Stoppard criticism is Charles A. Carpenter's 'Bond, Shaffer, Stoppard, Storey: An International Checklist of Commentary', in *Modern Drama* XXIV (1981), pp. 546–56. The chief difference between our lists is that Professor Carpenter omits all 'reviews of performances, career summaries and other ephemerae', whereas I include from these categories a few items which seem to me to have special merit—often because they are based on discussions with Stoppard himself. Professor Carpenter's annual update of his checklist (in the June number of *Modern Drama*) should provide a reliable guide to Stoppard criticism in the future.

'Ambushes for the Audience: Towards a High Comedy of Ideas'. *Theatre Quarterly* IV/xiv (1974), pp. 3–17.

Amory, Mark. 'The Joke's the Thing'. *Sunday Times Magazine* (9 June 1974), pp. 65–75.

Asmus, Walter D. '*Rosencrantz and Guildenstern Are Dead*'. *Shakespeare Jahrbuch* CVI (1970), pp. 118–31.

Atticus (Ray Connolly). 'Stoppard in Greeneland'. *Sunday Times* (20 January 1980), p. 32.

Ayer, A. J. 'Love Among the Logical Positivists'. *Sunday Times* (9 April 1972), p. 16.

Babula, William. 'The Play-Life Metaphor in Shakespeare and Stoppard'. *Modern Drama* XV (1972), pp. 279–81.

Bailey, John A. '*Jumpers* by Tom Stoppard: The Ironist as Theistic Apologist'. *Michigan Academician* XI (1979), pp. 237–50.

Barker, Clive. 'Contemporary Shakespearean Parody in British Theatre'. *Shakespeare Jahrbuch* CV (1969), pp. 104–20.

Bassnett-McGuire, Susan. 'Textual Understructures in Jean-Louis Barrault's *Rabelais* and Tom Stoppard's *Rosencrantz and Guildenstern Are Dead*'. *Comparison* I (1975), pp. 102–40.

Baumgart, Wolfgang. 'Hamlet's Excellent Good Friends: Beobachtungen zu Shakespeare und Stoppard'. In Rudolf Sühnel and Dieter Riesner (edd.), *Englische Dichter der Moderne* (Berlin, 1971), pp. 588–98.

Bennett, Jonathan. 'Philosophy and Mr Stoppard'. *Philosophy* L (1975), pp. 5–18.

Berkvist, Robert. 'This Time, Stoppard Plays It (Almost) Straight'. *New York Times* (25 November 1979), Section II, pp. 1, 5.

Berlin, Normand. '*Rosencrantz and Guildenstern Are Dead*: Theater of Criticism'. *Modern Drama* XVI (1973), pp. 269–77.

Bigsby, C. W. E. *Tom Stoppard* (2nd edition). Harlow, 1979.

Billman, Carol. 'The Art of History in Tom Stoppard's *Travesties*'. *Kansas Quarterly* XII (1980), pp. 47–52.

Blumenfeld, Y. 'The Dramatic Relationship Between Soccer and Freedom'. *Horizon* XXI (1978), pp. 90–92.

Brassell, Tim '*Jumpers*: A Happy Marriage?'. *Gambit* XXXVII (1980), pp. 43–59.

Brater, Enoch. 'Parody, Travesty and Politics in the Plays of Tom Stoppard'. In Hedwig Bock and Albert Wertheim (edd.), *Essays on Contemporary British Drama* (Munich, 1981), pp. 117–30.

Broich, Ulrich. 'Das englische historische Drama der Gegenwart'. *Anglia* XCVIII (1980), pp. 357–82.

Brustein, Robert. 'Waiting for Hamlet'. *New Republic* IV (1967), pp. 25–26. Reprinted in *Plays and Players* XV (January 1968), pp. 51–52, and in Brustein, *The Third Theatre* (London, 1970), pp. 149–53.

Buhr, Richard J. 'Epistemology and Ethics in Tom Stoppard's *Professional Foul*'. *Comparative Drama* XIII (1979), pp. 320–29.
——'The Philosophy Game in Tom Stoppard's *Professional Foul*'. *Midwest Quarterly* XXII (1981), pp. 407–15.
Burton, Deirdre. 'Dialogue and Discourse in Tom Stoppard'. *Nottingham Linguistic Circular* IV (1977), pp. 28–49.
Cahn, Victor L. *Beyond Absurdity: The Plays of Tom Stoppard*. Rutherford, N. J., 1979.
Callen, Anthony. 'Stoppard's Godot: Some French Influences on Post-War English Drama'. *New Theatre Magazine* X (1969), pp. 22–30.
Camroux, David. 'Tom Stoppard: The Last of the Metaphysical Egocentrics'. *Caliban* XV (1978), pp. 79–84.
Cardenas de Becu, Isabel. *Teatro de Vanguardia: Polémica y Vida*. Buenos Aires, 1975.
Carroll, Peter. 'They Have Their Entrances and Their Exits: *Rosencrantz and Guildenstern Are Dead*'. *Teaching of English* XX (1971), pp. 50–60.
Clum, John M. 'Religion and Five Contemporary Plays: The Quest for God in a Godless World'. *South Atlantic Quarterly* LXXVII (1978), pp. 418–32.
Cohn, Ruby. *Modern Shakespeare Offshoots*. Princeton, N. J., 1976.
——'Tom Stoppard: Light Drama and Dirges in Marriage'. In C. W. E. Bigsby (ed.), *Contemporary English Drama* (London, 1981), pp. 109–20.
Colby, Douglas. *As the Curtain Rises: On Contemporary British Drama 1966–76*. Rutherford, N. J., 1978.
Combs, Richard. 'Losey, *Galileo* and *The Romantic Englishwoman*'. *Sight and Sound* XLIV (1975), pp. 139–43.
Cook, B. 'Tom Stoppard: The Man Behind the Plays'. *Saturday Review* (8 January 1977), pp. 52–53.
Cooke, John William. 'The Optical Allusion: Perception and Form in Stoppard's *Travesties*'. *Modern Drama* XXIV (1981), pp. 525–39.
Corballis, Richard. 'Extending the Audience: The Structure of *Rosencrantz and Guildenstern Are Dead*'. *Ariel* XI (1980), pp. 65–79.
—— 'Hints on Teaching *Rosencrantz and Guildenstern Are Dead*'. *English in New Zealand* (April, 1978), pp. 27–33.
Crick, Bernard. '*Travesties*'. *Times Higher Educational Supplement* (2 August 1974), p. 13.
Crossley, Brian M. 'An Investigation of Stoppard's "Hound" and "Foot"'. *Modern Drama* XX (1977), pp. 77–86.
Crump, G. B. 'The Universe as Murder Mystery: Tom Stoppard's *Jumpers*'. *Contemporary Literature* XX (1979), pp. 354–68.

Davidson, Mary R. 'Historical Homonyms: A New Way of Naming in Tom Stoppard's *Jumpers*'. *Modern Drama* XXII (1979), pp. 305–13.

Dean, Joan Fitzpatrick. *Tom Stoppard: Comedy as a Moral Matrix.* Columbia, Mo., 1981.

Delaney, Paul. 'The Flesh and the Word in *Jumpers*'. *Modern Language Quarterly* XLII (1981), pp. 369–88.

Djordjevic, Jelena. 'Tri Drame Toma Stoparda: Nacelo Ironije'. *Savremenik* XXV (1979), pp. 529–41.

Dobrin, David N. 'Stoppard's *Travesties*'. *Explicator* XL/i (1981), pp. 63–64.

Donaldson, Ian. 'The Ledger of the Lost-and-Stolen Office'. *Southern Review* XIII (1980), pp. 41–52.

Draudt, M. '"Two Sides of the Same Coin, or . . . the Same Side of Two Coins": An Analysis of Tom Stoppard's *Rosencrantz and Guildenstern Are Dead*'. *English Studies* LXII (1981), pp. 348–57.

Duncan, Joseph E. 'Godot Comes: *Rosencrantz and Guildenstern Are Dead*'. *Ariel* XII (1981), pp. 57–70.

Durham, Weldon B. 'Symbolic Action in Tom Stoppard's *Jumpers*'. *Theatre Journal* XXXII (1980), pp. 169–79.

Egan, Robert. 'A Thin Beam of Light: The Purpose of Playing in *Rosencrantz and Guildenstern Are Dead*'. *Theatre Journal* XXXI (1979), pp. 59–69.

Ellmann, Richard. 'The Zealots of Zurich'. *Times Literary Supplement* (12 July 1974), p. 744.

Farish, Gillian. 'Into the Looking-Glass Bowl: An Instant of Grateful Terror'. *University of Windsor Review* X (1975), pp. 14–29.

Funke, Lewis. *Playwrights Talk About Writing.* Chicago, 1975.

Gabbard, Lucina P. 'Stoppard's *Jumpers*: A Mystery Play'. *Modern Drama* XX (1977), pp. 87–95.

Gale, John. 'Writing's My 43rd Priority, Says Tom Stoppard'. *Observer* (17 December 1967), p. 4.

Gardner, C. D. '*Rosencrantz and Guildenstern Are Dead*'. *Theoria* XXXIV (1970), pp. 83–84.

Gaskell, Philip. *From Writer to Reader: Studies in Editorial Method.* Oxford, 1978.

Geraths, Armin. 'Geschichte und Geschichtskritik in Tom Stoppards "Ideen-Komödie" *Travesties*'. *Anglistik und Englischunterricht* VII (1979), pp. 89–101.

—— 'Rosenkranz und Güldenstern: *Hamlet*-Varianten bei William Schwenk Gilbert und Tom Stoppard'. In Horst Priessnitz (ed.), *Anglo-Amerikanische Shakespeare-Bearbeitungen des 20 Jahrhunderts* (Darmstadt, 1980), pp. 251–74.

Gianakaris, C. J. 'Absurdism Altered: *Rosencrantz and Guildenstern Are Dead*'. *Drama Survey* VII (1968–69), pp. 52–58.

Gitzen, Julian. 'Tom Stoppard: Chaos in Perspective'. *Southern Humanities Review* X (1976), pp. 143–52.

Gold, Margaret. 'Who Are the Dadas of *Travesties?*'. *Modern Drama* XXI (1978), pp. 59–65.

Goldstein, Leonard. 'A Note on Tom Stoppard's *After Magritte*'. *Zeitschrift für Anglistik und Amerikanistik* XXIII (1975), pp. 16–21.

Gollob, David and Roper, David. 'Trad Tom Pops In'. *Gambit* XXXVII (1980), pp. 5–17.

Gordon, Giles. 'Interview with Tom Stoppard'. *Transatlantic Review* XXIX (1968), pp. 17–25. Reprinted in Joseph F. McCrindle (ed.), *Behind the Scenes: Theatre and Film Interviews from the 'Transatlantic Review'* (New York, 1971), pp. 77–87.

Grant, Steve. 'Serious Frivolity'. *Time Out* (18 June 1976), p. 7.

Griffiths, Gareth. 'New Lines: English Theatre in the Sixties and After'. *Kansas Quarterly* III (1971), pp. 77–88.

Gruber, William E. '"Wheels Within Wheels, etcetera": Artistic Design in *Rosencrantz and Guildenstern Are Dead*'. *Comparative Drama* XV (1981–82), pp. 291–310.

Gussow, Mel. '*Jumpers* Author is Verbal Gymnast'. *New York Times* (23 April 1974), p. 36.

—— 'Playwright, Star Provide a Little Curtain-Raiser'. *New York Times* (31 October 1975), p. 21.

—— 'Stoppard Refutes Himself, Endlessly'. *New York Times* (26 April 1972), p. 54.

—— 'Stoppard's Intellectual Cartwheels Now With Music'. *New York Times* (29 July 1979), Section II, pp. 1, 22.

Halton, Kathleen. 'Tom Stoppard'. [*American*] *Vogue* (15 October 1967), p. 112.

Hardin, Nancy Shields. 'An Interview with Tom Stoppard'. *Contemporary Literature* XXII (1981), pp. 153–66.

Harper, Keith. 'The Devious Route to Waterloo Road'. *Guardian* (12 April 1967), p. 7.

Harris, Wendell V. 'Stoppard's *After Magritte*'. *Explicator* XXXIV (1976), item 40.

Hayes, Ann. 'A Note on *Travesties*, the New Stoppard Play'. *Sycamore* I (1977), pp. 5–9.

Hayman, Ronald. *British Theatre Since 1955: A Reassessment*. Oxford, 1979.

—— 'Double Acts: Tom Stoppard and Peter Wood'. *Sunday Times Magazine* (2 March 1980), pp. 29–31.

—— 'Profile 9: Tom Stoppard'. *New Review* I/ix (1974), pp. 15–22.

—— *Theatre and Anti-Theatre: New Movements Since Beckett*. London, 1979.

—— *Tom Stoppard* (4th edition). London, 1982.

Hidalgo, Pilar. *La Ira y la Palabra: Teatro Inglés Actual*. Madrid, 1978.

Hill, Frances. 'Quarter-Laughing Assurance'. *Times Educational Supplement* (9 February 1973), p. 23.

Hindin, Michael. '*Jumpers*: Stoppard and the Theatre of Exhaustion'. *Twentieth Century Literature* XXVII (1981), pp. 1–15.

Hunter, Jim. *Tom Stoppard's Plays*. London, 1982.

Jama, Virginia, 'The Image of the African Leader in Recent Western Fiction'. *Horn of Africa* III (1980), pp. 43–45.

James, Clive. 'Count Zero Splits the Infinite: Tom Stoppard's Plays'. *Encounter* XLV (November 1975), pp. 68–76.

Jensen, Henning. 'Jonathan Bennett and Mr Stoppard'. *Philosophy* LII (1977), pp. 214–17.

Johnson, Paul. *Enemies of Society*. London, 1977.

Kahn, Coppelia. '*Travesties* and the Importance of Being Stoppard'. *New York Literary Forum* I (1978), pp. 187–97.

Kennedy, Andrew. 'Natural, Mannered and Parodic Dialogue'. *Yearbook of English Studies* IX (1979), pp. 28–54.

—— 'Old and New in London Now'. *Modern Drama* XI (1969), pp. 437–46.

Kerensky, Oleg. *The New British Drama: Fourteen Playwrights Since Osborne and Pinter*. London, 1977.

Kerr, Walter. *Thirty Plays Hath November*. New York, 1969.

Keyssar-Franke, Helene. 'The Strategy of *Rosencrantz and Guildenstern Are Dead*'. *Educational Theatre Journal* XXVII (1975), pp. 85–97.

Killinger, John. *World in Collapse: The Vision of Absurd Drama*. New York, 1971.

King, Kimball. *Twenty Modern British Playwrights*. New York, 1977.

Kruse, Axel. 'Tragicomedy and Tragic Burlesque: *Waiting for Godot* and *Rosencrantz and Guildenstern Are Dead*'. *Sydney Studies in English* I (1980), pp. 76–96.

Kuurman, Joost, and others. 'An Interview with Tom Stoppard'. *Dutch Quarterly Review of Anglo-American Letters* X (1980), pp. 41–57.

Lee, R. H. 'The Circle and Its Tangent'. *Theoria* XXXIII (1969), pp. 37–43.

Leech, Michael. 'The Translators'. *Plays and Players* XX (April 1973), pp. 36–38.

Leonard, John. 'Tom Stoppard Tries on a "Knickers Farce"'. *New York Times* (9 January 1977), Section II, pp. 1, 5.

Leonard, Virginia E. 'Tom Stoppard's *Jumpers*: The Separation From Reality'. *Bulletin of the West Virginia Association of College English Teachers* II (1975), pp. 45–56.

Levenson, Jill. 'Views from a Revolving Door: Tom Stoppard's Canon to Date'. *Queen's Quarterly* LXXVIII (1971), pp. 431–42.

Levy, R. S. 'Serious Propositions Compromised by Frivolity'. *Critical Quarterly* XXII (1980), pp. 79–85.

Londré, Felicity Hardison. *Tom Stoppard*. New York, 1981.

―― 'Using Comic Devices to Answer the Ultimate Question: Tom Stoppard's *Jumpers* and Woody Allen's *God*'. *Comparative Drama* XIV (1980), pp. 346–52.

Longman, Stanley V. 'The Spatial Dimension of Theatre'. *Theatre Journal* XXXIII (1981), pp. 46–59.

Ludlow, Colin. 'Marriage Lines'. *London Magazine* XVIII/xi (1979), pp. 91–99.

McMillan, Dougald. 'Dropping the Other Boot, or Getting Stoppard out of Limbo'. *Gambit* XXXVII (1980), pp. 61–76.

Mansat, A. '*Rosencrantz et Guildenstern Sont Morts*'. *Langues Modernes* LXIV (1970), pp. 396–400.

Marowitz, Charles. *Confessions of a Counterfeit Critic: A London Theatre Notebook 1958–1971*. London, 1973.

―― 'Tom Stoppard—The Theatre's Intellectual P. T. Barnum'. *New York Times* (19 October 1975), Section II, pp. 1, 5.

May, Clifford D. and Behr, Edward. 'Master of the Stage'. *Newsweek* (15 August 1977), pp. 35–40.

Mehl, Dieter. 'Stoppard: *Rosencrantz and Guildenstern Are Dead*'. In Mehl (ed.), *Das englische Drama: vom Mittelalter bis zur Gegenwart* (Düsseldorf, 1970), pp. 336–46.

Miner, Michael D. 'Grotesque Drama in the '70s'. *Kansas Quarterly* XII (1980), pp. 99–109.

Morwood, James. '*Jumpers* Revisited'. *Agenda* XVIII/iv-XIX/i (Winter–Spring 1981), pp. 135–41.

Neil, Boyd. 'Green Room: *Travesties* and Translation'. *Plays and Players* XXVI (December 1978), pp. 8–9.

Neri, Nicoletta. *Aspetti e Figure del Teatro Inglese Contemporaneo*. Turin, 1971.

Nitzsche, J. C. 'McLuhan's Message and Stoppard's Medium in *Rosencrantz and Guildenstern Are Dead*'. *Dutch Quarterly Review of Anglo-American Letters* X (1980), pp. 32–40.

Norman, Barry. 'Tom Stoppard and the Contentment of Insecurity'. *Times* (11 November 1972), p. 11.

Pache, Walter. 'Pirandellos Urenkel: Formen des Spiels im Spiel bei Max Frisch und Tom Stoppard'. *Sprachkunst* IV (1973), pp. 124–41.

Pasquier, Marie-Claire. 'Shakespeare ou le Lieu Commun: A

Propos de *Rosencrantz and Guildenstern Are Dead* de Tom Stoppard'. *Recherches Anglaises et Americaines* V (1972), pp. 110–20.

Pearce, Howard D. 'Stage as Mirror: Tom Stoppard's *Travesties*'. *Modern Language Notes* XCIV (1979), pp. 1139–58.

Peereboom, J. J. 'The Political Wave: The London Drama Scene'. *Dutch Quarterly Review of Anglo-American Letters* X (1980), pp. 59–72.

Pendennis. 'Dialogue with a Driven Man'. *Observer* (30 August 1981), p. 18.

'Playwright-Novelist'. *New Yorker* (4 May 1968), pp. 40–41.

Plett, Heinrich F. 'Tom Stoppard: *Travesties*'. In Rainer Lengeler (ed.), *Englische Literatur der Gegenwart 1971–1975* (Düsseldorf, 1977), pp. 81–93.

Prideaux, Tom. 'Uncertainty Makes the Big Time'. *Life* (9 February 1968), pp. 72–76.

Pritchard, R. 'Rosencrantz and Guildenstern'. *English in New Zealand* (September 1978), pp. 34–36.

Quinn, James E. 'Rosencrantz and Guildenstern Are Alive and Well in the Classroom'. *Missouri English Bulletin* XXVI (October 1970), pp. 16–19.

Rabinowitz, Peter J. '"What's Hecuba to Us?" The Audience's Experience of Literary Borrowing'. In Susan R. Suleiman and Inge Crosman (edd.), *The Reader in the Text: Essays on Audience and Interpretation* (Princeton, 1980), pp. 241–63.

Riehle, Wolfgang. 'Tom Stoppard's *Jumpers*: Gedanken zu einer Interpretation'. *Archiv* CCXVI (1979), pp. 280–90.

Riley, Carolyn (ed.). *Contemporary Literary Criticism: Excerpts from Criticism of the Works of Today's Novelists, Poets, Playwrights and Other Creative Writers*. Detroit, 1975.

Roberts, Philip. 'Tom Stoppard: Serious Artist or Siren?' *Critical Quarterly* XX (1978), pp. 84–92.

Robinson, Gabriele Scott. 'Nothing Left But Parody: Friedrich Dürrenmatt and Tom Stoppard'. *Theatre Journal* XXXII (1980), pp. 85–94.

—— 'Plays Without Plot: The Theatre of Tom Stoppard'. *Educational Theatre Journal* XXIX (1977), pp. 37–48.

Rodway, Alan. *English Comedy: Its Role and Nature from Chaucer to the Present Day*. London, 1975.

—— 'Stripping Off'. *London Magazine* XVI (1976), pp. 66–72.

Rothstein, Bobbi. 'The Reappearance of Public Man: Stoppard's *Jumpers* and *Professional Foul*'. *Kansas Quarterly* XII (1980), pp. 35–44.

Ruiz Ruiz, José M. '*Travesties*: Lenin, James Joyce y Tristan Tzara en escena'. *Letras De Deusto* IX (1979), pp. 137–56.

Ryan, Pat M. 'Tom Stoppard's Cryptic *R & G*'. *Theatre Journal* X (1971), pp. 3–9.

Ryan, Randolph. 'Theatre Checklist No 2: Tom Stoppard'. *Theatrefacts* II (May–July 1974), pp. 2–9.

Salmon, Eric. 'Faith in Tom Stoppard'. *Queen's Quarterly* LXXXVI (1979), pp. 215–32.

Salter, Charles H. '*Rosencrantz and Guildenstern Are Dead*'. In Hermann J. Weiand (ed.), *Insight IV: Analyses of Modern British and American Drama* (Frankfurt, 1975), pp. 144–50.

Schlueter, Jane. *Metafictional Characters in Modern Drama*. New York, 1979.

Schwanitz, Dietrich. 'The Method of Madness: Tom Stoppard's *Theatrum Logico-Philosophicum*'. In Hedwig Bock and Albert Wertheim (edd.), *Essays in Contemporary British Drama* (Munich, 1981), pp. 131–54.

Schwartz, Alfred. *From Büchner to Beckett: Dramatic Theory and the Modes of Tragic Drama*. Athens, 1978.

Schwartzman, Myron. 'Wilde About Joyce? Da! But My Art Belongs to Dada!'. *James Joyce Quarterly* XIII (1975), pp. 122–23.

Self, David. 'On the Edge of Reality: Some Thoughts on the Studying of Tom Stoppard'. *The Use of English* XXVI (1975), pp. 195–200.

Semple, Robert B. Jr. 'How Life Imitates a Stoppard Farce'. *New York Times* (21 June 1976), p. 45.

Shulman, Milton. 'The Politicizing of Tom Stoppard'. *New York Times* (23 April 1978), Section II, pp. 3, 27.

Simon, John. 'Theatre Chronicle'. *Hudson Review* XX (1967–68), pp. 664–65.

—— 'Theatre Chronicle'. *Hudson Review* XXIX (1976–77), pp. 79–84.

Simons, Judy. '*Night and Day*'. *Gambit* XXXVII (1980), pp. 77–86.

Stajkov, Dimitar. 'Dramaturgijata na Tom Stoppard'. *Teatar* XXXII (1976), pp. 50–54.

Stern, J. P. 'Anyone for Tennis, Anyone for Death? The Schnitzler/Stoppard *Undiscovered Country*'. *Encounter* LIII (October 1979), pp. 26–31.

Styan, J. L. 'High Tide in the London Theater: Some Notes on the 1978–9 Season'. *Comparative Drama* XIII (1979), pp. 252–57.

Sullivan, Dan. 'Young British Playwright Here for Rehearsal of *Rosencrantz*'. *New York Times* (29 August 1967), p. 27.

Taylor, John Russell. *Anger and After: A Guide to the New British Drama* (revised edition). London, 1969.

—— 'The Road to Dusty Death'. *Plays and Players* XIV (June 1967), pp. 12–15.

—— The Second Wave: British Drama of the Sixties (revised edition). London 1978.

—— 'Tom Stoppard—Structure + Intellect'. Plays and Players XVII (July 1970), pp. 16–18, 78.

Thomsen, Christian W. 'Tom Stoppard, Rosencrantz and Guildenstern Are Dead: Spiel vom Sterben,' Spiel vom Tod im Leben'. Maske und Kothurn XXIV (1978), pp. 230–43.

Toebosch, Guillaume. "Les Jeunes Gens en Colère: Le Théâtre Anglais d'Après-Guerre et Tom Stoppard'. Cahiers du Rideau VIII (1978), pp. 7–16.

Treglown, Jeremy. 'Shakespeare's Macbeths: Davenant, Verdi, Stoppard and the Question of Theatrical Text'. English XXIX (1980), pp. 95–113.

Tynan, Kenneth. 'Withdrawing with Style from the Chaos'. New Yorker (19 December 1977), pp. 41–111. Reprinted in Tynan, Show People: Profiles in Entertainment (London, 1980), in Gambit XXXVII (1980), pp. 19–41 and (as 'The Man in the Moon') in Sunday Times (15 January 1978), pp. 33–34.

Varey, Simon. 'Nobody Special: On Rosencrantz and Guildenstern Are Dead'. Dutch Quarterly Review of Anglo-American Letters X (1980), pp. 20–31.

Vickery, D. J. Brodie's Notes on Tom Stoppard's 'Rosencrantz and Guildenstern Are Dead'. London, 1980.

Vos, Jozef de. 'Rosencrantz and Guildenstern Are Dead: Tom Stoppard's "Artistic Failure"'. Neophilologus LXI (1977), pp. 152–59.

Wardle, Irving. 'A Grin Without a Cat'. Times (22 June 1968), p. 19.

Watts, Janet. 'Tom Stoppard'. Guardian (21 March 1973), p. 12.

Weber, Hans. 'Tom Stoppard: Where Are They Now? (1970)'. In Horst Priessnitz (ed.), Das englische Hörspiel (Düsseldorf, 1977), pp. 319–31.

Weightman, John. 'Art Versus Life'. Encounter XLIII (September 1974), pp. 57–59.

—— 'A Metaphysical Comedy'. Encounter XXXVIII (April 1972), pp. 44–46.

—— 'Mini-Hamlets in Limbo'. Encounter XXIX (July 1967), pp. 38–40.

Weikert, Heidrun-Edda. Tom Stoppards Dramen: Untersuchungen zu Sprache und Dialog. Tübingen, 1982.

Weise, Wolf D. 'Tom Stoppard: Albert's Bridge (1967)'. In Horst Priessnitz (ed.) Das englische Hörspiel (Düsseldorf, 1977), pp. 291–305.

Werner, Craig. 'Stoppard's Critical Travesty, or Who Vindicates Whom and Why'. Arizona Quarterly XXXV (1979), pp. 228–36.

Whitaker, Thomas R. *Fields of Play in Modern Drama*. Princeton, 1977.

—— 'Notes on Playing the Player'. *Centennial Review* XVI (1972), pp. 1–22.

Wilcher, Robert. 'The Museum of Tragedy: *Endgame* and *Rosencrantz and Guildenstern Are Dead*'. *Journal of Beckett Studies* IV (1979), pp. 43–54.

Zeh, Dieter. 'Tom Stoppard: *Rosencrantz and Guildenstern Are Dead* (1967)'. In Klaus D. Fehse and Norbert Platz (edd.), *Das zeitgenössische englische Drama* (Frankfurt, 1975), pp. 229–46.

Zeifman, Hersh. 'Tomfoolery: Stoppard's Theatrical Puns'. *Yearbook of English Studies* IX (1979), pp. 204–20.

Zimmerman, Heinz. 'T. Stoppards Publikumsverwirrung: Zu Rezeption und Sinn von *Rosencrantz and Guildenstern Are Dead*'. *Shakespeare Jahrbuch* CXIV (1978), pp. 184–200.